Confidentiality

Confidentiality
Ethical Perspectives and Clinical Dilemmas

Edited by

Charles Levin
Allannah Furlong
Mary Kay O'Neil

THE ANALYTIC PRESS

2003   Hillsdale, NJ   London

Published by
The Analytic Press, Inc., Publishers
    Editorial Offices:
    101 West Street
    Hillsdale, NJ 07642

    www.analyticpress.com

    Designed and typeset by EVS Communications, Point Pleasant, NJ.

Library of Congress Cataloging-in-Publication Data

    Confidentiality : ethical perspectives and clinical dilemmas / edited by Charles Levin, Allannah Furlong, Mary Kay O'Neil.
        p. cm.
    Includes bibliographical references and index.
    ISBN 0-88163-355-0
    1. Psychotherapist and patient—Moral and ethical aspects.
    2.Psychoanalysis—Moral and ethical aspects. 3. Confidential
    communications—Physicians. I. Levin, Charles II. Furlong, Allannah.
    III. O'Neil, Mary Kay.

    RC480.8.C655 2003
    616.89'14—dc21

                                 2003049640

Printed in the United States of America

10 9 8 7 6 5 4 3 2 1

Contents

$\mathcal{CSO}$

Acknowledgments

T he thanks we owe as editors really begin with those who gave us the confidence to pursue the question of confidentiality in the first place and to help place it on the international agenda. Lise Monette, as President-Elect and then President of the Canadian Psychoanalytic Society, encouraged us to raise the issue and to explore it in every way possible. Eva Lester put us in touch with Sara Zac de Filc of the International Psychoanalytic Association Committee on Inter-Regional Conferences, and both helped us to steer the idea of an interdisciplinary conference through the upper echelons of the IPA, with the assistance of Stephen Firestein, Otto Kernberg, and Moises Lemlij, among others. Of the many who offered crucial support in the early stages, we should also mention, at the very least, Andrew Brook, Guy Da Silva, Marcella Evan-Grenier, David Iseman, Arthur Leonoff, Elyse Michon, Anne Marie Pons, Dominique Scarfone, Sam Stein, and Hélène Tessier. All the many participants in the "Confidentiality and Society" conference helped to determine the eventual shape of this book, but we have space to mention only a few who may not realize how grateful we are: Paul Beaudry; Ron Brown; William Bukowski, Chair, Department of Psychology, Concordia University; Howard Levine; Frederick Lowy, Rector and Vice-Chancellor of Concordia University; Yves-Marie Morissette, McGill Faculty of Law; Paul Mosher; Danielle Ros; and David Weisstub, Faculty of Law, Université de Montréal.

Yet *Confidentiality: Ethical Perspectives and Clinical Dilemmas* is not a conference book. Only one or two of the chapters resemble papers previously presented. While three-quarters of our contributors participated in the conference, the majority of them wrote entirely original work for this volume. Each chapter represents a vital strand in the evolution and refinement of a complex debate. We count ourselves extraordinarily lucky to have worked with so brilliant and distinguished a group of contributors, all of whom have been very generous with their time, thought, knowledge, guidance, and advice. If *Confidentiality* as a collective work possesses intellectual coherence and depth, it is in large part owed both to the individual contributions of our authors and to their supplementary care for the quality of this project as a whole. This happy result might have been quite different, however, without the timely advice of Donald Campbell, then president of the British Psycho-Analytical Society. And it would certainly never have come to pass if we had not had the good fortune to benefit from the experience and vision of John Kerr of The Analytic Press. John not only kept us on the right track in what might otherwise have been a frustrating labyrinth; he also influenced our editorial conception of the book significantly for the better. The confidence that he and Paul Stepansky, Managing Director of The Analytic Press, have shown in our work has sustained us throughout. We are also pleased to mention the cheerfully meticulous professionalism of the always helpful staff at The Analytic Press, especially Nancy Liguori, Senior Production Manager, and Joan Riegel, Promotion Manager.

Finally, each of us deeply appreciates the support and understanding not only of his or her own spouse, but of all three of them—Christine Ury, Thomas Milroy, and Frederick Lowy—whose patience and intelligence have enhanced this book at every phase and level of its becoming.

Introduction

Charles Levin
Allannah Furlong
Mary Kay O'Neil

*T*he International Psychoanalytical Association (IPA) Interregional Conference on Confidentiality and Society, held in Montreal in October 2000 and hosted by the Canadian Psychoanalytic Society, symbolized a new era in the history of psychoanalytic ethics.[1] Psychoanalysts entered into direct public dialogue with lawyers, judges, politicians, ethicists, social scientists, and other psychotherapists, introducing a specialized psychoanalytic issue as a matter of public concern. The principle organizers of the conference, the editors of this volume, argued at the time that confidentiality is more than an ethical or legal concept. Confidentiality is also a complex form of professional practice, with multidisciplinary implications, linking the most abstract dimensions of the "social contract," such as privacy and freedom of thought, with the heart of clinical practice, the concrete and intimate details of the psychoanalytic encounter and its essential methodology.

The aims of the Montreal conference were essentially threefold, and these have remained the motivating objectives of this volume: to call attention to developments in the law and the health-care industry that threaten to undermine the credibility of the professional promise of confidentiality, to explore the specific meaning of confidentiality

---

[1] Confidentiality and Society: Psychotherapy, Ethics and the Law—Social, Philosophical and Psychoanalytic Perspectives, October 13–15, 2000, Montreal, Quebec, Canada. In addition to IPA funding, the conference also received financial support from the Social Science and Humanities Research Council of Canada, Justice Canada, the Law Commission of Canada, Heritage Canada, Government of Quebec, Concordia University, McGill Faculty of Law, and the Canadian Psychoanalytic Society.

in the psychoanalytic context, and to invite public debate and research about confidentiality and its ethics.

What is sometimes described with alarm as the "crisis of confidentiality" has been brewing for some years; but there has also been a concomitant trend that is equally alarming: the flaccid response of the mental-health professions themselves. The sense that psychoanalysts in particular, who tend to be so knowing about the importance of confidentiality, were missing the boat on this issue was an important spur to the decision by the IPA and the Canadian Psychoanalytic Society to cosponsor a conference sharing the podiums and the workshops with professionals and academics from other fields, on an equal footing. Participants from other fields included a justice of the Supreme Court of Canada, the president of the Law Commission of Canada, the presidents of the Human Rights Commission and of the Information Access Commission of Quebec, members of Parliament, the Rector and Vice-Chancellor of Concordia University, the McGill University ombudsperson, the privacy advocate of the U.S. Department of Health and Human Services, the chief ethicist of the Canadian Medical Association, representatives from major law firms, administrators and legal representatives of public and parapublic social-service organizations, prominent legal scholars from all across North America, and philosophers and ethicists from North America, Europe, and Israel.

Thinking in public about the conditions of its own practice is relatively new for psychoanalysis. Critics of psychoanalysis have tended to characterize it as a secretive "movement," pointing to the "apostolic" nature of its early organizational structure and to its still relatively exclusive system of training (Gellner, 1985). These criticisms have been echoed in recent years by psychoanalysts themselves (Kernberg, 1986; Eisold, 1994). Among outside critics, moreover, there is a widespread, related perception of confidentiality as a disingenuous ethical rationale for evading scientific and public scrutiny. To overcome these not entirely unjustified impressions, psychoanalysis has had to recognize and to acknowledge its somewhat eccentric and therefore vulnerable status within the world of science and society.

The challenge will be to give a credible accounting of this eccentricity without retreating once again into passive isolation and defensive hermeticism. The task is hard because the material with which psychoanalysts work tends to fall outside the conventional domain of scientific and commonsense objects, gravitating to areas of subjective experience traditionally associated with notions of romantic inspiration, "madness," and the soul. In premodern societies, these domains were the preserve of bards, seers, mystics, and priests, liminal figures who normally acted under cover of poetic license or divine authority. In sharp contrast, psychoanalysis provides no such exculpating disclaimer, preferring to stand or fall on its own merits as an integral part of the contemporary-knowledge project in the ordinary enlightenment sense. It is a difficult area in which to do research and practice—a field in which the intimacy of the clinical encounter generates very particular and odd ethical requirements. Yet the profession does not present itself as an unfathomable mystery about which noninitiates have nothing worthwhile to say.

Robert Wallerstein (1976) once remarked on the "inextricable intertwining of scientific endeavour with ethical and moral presuppositions and implications" (p. 369). Such intermingling may be generally true of all fields of inquiry, but there are reasons to think that it is a special problem for psychoanalysis. Normally, the intertwining of which Wallerstein spoke is not so "inextricable" that technical or scientific arguments and reasons cannot be distinguished fairly clearly from ethical arguments and reasons. This is not so easy to do in psychoanalysis. The relationship between clinical and ethical considerations in psychoanalysis seems to be so symbiotic that an analyst is likely to find himself offering clinical rather than ethical reasons for making an ethical decision. This reliance on clinical justifications for ethical precepts is typical of the in-house debates over confidentiality. Because ethical guidelines in psychoanalysis tend be derived from the clinical specifics of psychoanalytic practice rather than from philosophical first principles, consistency in the terms of debate is difficult to achieve. For example, sharply contrasting positions on the ethics of reporting analyses in psychoanalytic training may be grounded in similar considerations of clinical effectiveness and responsibility. Therapeutic and scientific arguments have been advanced both in opposition to and in favor of obtaining informed consent for the publication of case material (Stoller, 1988).

If the deciding factor in the ethics of psychoanalysis is often the clinical implications of the decision rather than its formal ethical significance, is the opposite ever true? Are clinical or scientific decisions made for primarily ethical reasons in psychoanalysis, as they often are in medical practice or physical research? The answer, here, is also less clear than it may be in other fields. To be sure, decisions about research in psychoanalysis have been profoundly affected by ethical considerations, but these in turn may have been generated by therapeutic factors, such as concerns about the effect of certain information-gathering methods, for example, the intrusiveness of tape recording, on the treatment process itself.

Another important example of ambiguity has to do with the "limits" of confidentiality itself: should confidentiality be broken in cases of danger to the patient or possible harm to another, such as suicide, homicide, or child abuse? The common strategy is to view this dilemma as a conflict between the interests of the individual (the patient) and the interests of society. This is not always helpful, though, because the patient's health should also count as a paramount interest of society, as does the security of the psychotherapeutic treatment (*Jaffee v. Redmond*, 1996). Moreover, restricting ourselves to the patient's interests is problematic since the patient may not know what his best interests are. A good example of just how ethically uncertain such apparently straightforward situations may be in psychotherapy is the famous Tarasoff case, which lies at the root of the existing reporting laws and informs legal notions of a psychotherapist's "duty to warn" and "duty to protect" in North America. It is not widely known that the Tarasoff decision never resulted in a trial; the parties settled out of court once the tribunal held that a therapist could in principle be held liable if he failed to warn a potential victim of a client's dangerous intentions. Even less well-known about this case is that the treating psychologist *did* in fact break confidentiality and report his patient's murder threats to the police, though not the victim to be (Slovenko, 1990). The patient left treatment as a result of this betrayal and committed the murder two months later. Would "society" have been better served if the patient's confidentiality had been respected and he had remained in treatment? Was the breach of confidentiality in this case actually in violation of all the significant values at stake: the aims of treatment (to heal), the interest of society (public safety), and the interest of the patient's victim (to remain alive)?

It is difficult to disentangle ethical and clinical reasoning in psychoanalysis for two main reasons, which distinguish psychoanalysis from virtually every other profession, even within the mental health field. First, the patient and the analyst are necessarily involved in an intense intersubjective relationship in which the roles of transference and countertransference cannot be set aside for treatment purposes because they are precisely the "stuff" of the treatment process. Second, the psychoanalyst is bound, clinically *and* ethically, to nurture the expression of unconscious mental life and to protect it. Both of these unique conditions tend to encourage a confusing, but in principle, defensible blending of the clinical and the ethical strands of reasoning in many vital areas of psychoanalytic work where confidentiality is concerned. The consequence, however, is that fundamental precepts and policies in psychoanalytic ethics remain provisional and highly controversial.

In the ethics of confidentiality, psychoanalysis is still at the "data-gathering stage." Indeed, as all the chapters in this volume make clear, psychoanalysis is still in the process of defining the terms and boundaries of the ethical debate. Numerous basic orientation questions remain unanswered. Is there an ethics intrinsic to psychoanalysis, and, if so, to what extent can it legitimately supersede more widely accepted bioethical principles and procedures of ethics? Can psychoanalysis be, in some limited but meaningful sense, outside the law? How can the inevitable tensions between professional ethics and public law best be adjudicated from a psychoanalytic point of view?[2] Moreover, what do psychoanalysts really mean when they say that treatment is confidential? Are they referring to a contract between two parties, and, if so, does the patient have the right to abrogate this contract? Does the contract imply ownership rights? Is confidentiality more like a sacred duty, as seems to be implied in the Hippocratic oath, a kind of mystical commitment to the patient about which only psychoanalysts can speak? Or is this esoteric connotation actually an allusion to much broader but hitherto poorly explicated notions about the conditions of professional life, a sort of "culture" of confidentiality whose parameters extend beyond the psychoanalytic dyad? Finally, whether confidentiality operates within or beyond the law, whether it is a form of contract, a moral obligation, or a professional ethos, why is it so important for psychoanalytic treatment? Is the need for the patient's trust a sufficient or credible explanation? What is the evidence for this claim, and how compelling is it to a disinterested observer? Does the practice of confidentiality have deeper roots in psychological development and even the biology of the brain? Does it in some way reflect the essential conditions of thought (Aulagnier, 1986)?

The editors of this volume and its contributors are not aware of

---

[2] In July 2000, the International Psychoanalytical Association Executive Council altered the statement "Psychoanalysts shall respect the confidentiality of their patients' information and documents," deleting the clause "within the contours of applicable legal and professional standards," thereby making it possible for the IPA to support members who choose to resist when ordered by law to disclose information on their patients.

any ideal method of ordering the many questions and topics that comprise the contemporary debate about confidentiality. To make things easier for the reader, we have supplied each chapter with a brief editorial note, an approach that seems less cumbersome than a lengthy summary of the entire book and all its varied contents. The chapters are grouped under four separate sections (Thinking about Confidentiality; Dilemmas in Treatment, Research, and Training; Clinical Practice; and Professional Ethics and the Law) that we hope are self-explanatory and thematically consistent. It was felt, however, that Section 3, Clinical Practice, deserved further contextualization. This section has been provided with a separate introduction of its own, in recognition of the vital role of research in ethics, and of the sensitive position in which clinical reporters place themselves when addressing the public.

The reader should not enter this volume expecting a consensus. Our history as a profession does not provide the prerequisites for such a simple state of affairs. In 1965, Anne Hayman of the British Psychoanalytical Society was ordered to testify about someone who was alleged to be her analysand. She refused even to state whether or not the individual in question was in treatment with her (Hayman, 1965). Sadly, her legendary example did not alter the disposition of the law, or even of the psychoanalytic profession, toward the question of confidentiality. The latter was not placed high on the psychoanalytic agenda of problems to be addressed until quite recently. The wake-up call came 30 years after Hayman's stand, mainly from two sources: the publication of a ground-breaking study by Christopher Bollas and David Sundelson, *The New Informants* (1995), and the American Psychoanalytic Association's amicus curiae brief to the United States Supreme Court in *Jaffee v. Redmond* (1996). Since then, much work has been accomplished; but if there is a consensus among the contributors to this book, it is that there is much work still to be done, not only in the form of research but also in terms of the internal organization of psychoanalysis, as well as in the appropriate public forums.

References

Aulagnier, P. (1986), Le droit au secret: Condition pour pouvoir penser. In: *Une interprète en quête de sens*. Paris: Payot.
Bollas, C. & Sundelson, D. (1995), *The New Informants*. Northvale, NJ: Aronson.

Eisold, K. (1994), The intolerance of diversity in psychoanalytic institutes. *Internat. J. Psycho-Anal.,* 75:785–800.

Gellner, E. (1985), *The Psychoanalytic Movement,* 2nd ed. London: Fontana.

Hayman, A. (1965), Psychoanalyst subpoenaed. *Lancet,* October 16:785–786.

Jaffee v. Redmond, 518 U.S. 1 (1996).

Kernberg, O. (1986), Institutional problems of psychoanalytic education. *J. Amer. Psychoanal. Assn.,* 34:799–834.

Slovenko, R. (1990), The Tarasoff progeny. In *Review of Clinical Psychiatry and the Law, Vol. 1,* ed. R. L. Simon. Washington, DC: American Psychiatric Press, pp. 177–190.

Stoller, R. (1988), Patients' responses to their own case reports. *J. Amer. Psychoanal. Assn.,* 36:371–391.

Wallerstein, R. (1976), Introduction to Symposium on "Ethics, Moral Values and Psychological Interventions." *Internat. Rev. Psycho-Anal.,* 3:369–372.

Contributors

Christopher Bollas, Ph.D. is a member of the British Psychoanalytical Association and author of many psychoanalytic articles and books, including *The Shadow of the Object, Hysteria,* and the forthcoming *The Return of the Oppressed.*

Ronald Britton, M.B. is president of the British Psycho-Analytical Society and vice-president of the International Psychoanalytical Association. His recent publications include *Belief and Imagination* and *Sex, Death and the Super-ego.*

Guy Da Silva, M.D. is associate professor of clinical psychiatry, Faculty of Medicine, Université de Montréal and training and supervising Analyst, Canadian Psychoanalytic Society and Institute.

John Forrester, Ph.D. is acting head of the Department of History and Philosophy of Science at the University of Cambridge, England. His writings include *Truth Games* and *Dispatches from the Freud Wars.*

D. Ray Freebury, M.B. is a training and supervising analyst at the Canadian Psychoanalytic Society and former chair of its Ethics Committee. He is also a member of the American Psychiatric Association Committee on International Abuse of Psychiatry and coauthor of a chapter *in Standards and Guidelines for the Psychotherapies.*

Allannah Furlong, Ph.D. (editor) is a member of the Société psychanalytique de Montréal in full-time private practice and coeditor of *Confidential Relationships: Psychoanalytic, Ethical and Legal Contexts.*

Robert M. Galatzer-Levy, M.D. is a training and supervising analyst at the Chicago Institute for Psychoanalysis. He is active in many areas of research. His two most recent books are *The Course of Gay and Lesbian Lives* and *The Scientific Basis of Child Custody Decisions.*

Penelope Garvey is a member of the British Psychoanalytical Society in private practice in Devon. She chaired the Ad Hoc Group on Confidentiality of the European Psychoanalytic Federation until 2002 and currently chairs the Steering Group of a research project on confidentiality with the British Institute of International and Comparative Law.

Anne Hayman, M.B. is a member and training analyst of the British Psychoanalytical Society (retired in 1998) as well as of the European Psychoanalytical Federation. Her numerous psychoanalytic publications include a chapter in *Within Time and Beyond Time: A Festschrift for Pearl King.*

Otto F. Kernberg, M.D., F.A.P.A. is past president of the International Psychoanalytical Association, professor of psychiatry at Cornell University, and director of the Personality Disorders Institute of the New York Presbyterian Hospital. He has published widely in the areas of psychoanalytic theory, technique, and research.

Claire L'Heureux-Dubé, LL.L. is a former member of the Supreme Court of Canada and past president of the International Commission of Jurists. She is the recipient of numerous awards and honorary doctorates in recognition of her many scholarly and judicial contributions to contemporary law and its reform.

Jonathan Lear, Ph.D. is John U. Nef Distinguished Professor in the Committee on Social Thought and the Department of Philosophy at the University of Chicago. His books include *Open Minded; Happiness, Death, and the Remainder of Life;* and *Therapeutic Action: An Earnest Plea for Irony.*

Charles Levin, Ph.D. (editor) is president of the Quebec English Branch of the Canadian Psychoanalytic Society; adjunct professor, Graduate Program in Art History and Communication Studies, McGill University; and coeditor of *Confidential Relationships: Psychoanalytic, Ethical and Legal Contexts.*

Robert Michels, M.D. is the Walsh McDermott University Professor of Medicine and University Professor of Psychiatry at Cornell University and supervising and training analyst at the Columbia University Center for Psychoanalytic Training. He has published numerous articles on psychoanalytic education, theory, and technique.

Arnold Modell, M.D. is clinical professor of psychiatry, Harvard Medical School and training and supervising analyst, Boston Psychoanalytic Institute. His many books include *Psychoanalysis in a New Context; The Private Self;* and *Imagination and the Meaningful Brain.*

Paul W. Mosher, M.D. is a psychoanalyst in private practice in Albany, New York and is the former chair of the Joint Committee on Confidentiality, and Executive Counsellor-at-Large of the American Psychoanalytic Association. He coordinated the amicus curiae brief to the U.S. Supreme Court by U.S. psychoanalytic organizations in *Jaffee v. Redmond.*

Mary Kay O'Neil, Ph.D. (editor), a supervising and training analyst of the Canadian Institute of Psychoanalysis, is in private practice in Montreal. She is active on ethics committees at the Canadian and international (IPA) levels. Her forthcoming book is *The Unsung Psychoanalyst.*

Robert Pyles, M.D. was president of the American Psychoanalytic Association and now chairs the International Psychoanalytical Association Committee on Professional Standards. He has campaigned widely on the subject of confidentiality and appeared as an expert witness in several landmark court cases.

Daniel Shuman is Professor of Law, Dedman School of Law at Southern Methodist University. He is the author of numerous books and articles including *The Psychotherapist-Patient Privilege; Law and Mental Health Professionals: Texas;* and *Psychiatric and Psychological Evidence.*

David Sundelson is an appellate lawyer in private practice in San Francisco and author (with Christopher Bollas) of *The New Informants: The Betrayal of Confidentiality in Psychoanalysis and Psychotherapy.* He has taught literature and psychoanalysis at S.U.N.Y., California Institute of Technology, and Claremont Graduate School.

Craig Tomlinson, M.D. is a psychiatrist and psychoanalyst in private practice in New York. He is also assistant clinical professor of psychiatry at Columbia University. Among his publications on the history of psychoanalysis are *Sándor Rado and Adolf Meyer* and *G. C. Lichtenberg: Dreams, Jokes, and the Unconscious in Eighteenth Century Germany.*

Confidentiality

SECTION 1

Thinking about Confidentiality

Introduction to CHAPTER 1

❦

Confidentiality as a Virtue

This chapter addresses the problem of threats to confidentiality that come from within the profession and during the ordinary course of good-enough analysis, particularly those related to the wish to publish. Jonathan Lear describes the existential complications for the patient and the analysis arising from the informed-consent solution, whether used during or after analysis. He advances the premise that analysis of the unconscious transference and maintenance of confidentiality are deeply interrelated constitutive principles of the analytic process and need to be enshrined as such in the training experience of candidates. Lear proposes that a psychoanalytic ethic needs to move away from contemporary Kantian universal laws toward a classical, Aristotelian concern with effective ways of building psychoanalytic *character*. In this light, confidentiality will be most meaningful when deeply internalized through successful initiation over time into the culture of psychoanalysis as a "master craft."

CHAPTER 1

❦

Confidentiality as a Virtue

Jonathan Lear

*A*lthough current concerns about confidentiality tend to focus on the intrusion of outside agencies, I focus here on a problem that is *internal* to psychotherapeutic and psychoanalytic practice. The question I raise is whether something is *inherently* unethical in the psychoanalytic situation. Here I am not talking about boundary violations or various forms of excess and bad behavior. I mean problems that arise even when we are on our best behavior.

The problem arises from a conflict between two important values. First, we need to transmit knowledge. We cannot train a new generation of psychoanalysts and psychotherapists, we cannot transmit new insights and improvements in technique, unless we can pass on what we know and what we learn. We also need structures of recognition—journals, professional organizations—in which true expertise can be recognized, and a class of teachers selected to impart knowledge to the next generation.

Second, there is a need to preserve confidentiality, a need that is special to psychoanalysis and psychotherapy.

In medicine, for example, there may be all sorts of reasons to keep, say, the results of an HIV blood test confidential. But a breach in confidentiality does not compromise the results of the blood test. In contrast, in psychoanalysis confidentiality is *constitutive* of the process.

I should like to dedicate this paper to Jay Katz, a wise and humane man who first taught me to think about psychoanalytic ethics.

Psychoanalysis is a response to a fascinating fact about the human psyche: it represses. The unconscious is constituted by repressing forces, and the analysis is a peculiar response to repression. It is an attempt to lift or modify repression under certain delicate conditions. Roughly speaking, an analysand enters analysis in a situation where he is keeping certain secrets from himself. The analysis is a transformation of a situation such that a person moves from a condition in which he is keeping secrets from himself into a condition in which he now has a private life. Now he is no longer keeping those secrets from himself, but he may choose to keep secrets from others. There is a movement, you might say, from secrecy to privacy. And the very existence of psychoanalysis depends on the kind of environment that will allow that process to occur.

As it turns out, breaching confidentiality breaches the process itself. Imagine a new reality-TV show, *Analysis!* in which people confess their inner secrets, try to free associate, and so on. There will be an "analyst" who makes some analytically minded comments from time to time. And we can tune in and watch the spectacle. Any clinician who has really worked with a person's defenses and resistances will see straightaway that this would be the expression of one more defense. In the name of "making the unconscious conscious," this kiss-and-tell would be one more way of keeping things repressed in the name of letting it all hang out.

The fact is, repressions don't get lifted on TV. One needs an environment of trust, and that trust is established in significant part by the maintenance of confidentiality. That is why, *in psychoanalysis, confidentiality is not just one value to be weighed against competing values, it is constitutive of the process itself.*

The issue does not simply arise because of the nature of repression. The mode of treating patients in analysis is the analysis of the transference. This is not just an analytic technique, it is constitutive of psychoanalysis. Now the idea that we are analyzing a transference rather than exploiting it, making suggestions, or engaging in hypnosis helps to define who we are and what we are doing. Not that we always succeed at our task, but we should always be trying. In this way, avoiding suggestion becomes a *constitutive ideal* of psychoanalysis. And there is a serious question whether this ideal is fatally compromised when confidentiality is violated.

One way to begin to see the problem is to consider the issue of informed consent. Three problems immediately present themselves. First, what could possibly count as informing a person? Second, how much of the analytic process would get disturbed by doing so? Third, who is giving the consent and for what is the consent being given?

When does one raise the issue of informed consent? If an analyst says at the very beginning, even before the analysis proper commences, that some of the information may be transmitted to colleagues or published in a professional journal, it is fair to say that the potential analysand has no real idea what his consent involves. And there really is no saying how much such a statement might disturb the unfolding of the analytic process. Nor could we predict what might never emerge precisely because there is an underlying concern that the situation is not sufficiently safe. It is easy enough to say "it's all grist for the mill," but it is simply not known how self-serving for analysts such a slogan is.

If one waits for the analysis to take hold before asking for consent, further problems arise. Suppose that there is a good working relation between analyst and analysand and the transference is well-established. If at this point the analyst introduces her own desire and makes a request of the analysand, this will obviously have significant transference implications. But let us suppose, for the sake of argument, that we could analyze all the transference and countertransference implications. (Obviously, this is unlikely to the point of being practically impossible.) The analysis would no longer unfold according to the patient's needs; it would unfold according to the analyst's desires. Of course, we should not be prisoners to a phony idealization of the analytic situation as having only to do with the analysand's wishes, fantasies, and conflicts. We can accept that the analyst is also a participant in the analytic situation. It is one thing to acknowledge this. It is quite another to use this acknowledgment as an excuse for taking over the analytic situation so that it is either spent dealing with the analyst's desires or it ends up in a defensive silence about them.

There would be a further complication for the analyst. The analyst would then act on a desire to communicate information and that is usually tied to powerful desire for professional recognition. As a profession, psychoanalysis is in many ways self-abnegating and, thereby, frustrating. Whatever good work you do is done in private. And it is critical to the analysis that our own sense of worth and good work is not overly dependent on the analysand's judgment or recognition. I do not have surveys to go on, but I do notice anecdotally among analysts who attend conferences that a certain hunger for recognition is not getting satisfied in the analytic situation. Fair enough; but there is then a question to what extent these desires are getting entangled in the countertransference. And what internal pressures are there to ignore the countertransference?

Certainly, these countertransference pressures can easily skew an analyst's view of the case. With some notable exceptions, a case that is a mess is not worthy of transmission. The generic analytic case history that one reads in a journal has this broad structure: the analyst spends some time in confusion; there are false starts and stops; there is an impasse or two; suddenly the analyst finds the impasse is broken and can see an interpretive and dynamic reason why; and then there is great progress. Is this really the way analytic stories unfold? Or has an analyst's own wishes helped to shape the story? And if an attuned analysand wants to gratify his analyst by presenting such a story, how many analysts are going to interpret that wish?

If that problem is put aside, there is yet another scenario. Assume the analysis is going well—the analyst is well aware of her countertransference wishes and is handling them well. In what seems like a good moment, the analyst asks the question in the most responsible way she knows how. In short, let us assume the best possible scenario for giving analytically informed consent. There is still going to be a problem of who (or what) is giving the informed consent and for whom or for what he is giving consent.

Precisely because the issue concerns the unfolding of the unconscious, if the process is working it unfolds in its own way, bypassing a person's conscious will. Here there is a question: to what extent can I speak for my own unconscious? From a psychoanalytic point of view, the answer must be: very little. The process of psychoanalysis—what Freud called making the unconscious conscious—is a process of accepting responsibility for one's unconscious.[1] It is precisely because I cannot speak for my unconscious that analysis is necessary. So if I stand up boldly and say, "I hereby give you informed consent to let the unfolding of my unconscious be public property," it is unclear what kind of gesture I am making. It is unclear of whom or for what I am speaking. And it is certainly unclear to what extent my supposed informed consent is actually disturbing the process over which I am supposedly giving informed consent. In the spirit of Rousseau, consider the man who sails his boat to the coast of an unknown land and who plants a stick and says, "I declare all this for King." What could he possibly mean by "all this"? What could this

---

[1] I discuss this in detail in my book *Love and Its Place in Nature* (Lear, 1998).

gesture possibly be? And yet, it may end up having the most disturbing effects on any poor souls who happen to be living in the region.

What about informed consent after a successful analysis? The
analysand is so grateful he wants the wisdom won from his analysis
to be transmitted. And the analysand now has the analytic skill to
know what he is talking about. He can continue his own self-analysis,
it is grist for his mill, and so on. Why not then? This is not to say an
analyst could never do this well. But, even here, there are serious
problems that tend to get overlooked.

Much significant analytic work is done after the analysis is officially over, in significant part around the question "what has my
analysis done for me?" The needs, desires, real-life and fantasied
quirks of the analyst are fading into the imaginative and symbolic
background, and the meaning of the analytic function, the meaning
of one's own past and future life, is coming into the foreground. It is
precisely then that the analyst injects his request. It is hard not to see
this as a disturbance of the postanalytic period, one that is induced
by the analyst's desire. (It is similar to approaching a close relative at
a funeral and asking a personal favor. Even if it is for a good cause,
it is not the right time. And if the issue is a charged one, then, however
worthy, it will of course disturb the mourning process.)

Either the analyst leaves the analysand to deal with the consent
request or invites him back to discuss the issue. Who is going to pay
for these sessions? Is this the appropriate time to have a discussion
about whether the analysand should or should not accede to the
analyst's requests?

So far, I've focused on the constitutive nature of confidentiality
for the analytic process. I now want to focus on the constitution of
the self. One of the psyche's fundamental meaning-making activities
is to construct stories about who one is and how one got to be how
one is. These stories occur at all sorts of levels, from primitive fantasies
to sophisticated narratives, and have many functions, some more
defensive than others. Still, it is crucial to its very constitution that the
self has certain self-defining narratives however distorted or rigid.
One of the values of analysis is to allow this narrative capacity to take
on less rigid, more imaginative, and responsive roles. Of course,
there are many potential problems here, and I think there are myriad
ways both analyst and analysand can defensively valorize the construction of narratives. In general, I am concerned that the analyst's
desire for a narrative can get in the way of the analytic process. But

I'll leave this problem aside and consider a different question: Who is this story *for* and, more important, *whose* story is it?

The answer ought to be that it is the analysand's story and it is for the analysand. But to what extent is this answer compromised by the analyst telling his or her story of the analysand's story? Isn't the analysis ideally supposed to be a place where the analysand works out *his own* story? Of course, the analysand needs the interpretive aid of the analyst. But the aid is supposed to facilitate *self*-knowledge, not the analyst's knowledge. And this self-constructive process does seem to be interfered with by any process in which the analyst is giving his own version—beyond, that is, the analytic activities of interpretation. This is another important reason for confidentiality: the analysand may wish to preserve the privacy of his story as a way of treating it as *his* story, not someone else's. For him, the privacy of his fundamental narratives may be constitutive to his own sense of self. Suppose an analysand treats the narratives constructed in analysis as essential to his sense of identity. And suppose it is important to him to keep that identity private. Must the analyst assume that this is necessarily an atavistic wish that needs to be analyzed *away?*

If the analysand knows that his analyst is going to be publishing material that includes his case history, that has to generate conflicts. In the first instance, if there is a prospect that the analyst will tell a different story from the analysand, would this put into question the story that he has been constructing in the analysis? But, if the stories should coincide, does that cast doubt on the story truly being the analysand's? Obviously, these are questions that can be addressed, issues that can be analyzed. But to take the issues seriously is to see them fanning out in all sorts of directions. And the question then becomes: to what extent is the analysis being hijacked by the analyst's desires?

These problems arise in an even more heightened form in training analyses. And training analysts who, as a group, are at the top of their profession are more likely to want to write up case material than are other clinicians. Now their material is, for the most part, coming from the analysis of candidates or from the supervision of cases presented by candidates. The pressures of their desires on candidates have not been sufficiently investigated. And there is a question as to what extent the training of the next generation is compromised by analyses in which very delicate issues are skated over.

In short, there is a tension between the demands of the profession and the demands of the art. Following the categories of the ancient world, I would say that psychoanalysis is a master craft rather than a science. (This is the sense in which medicine is a master craft, not a science.) It applies very complicated knowledge in peculiar ways with the aim of helping people in peculiar ways. To what extent has the professionalization of the craft gotten in the way of the craft?

Are there ways to deal with these problems? Or, do we have to accept with Freud and Janet Malcolm that psychoanalysis is an "impossible profession"? Is the conflict I have been delineating irresolvable? Psychoanalysts ought to be well equipped to think about compromises, to think about better and worse approaches to a conflict. I want to go back to one of my heroes, Aristotle, because a feature of ancient Greek ethics may be of help.

The psychoanalytic profession has unwittingly approached ethics from one particular point of view and ignored another. It starts with Freud. It is striking that when Freud was interested in myth he went to the Greeks but when he was interested in ethics he went to the Jews and Christians. For him, ethics was the Judeo-Christian tradition, and that tradition was the tradition of the Law. That is one of two vibrant approaches to ethics in the western tradition, but it is a tradition of *thou shalt* and *thou shalt not.*

The ethics of the Judeo-Christian tradition is an ethics of absolutes and laws. This is certainly what concerned Freud. He was especially concerned with how these absolutes emerged in a cruel and punishing superego. But there is another rich ethical tradition, which begins with Socrates, Plato, and Aristotle, and it stands in healthy contrast with the Judeo-Christian tradition. As an ethical tradition, it has been ignored in psychoanalysis.

Socrates, Plato, and Aristotle are all concerned with the virtues or excellences of the human psyche. They want to know what kind of character leads to the living of a full, rich, happy life, and they want to know how to instill that character. This is of ethical significance. In the *Nicomachean Ethics*, Aristotle makes it clear that laws and rule books are not themselves sufficient for an ethical life. Consider a virtue like courage. Aristotle makes it clear that there isn't going to be any rule book for courage, nor will there be any contentful law to obey. There are certain times when the courageous thing to do is to retreat, other times when the courageous thing to do is to keep on analyzing. Given any purported rule—"stand fast in front of the enemy" or "always say what you think"—there are going to be circumstances in which following the rule is foolhardy, immature, or rash, certainly not courageous. A courageous person, with a certain sensitivity to the situations in which she finds herself, will have certain motivations to act on that sensitivity. She will know when to step forward and when to step back, and why. There won't be a hard-and-fast rule; there will be a sensitivity to life's changing circumstances.[2]

This is of course relevant to the analytic situation. For an analyst must have the sensitivity to know when it is time to step in with an appropriate interpretation and when it is appropriate to step back and let the analysand carry on his own analytic work.

Are there ways to build up good analytic characters? Do we need to build up analytic wisdom or good judgment? Aristotle had a word for this, the *phronimos*, which means the person of overall good judgment, the practically wise person. Aristotle needed to concentrate on the *phronimos* because courage isn't the only virtue; it is one among others. There is also, for example, generosity. In a particular set of circumstances, the disposition toward courage will tell you what the courageous thing to do is, and the disposition toward generosity will tell you what the generous thing to do is. But one needs to know overall what the best thing to do is. That is what the *phronimos* knows. And that is what she wants to do.

What kind of training will produce an analytic *phronimos*, that is, an analytically wise person? That question is too big to address here, but it is one well worth asking. I want to concentrate here on the smaller question of what it might be like to instill confidentiality as virtue. That is, what kind of training, what kinds of procedures, should we have in analytic institutes and in our professional organizations so that we instill in our own psyches a disposition toward confidentiality, and good judgment when it comes to all the particular complexities of confidentiality that might arise? Can confidentiality be a disposition or character trait of the soul? Can confidentiality become a part of us, a part of the way we see the world, a source of judgment that flows from deep within us?

This question looks difficult to tackle. A tip of the trade I learned from Aristotle is that when a question looks overwhelming, try to break it down into its constituent parts, try to see how it might apply to particular cases. If we are thinking about building up confidentiality as a virtue in the *analyst's* psyche, then we have to think about what we already know is crucial to analytic training.

---

[2]See McDowell (1998, pp. 3–22).

In psychoanalytic training, the case study is crucial. On one hand, it is a peculiar form of transmission of knowledge, needed because the level of understanding psychoanalysts are concerned with involves complicated and hidden dynamics of an individual human being. On the other hand, it is also important to realize that there is such a thing as too much detail and unnecessary detail. Psychoanalytic writers like Hans Loewald and D. W. Winnicott are able to bring clinical material alive, but they do it with thumbnail sketches, and they tend to avoid the form of case presentation.

Within the analytic world, in institutes, on editorial boards, at conferences, there always and everywhere should be this question: is a case study necessary to transmit this particular knowledge? Of the clinical material that really is of value in this case study, might it be communicated in some other way? Sometimes the answer will be no, but it ought to be a question we are asking and answering before we simply present clinical material to each other. We ought not simply to assume without question that the case study is an absolutely privileged form of transmitting knowledge.

There is one important benefit of this process that has nothing to do with confidentiality. If we know that the published case history we are reading has really passed the test, then we know it is there for a reason. We know the author and editors have gone through the process of asking, "Is this case history *really* needed?" and this gives us reason to pay attention. As readers, we will assume that potentially everything about the case is there to expand our knowledge and understanding.

One also must keep in mind that there are intermediate cases. For example, often what one needs is a particular clinical vignette. One does not need to locate that vignette in a larger case study. We tend to take it as an unquestioned good to locate a vignette in its larger context, for only by seeing the overall case do we really grasp the whole meaning of the vignette. Obviously, there is some truth to this. But rather than treat this as an absolute or unquestioned good, we should think of this as one good among others. Another good is striving to preserve confidentiality. One virtue of removing a vignette from a larger context is that it helps to preserve confidentiality. There is not going to be a hard-and-fast rule; on any occasion, there will be various relevant considerations. So we need to think about promoting analytic virtues rather than enforcing particular rules.

Here is one example of how I have dealt with this problem. In the preface to my book *Love and Its Place in Nature* (1998), I wrote:

People tend not to understand how unconscious meanings extend to the tips of their fingers. In the thousands of occasions in which an analysand has come to my office, I doubt there has been one in which the physical act of opening or closing the outer door has not been fraught with meaning. One analysand, as he entered my office for the beginning of a session, would leave the outer door a fraction of an inch ajar. As his hand let the door handle go, it would make a gesture as delicate as any I have seen in a ballet. The next step in the *pas de deux* was being turned over to me: his fingers *told me* to finish the job and close the door. I, of course, said nothing; but as time passed and the analysand relaxed into his analysis, he eventually became puzzled by this gesture. Here is a small selection of the meanings that began to emerge as he associated to it: He liked getting me to do something; he enjoyed the feeling of control over me, for he knew that I would have to close the door. Leaving the door ajar meant that nothing he was going to say was going to be so important or private that it should not be heard by someone outside. He longed for us to be working together on a collaborative project, and if we both closed the door, we were a team. My noticing that he left the door ajar meant that I was sensitive. He was scared of what might happen inside the room and wanted to know that the emergency exit was open and ready for an escape. He was afraid that I might try to rape him from behind and he wanted to be sure that people outside could hear his screams. He was hoping that others might accidentally come into my office and then he would get a glimpse of what the rest of my life was like. He was hoping that others would come in and that he would be the object of their voyeuristic pleasure. He wanted others to know we were a couple. He wanted to be the star in a porno movie. He was teasing me, setting up a game that involved his wondering whether I would ever ask him about it. He was testing my analytic resoluteness. Closing the door meant sealing his fate. Closing the door meant there was no escape from facing his own mind. And so on [pp. x–xi].

Here is my thinking about this example. First, it seemed to me that it was important to provide some clinical material to illustrate the general point that the slightest bodily movement can be fraught with meaning. My claim alone that people in general do not understand how meaning extends to their fingertips will not be concrete enough for readers to understand. On its own, the claim is an abstract and empty phrase. Second, I was able to provide clinical material in isolation from the larger case history in which it is embedded. And so there is nothing in this fragment that picks out this one analysand from countless other analysands who give open doors meaning. Yet the particularity of the material adds life to the example. A reader can start to get a lively sense of the myriad directions in which an analysis might branch out in relation to one tiny symptom. This, I think, helps to bring the analytic process to light. Third, all the associations here are the analysand's. It is true that I collected them over years, and I am bringing them together to make a point. But it is not my narrative, nor do I disclose the larger narrative in which these associations are embedded. So, although there seems to be great particularity to the example, and thus a sense of clinical reality, there is nothing about the vignette that necessarily attaches it to a particular person. Many people could have come up with these associations or associations like them. (It is almost like looking at the x-ray of a finger: one has no idea whose finger it is, nor can one glean much of an idea of the larger skeleton to which the finger is attached. Still, there may be all kinds of things one can learn about fingers by looking at that particular x-ray.)

I do not pretend that this reasoning is not open to objection, nor do I think it complete, nor do I think that all clinical examples should be like this. But I do think that all clinical examples should be preceded by careful consideration of confidentiality before the analyst goes ahead. I simply give an example of the kind of reasoning that went into my decision.

Let me close with some suggestions for institutional reform. First, every institute should have an advanced course in ethical problems in psychoanalytic technique. This ought to be a problem-solving course, directed to specific cases and specific problems arising in the case. It should not simply be about generalizations concerning good behavior. And it ought to address in specific ways problems that arise around the issue of confidentiality. We develop good judgment about confidentiality both as individuals and as a profession by having continual discussion about how to resolve difficult cases. Not that there is necessarily one right answer about each case but that we cultivate a sensitivity and sensibility by trying out our judgments, by giving reasons to ourselves and our colleagues, and by listening to how others go through the process.

Second, there ought to be norms in the profession such that if a person is going to give a paper that involves a case presentation she has to explain why that method is needed. No doubt there are times when we have to pass on information to each other that does threaten the confidentiality of an analysis. But we should never take the threat for granted. It should be part of our professional lives that we assume that whenever there is such a threat to confidentiality there is also a requirement to provide an explanation and defense.

Third, as professionals, we need to come up with alternative forms of recognition. Analysts have narcissistic needs too, and there ought to be institutional ways of gratifying those needs without the analyst feeling pressure to compromise her own commitment to preserving confidentiality. To give one example: one ought to be able to understand from one's colleagues, one's institute, and the larger professional organization that one is regarded as an *outstanding* analyst without feeling pressure to make a contribution to knowledge. The truth is that only a handful of people ever make a contribution to knowledge and most journal articles appear mainly to promote the career of the author. Of course, as long as there are professions, the world is going to have to tolerate mediocre journal articles. That is professional life. But we ought not to be promoting articles that threaten confidentiality. And we ought to be thinking of alternative forms of recognition.

My other calling is philosophy. And philosophy, too, has become a profession. But within that profession there lives the model and ideal of Socrates, certainly one of the greatest, if not the greatest, philosopher of all time. There is reason to think that, today, Socrates could not get tenure in any philosophy department in America or Canada. After all, he never published. His idea of philosophy was to go to the town square and talk philosophy with all comers. It seems to me quite a healthy reminder within the profession of philosophy, a thought that combats pride and arrogance, to realize that the greatest of our practitioners would not make it in the profession as it is structured today.

Might there not be a similar ideal available for analysts? One might begin by wondering: why are meetings at psychoanalytic institutes called "scientific meetings"? What is the felt need to see these meetings as "scientific"? When physicists meet, they do not call their meeting "scientific"; it is just a meeting. They do not need to call it scientific because there is no question as to whether it could be anything else. Whence the anxiety about being scientific? I am not sure of the answer, but I suspect that it derives from the fact that, until recently, the psychoanalytic profession in North America has been exclusively directed by medical doctors. And medical doctors as a group do tend to experience some ambivalence and anxiety about whether their profession is a science. At the heart of medicine, there is the art of making people better, promoting health. Of course, this activity requires expert knowledge but, in general, the activity of medicine is not that of acquiring knowledge, but of applying already acquired knowledge in the practical activity of promoting health. Something about this makes doctors uncomfortable, and it leads to the promotion of a scientific self-image.

However that may be, as soon as one characterizes one's meetings as "scientific meetings," there is already linguistic pressure to conceive of the activity as one of passing on knowledge. There is pressure to conceive of ourselves as passing on facts, newly discovered items of knowledge. In this way, the scientific self-image of psychoanalysis encourages us to pass over important questions of confidentiality.

Obviously, one needs to keep up the most rigorous standards of inquiry and thought. By bringing the term "science" into question, I am not at all joining up with relativists or nonobjectivists. I am just pointing out how a word can have its peculiar defensive influences within a profession. And this should give us reason to become more conscious about how we can rigorously transmit knowledge without having to fall unconsciously into clichés about what knowledge transmission consists of.

After a word of caution, the most important point I want to make is not a specific recommendation but an expression of hope. Here is the preliminary word of caution. Even when one talks about how to promote analytic virtues, there is a danger of complacency. The problem is that if you really do believe that in the end there is no rule book but that you must trust the good judgment of wise people, then the wise people may complacently overlook something they ought to be attending to. So, to take a notorious example, Aristotle formulated his theory of the virtues in the midst of a culture of masters and slaves. He even devoted several chapters in the *Politics* justifying a certain type of slavery.[3] Complacency is a very important problem, and I see no alternative but to try to live with it in as vibrant a way as we can. Again, there is no rule book for overcoming complacency.

Alas, neither is there any Archimedean point totally outside the universe of human foibles, vanity, and prejudice—one from which one can stand and absolutely determine which judgments are good judgments. Consider the psychoanalytic profession's struggle with

---

[3] See Aristotle (1984, I, 4–7).

the question of whether or not homosexuality is a disease. What a marvelous mess! Professions exist to ensure a certain standard of training and good judgment. They do this up to a point, but groups by nature will also tend to promote the prejudice of the day, allow unwise people to acquire undo influence, squelch originality, and so on. There is no magical antidote. The best one can do is the best one can do.

Now for the expression of hope. To live within the human realm is to live with these sorts of problems. Of course, we can ignore them. But there is no good alternative to thinking as hard as we can about what it would be to train analysts well. There is no good alternative to thinking hard about how we might build up a good analytic character. To direct ourselves toward instilling confidentiality as a virtue in the psyche is, I think, an incredibly hopeful activity. For to think that confidentiality might be a virtue is to express trust in the judgment of those who do have this virtue. For it commits us to this idea: if you want to know what is the right thing to do in a particular set of circumstances, from the point of view of confidentiality, ask the person who has the virtue. And if you have the virtue, you can turn to your own judgment and to the opinions of those you respect. There is no higher authority.

This simple idea commits us to hope for the future. For even if we do not know all the answers to the myriad problems of maintaining confidentiality while transmitting knowledge, maybe the next generation will be in a position to know better. For if we do our best to instill confidentiality as a virtue in the upcoming generation of analysts, then we can legitimately hope that the sensitivities and judgment they develop will outstrip our own. It is always a pleasure when one feels one can trust the judgment of another. It is a special delight when one can feel that amidst the vagaries of human existence, amidst all the ignorance in which we live, one is nevertheless helping to train judgment in which one can trust.

References

Aristotle (1984), Politics. In: *The Complete Works of Aristotle: Revised Oxford Translation,* ed. J. Barnes. Princeton: Princeton University Press.

Lear, J. (1998), *Love and Its Place in Nature.* New Haven: Yale University Press.

McDowell, J. (1998), The role of Eudaimonia in Aristotle's ethics. In: *Mind, Value and Reality.* Cambridge: Harvard University Press.

Introduction to CHAPTER 2

❧

Trust, Confidentiality, and the Possibility of Psychoanalysis

Discussion of psychoanalytic confidentiality frequently predicates its value on the need to secure the patient's trust. In this chapter, psychoanalytic historian John Forrester questions the wisdom of this seemingly commonsensical approach. Rather than trust, Forrester bases the specifically psychoanalytic need for confidentiality on its creation of a "shadow relationship" in which words are separate from actions and lifted from their everyday performative context as speech acts. He argues that confidentiality is a function of the wider principle of the analyst's abstinence, fundamental to the analytic situation, which invites not just the trusting but also the negative transference and sustains the possibility of its analysis.

CHAPTER 2

∞

Trust, Confidentiality, and the Possiblity of Psychoanalysis

John Forrester

*T*he issue of confidentiality is one in which social and philosophical issues cross, where issues of psychoanalytic technique mesh with its theory, and where powerful political and legal forces put into question the very legitimacy of psychoanalysis. This is not a radical, original, novel, or even unorthodox view. Let me quote Kurt Eissler (1974), not known to the psychoanalytic world as a rebel against psychoanalytic orthodoxy or a subversive spirit, writing a long time ago:

> The psychoanalytic situation is a model situation, which is essentially historically not subject to variation. As far as I can see, only two societal factors must be fulfilled: first, the confidentiality of the analysand's communications must be guaranteed beyond any doubt—that is to say, no government power must be given the right to force an analyst to testify in matters concerning his patient (this possibly makes the practice of psychoanalysis under a dictatorship impossible). Secondly, a certain level of self-observational ability must have been reached within society [p. 99].

The first condition is entirely clear: absolute confidentiality is the first and principal social condition for psychoanalysis. Historically, Eissler was right: wherever the conditions for confidentiality were lost, as in Nazi Germany or Soviet Russia, psychoanalysis withered away.[1] It is the possibility that the corrosion of absolute confi-

---

[1] Whether or not psychoanalysis was feasible under the South American dictatorships of the latter third of the twentieth century is still a disputed matter.

dentiality in other countries that are not plausibly described as dictatorships, such as the United States, that prompts us now to recon-
sider the relationship between confidentiality and society from the
standpoint of psychoanalysis. That this corrosion is vigorous and that
it constitutes a real threat to the existence of psychoanalysis is, to my
mind, convincingly documented in Bollas and Sundelson's book, *The
New Informants.* Despite my respect for that book and my admiration for the courage and logic of its authors, I think there are still
things to be said, in particular on the question of why confidentiality
is so elemental a part of psychoanalysis. I have a number of entirely
different arguments I would like to make but will restrict myself to
one principal argument concerning the rationale for the confidentiality
of psychoanalysis.

Since the 1960s, when American courts put the previously little
contested "privilege" of the confidentiality of psychotherapeutic communications under increasing pressure, there have been legal attempts
to define what this rationale is. Let me take as a typical example the
Amici brief submitted by the American Psychoanalytic Association
and other organizations on January 2, 1996 concerning the case of
Redmond in the Seventh Circuit Court of Appeals. The brief argued
that confidentiality "is critical to building the patient's trust in the
psychotherapist and thereby fosters the 'therapeutic alliance.'" The
brief went on to reiterate this view in stating: "The possibility that a
therapist might reveal in a court of law a patient's most troubling
inner secrets would stand as a permanent obstacle to development
of the necessary degree of patient trust in the therapist and would
pose a significant, and for many patients an insurmountable, barrier
to effective treatment." I argue that this is precisely the wrong basis
for defending the practice of absolute confidentiality in psychoanalysis.
It is wrong because it assimilates psychoanalysis to other professional
relationships, such as those with lawyers, doctors, or therapists, and
does not offer a distinctively psychoanalytic account or a distinctively psychoanalytic rationale. To put this another way, one can
practice as a doctor or a lawyer under a dictatorship, but one cannot,
as Eissler pointed out, practice psychoanalysis. That indicates that
the condition of confidentiality is not just a supplement to the practice
of psychoanalysis, as it is to the practice of law or medicine; it is
constitutive of the very possibility of psychoanalysis.

To prepare my argument, I will make some historical remarks.
The word "confidentiality" is nowhere to be found in the early English-
language psychoanalytic literature; the word is not to be found in

any psychoanalytic journal in English before 1961. Before 1940, the word "confidential" was used principally to mean "confiding"—in other words, it was intended to describe a mode of expression, as when one says, "He leaned forward and, in a confiding voice, told me the size of his salary." I think we can conclude what we might have guessed at anyway: that the development of a self-conscious ethic of confidentiality in psychoanalytic writing emerged at the same time that medical ethics underwent a revolution, that is, in the 1960s.

This does not mean that a realization of the importance of confidentiality cannot be found in the early psychoanalytic literature. Far from it: the essence of psychoanalysis is the speaking of the unspeakable secret, and the respect for that secret goes without saying in Freud's early practice (though, as usual, Freud is as active in the transgression of his own implicit rules, for his own good reasons, as he is in their observance). But as well as being taken for granted, confidentiality is seen by some analysts as a useful technical ploy.

Take Franz Alexander (1933), writing about his work with criminals in Chicago:

> The only way to gain the confidence of the criminals is to eliminate from the analytical situation the usual attitude of discrimination against this group of individuals, as if they were different human beings. At the very beginning of my criminal work, I learned the importance of this principle. In the case of a twenty-one-year-old delinquent boy, I succeeded at the first meeting in gaining his full confidence and was myself astonished at the amount of confidential material obtained compared with the results of the two court psychiatrists who had investigated him before. To my question "Why didn't you tell any of these things to the other doctors? That would have helped you very much," he answered that it was impossible for him to talk freely to them because their psychiatric investigation reminded him so much of the investigation of the police and of the judge. "But you talk with me," he said, "as with a human being, and I do not even feel that you think I did something wrong" [pp. 189–190].

Alexander's conception of what he is doing combines two very different projects. On the one hand, he is acting just like a forensic investigator but has discovered that working psychoanalytically—in a nonadversarial, ruminative, and nondirected manner—is a more efficient way of eliciting confidential material. But it is not clear whether the position he takes—eliminating his prejudice against criminals—is a purely pragmatic ploy or what. On the other hand, he recognizes that this method of investigation involves putting into abeyance for an indefinite period of time the judgments of right and wrong and of discrimination between criminals and noncriminals. What is crucial, he underlines, is the "gaining of confidence," that is, trust.

But, to go back to my earlier comment: Is the gaining of trust what psychoanalysis, as opposed to psychoanalytically informed forensic inquiry, is about? Let us change the perspective somewhat. Say a clinical seminar is hearing about a case from an analyst in training, who describes the patient as "very trusting," or equally provocatively, as "having complete confidence in me and the powers of analysis." We know very well what the clinical seminar will telegraphically call this: the positive transference. And achieving a positive transference, especially the general relationship of trust between a client and a professional, is not even the end of the beginning of the analytic process, let alone the beginning of the end. That's because equally important, if not more important, is the negative transference.

I'll make a very brief digression to remind you that psychoanalysts would be well-advised not to base the defense of their discipline on the relationship of trust that develops between therapist and client. From the scientific, as opposed to the therapeutic, point of view, it is this relationship of trust—implying a mutuality antithetical to the ideal of the detached, objective observer—that leads many of those suspicious of psychoanalysis to see all psychoanalytic effects as produced by suggestion. In the extreme version of this vision, psychoanalysis is a covert form of hypnotism, in which patients come entirely under the power of their analysts and produce all the interesting phenomena of psychoanalysis in a state of extreme pliancy to the suggestions of the analyst. Such a vision might even draw upon Freud's own account of the hypnotic relationship as consisting of a group of two, that is, two lovers. Freud was in no doubt about the libidinal foundation of the positive transference—that blind trust in the rightness, virtuousness, and even heroism of the analyst. He called psychoanalysis a cure through love, meaning its final efficacy was founded on the positive transference. And he had no illusions about the specificity of this positive transference: such a method of cure was to be found in many places, particularly in hypnotism and nonanalytic psychotherapy. "[Bernheim's concept of] suggestibility was nothing other than the tendency to transference, somewhat too narrowly conceived, so that it did not include negative transference" (Freud, 1916–17, p. 446). In explicit contrast to this therapy founded on positive transference, on trust, Freud asserted that the distinctive feature of psychoanalysis lay in its analysis of the transference, in particular of the negative transference: "In every other kind of suggestive treatment, the transference is carefully preserved and left untouched; in analysis it is itself subject to treatment [*Behandlung*] and is dissected in all the shapes in which it appears" (Freud, 1916–17, p. 453).

Given the crucial significance of the negative transference for the characterization of the psychoanalytical relationship and its development, I therefore think it unwise to base the rationale for confidentiality on the basis of "a rational, trusting therapeutic alliance" (Kaplan and Sadock, 1995, p. 1775). Psychoanalysts are in fact distinguished by the neutral equanimity with which they respond both to trust and intimacy or mistrust and coldness. Not only do I think the rationale for confidentiality based on trust is misleading, I also think it is giving hostages to fortune. If psychoanalysts sell themselves as the guardians and indeed devotees of such trusting relationships, they will never be able to respond effectively to the charge that psychoanalysis is, from a scientific point of view, a folie à deux.

So what is the specifically psychoanalytic foundation for the absolute confidentiality that is constitutive of psychoanalysis? I offer the following hypothesis. The essential feature of the analytic relationship is that it engenders a shadow relationship, which is neither real nor imaginary. From this arises the lack of "probative value" we should accord "evidence" from psychoanalysis. However, this "shadow relationship" is thus far very little understood by the public or by the legal system. As the famous oft-quoted passages from Freud indicate, "we have no right to dispute that the state of being in love which makes its appearance in the course of analytic treatment has the character of a 'genuine' love" (Freud, 1915, p. 168). And yet the "new edition" of the prototype text that is the transference must be *treated*, albeit with great tact and sensitivity, as the latest version of the neurotic structures the analysis is meant to dissolve: the analyst must abstain from supplying what Freud called the "surrogate" satisfactions the patient demands. Hence the transference as it develops and envelops the analyst is an "artificial illness which is at every point accessible to our intervention. [It is a] "piece of real experience . . . of a provisional nature" (Freud, 1914, p. 154). It is both real (as opposed to imaginary) and artificially induced—in the sense, perhaps, in which the use of radioactive tracers in the brain induces a potentially visible tracery that can be mapped by brain scans of one sort or another.

Thus the trick—or the skill, or the virtuosity—of maintaining an analytic relationship is to be positioned exactly in the shadowlands, halfway between the real and the repeated, between substance and absence. The basic rule for achieving this is to maintain the entire content of the relationship in a reversible (because it is nonmaterial) mode—in other words, in words. Words here are contrasted with actions. We can contrast psychoanalytic language with the performative function of speech in court testimony, where words are bonds and declarative acts. In ordinary life, words *do* things as well as *say* things— they perform. What the analyst says has the peculiar character of not belonging to the ordinary world of performative speech—no promises, no exclamations, and no declarations but many comments, quizzical noises, sympathetic queries, and multiple versions of what the patient has said, all jumbled up and rearranged to make a different pattern. The basic principle here is the rule of abstinence that, I insist, applies to both patient and analyst. The rule of abstinence for the analyst is: the analyst never acts, she only speaks or communicates. As I wrote in *The Seductions of Psychoanalysis* (1990, p. 83): "The analytic position is one which accepts the patient's feelings, beliefs, perceptions as genuine but which does not *engage* with them."

This rule of nonaction does require the analyst to use every means available to maintain the "shadow" or transitional environment in which analysis takes place. One might say that the rule of nonaction flows from this requirement to ensure that speech never becomes act. It also follows that communicating with a third party about the patient is a violation of the rule—professional communication is the analyst's version of acting out (Forrester, 1990, p. 253). If one needs an indication of how crucial the question of communication with third parties is to those in analysis, all one needs do is consider the havoc this question can play with the training of psychoanalysts. A state of absolute and complete paranoia is regularly induced in such trainees around the issue of whether the analyst communicates anything at all about the progress of the candidate to the training institution. And, to conduct a thought experiment that indicates how potent this sense of violation by communication with third parties can be, let us imagine an analysand who is the CEO of a major corporation who one day tells his analyst that next day there will be a take-over bid of his corporation by a major Japanese bank.

If the analyst phones her stockbroker later that day to invest a few hundred thousand dollars in the corporation, I for one think she is breaking the rule of confidentiality even though she has informed no one, and certainly not her stockbroker, about the prospective take-over bid. Her investment is an act in the real instigated by the analytic process. Any action in the real as a result of, or in connection with, the analysis of a patient is a similar violation. One need only recognize how, in this imaginary instance, the analyst's stockmarket speculations would always have to be examined for their degree of *unconscious* seduction into and collusion in the patient's imaginary world. Therefore, even if the patient consented to this use of confidential communications, the analyst should not, for analytic reasons, be free to do so—should not, that is, enact the private theatrical scene the patient is enticing him into. The analyst is no more free to break the rule of confidentiality than he is able to waive the fundamental rule of analysis. As Freud remarked concerning this latter waiver, when asked by the patient known as the Ratman if he could be spared the recital of all the gory details of an imagined torture: "Naturally I could not grant him something which was beyond my power. He might just as well ask me to give him the moon. The overcoming of resistances was a law of the treatment, and on no consideration could it be dispensed with" (Freud, 1909, pp. 221–2).

So my new formulation of the confidentiality condition of psychoanalysis makes it a consequence of a broader principle, that of the abstinence of the analyst, which is fundamentally linked to the manner in which the psychoanalytic situation first provokes and then analyzes the transference. In this way, confidentiality is not just a privilege that the analyst grants to the patient (and which she is granted by rules of evidence or legal precedent); it is constitutive of the possibility of psychoanalysis.

References

Alexander, F. (1933), On Ferenczi's relaxation principle. *Internat. J. Psycho-Anal.*, 14:183–192.

Eissler, K. R. (1974), On some theoretical and technical problems regarding the payment of fees for psychoanalytic treatment. *Internat. J. Psycho-Anal.*, 1:73–101.

Forrester, J. (1990), *The Seductions of Psychoanalysis. Freud, Lacan and Derrida.* Cambridge, MA: Cambridge University Press.

Freud, S. (1909), Notes upon a case of obsessional neurosis. *Standard Edition,* 10:155–318. London: Hogarth Press, 1957.

———— (1914), Remembering, repeating and working-through (Further recommendations on the technique of psycho-analysis: Part II). *Standard Edition,* 12:145–156. London: Hogarth Press, 1958.

———— (1915), Observations on transference-love (Further recommendations on the technique of psycho-analysis: Part III). *Standard Edition,* 12:157–171. London: Hogarth Press, 1958.

———— (1916–1917), Introductory lectures on psycho-analysis: Part III. General theory of the neuroses. *Standard Edition,* 16:243–463. London: Hogarth Press, 1963.

Jaffee v. Redmond (1996), Amici Brief, see: http://www.apsa.org/pubinfo/redmond.htm.

Kaplan, H. & Sadock, B. (1995), *Comprehensive Textbook of Psychiatry,* 6th ed. Philadelphia, PA: Lippincott, Williams, & Wilkins.

Introduction to CHAPTER 3

❧

Having a Thought of One's Own

Arnold Modell's exploration of the emotional significance of the private self and its unconscious dimensions can be traced back nearly forty years to his classic paper "Having Right to a Life." In this chapter, he further develops ideas concerning invariant aspects of the human need for privacy and its social prerequisites. Although privacy may seem in many ways an abstract concept, Modell shows how it is rooted metaphorically in the body and expresses a profound neurobiological disposition. Analytic confidentiality emerges as a therapeutic and ethical response to this fundamental human need.

CHAPTER 3

❦

Having a Thought of One's Own

Arnold H. Modell

*H*aving a thought of one's own means having a thought that can be safeguarded from the influence of others. This then leads us directly to the subject of the privacy of the self. What is at stake when our sense of self feels intruded upon? How do we understand our need for the privacy of the self? There is a paradox that is at the heart of the psychology of the self. Throughout our lives, we maintain a sense of self-coherence that must be protected from outside intrusion; yet at the same time, we are exquisitely dependent on others for self affirmation—an issue I have discussed in *The Private Self* (Modell, 1993). This quandary can be observed first in infancy and remains with us all of our lives. The paradoxical nature of the self is, I suggest, a fundamental aspect of human nature, a paradox that is not resolvable. We are all literally self-created individuals, we bootstrap ourselves from within, yet at the same time we are exquisitely dependent on others for our sense of self, for our sense of worth and value. This means that our preferred view of ourselves, that we have so assiduously created and that we strive so hard to maintain, can easily be disrupted.

There is a certain group of patients who, in the initial stage of psychoanalysis, defend themselves from the analyst's intrusion by maintaining a state of nonrelatedness. I have described this as a "cocoon transference"(Modell, 1976), analogous to a fortress where nothing leaves and nothing enters. I have understood this defense as a means of warding off the analyst's intrusive comments and interpretations. The cocoon transference is an attempt to maintain the integrity of a fragile sense of self, to preserve one's own thoughts. It also implies an attachment to the other; the patient is reassured by the fact that an attachment to the analyst does not necessarily disrupt their own network of beliefs.

The Biology of the Self

That we create ourselves from within is not simply a romantic notion but an observation of neuroscience. Neuroscience has established the fact that our brains are unique organs. Brains are different from livers or kidneys in that the brain's structure is formed not only by genetic instruction but also as a result of experience. Our brains create structures as a consequence of experience. The brain requires self-activation for its own development. This can be expressed by the aphorism "neurons that fire together wire together." This under-standing of the brain's function was suggested as long ago as 1949 by the Canadian psychologist Donald Hebb (Hebb, 1949). The process that occurs when neurons fire together is called binding. As the neuroscientist Rodolfo Llinas observed, "binding events comprise the substrate of the self" (Llinas, 2001). The self, as is true of the brain, can also be thought of as an emergent construction that bootstraps itself from within yet is exquisitely dependent on the experience derived from the other.

Every organism from mice to men is biologically unique. Unlike the liver or the kidney, the unique individuality of the human brain has a special role in relation to its function. Although the brain's structure is genetically determined, at the neuronal level there is sig-nificant individual variability in the structure of neurons (Edelman 1987). The fact that each brain is uniquely different from any other brain is the engine that drives a selective process that organizes the brain's development. The Nobel Prize–winning neurobiologist Gerald Edelman's theory is based on the assumption that individual differ-ences in brain development operate at a somatic level in a manner that is analogous to the use that Darwinian evolution makes of selec-tion based on individual differences between organisms (Edelman 1987, 1989, 1992).

Having one's own thoughts, which define one's individuality, is deeply rooted in our biology. From a biological perspective, I have suggested that the self, as personhood, monitors a sense of psycho-logical continuity that is analogous to the body's monitoring of homeo-stasis (Modell 1993, 2003). This means that safeguarding the coherence and continuity of the private self is a vital function.

Identical twins have very different brains. There is no way other than through experience that our limited number of genes can program the brain's complexity. In other words, the psyche is tailor-made. The way we feel, the way we create meanings, and how we construct the world are exclusively our own, and we need to preserve this uniqueness of our perceptions. The narrative lines of our biographies are exclusively our own, and no single person's experience can be duplicated. The poet William Blake captured this when he observed, "A fool sees not the same tree that a wise man sees."

Protecting the Self's Autonomy

The need to preserve the uniqueness of inner experience from intrusion begins in infancy. Donald Winnicott (1960) stressed the importance of the mother not intruding on the infant's creative apperception of the world. He described the infant's spontaneous gesture, which a sensitive mother will meet without attempting to substitute her own gesture. When a mother forces her own gesture, preempting that of the infant, Winnicott saw the beginnings of compliance and the future development of a false self designed to protect this inner core of experience.

We know that the infant does not construct the self entirely from within. We also know that the sense of coherence of the self requires empathic attunement, a fitting in from the other, from caretakers. Infant researchers Beatrice Beebe and Edward Tronick believe that the mother and infant together form a homeostatic system, a mutually regulated, self-organizing system consisting of a shared intersubjectivity, a shared consciousness (Tronick, 1989; Beebe, Lachmann, and Jaffe, 1997; Tronick et al., 1998). At the same time that the infant experiences a shared consciousness, the infant also develops a sense of autonomy that requires periods of disengagement from his or her mother. The infant researcher Louis Sander (1983) observed that by the third week of life the mother responds to the infant's need by providing periods of relative disengagement. Intuitive mothers provide their infants with "open space," which Sander sees as the infant's opportunity to exercise an idiosyncratic and selective volitional initiative. Our biology is one of individual differences. The infant is free to follow his or her own interests, which may involve self-exploration or responses to low-level stimuli. Disengagement, a private time, has a place of singular importance that complements the infant's need for attachment.

If we take a big developmental jump ahead and move from infancy to adolescence, we can again observe the impossible dilemmas that result from the paradoxical nature of the self. The adolescent faces the daunting problem of mastering the quandary of discovering one's uniqueness, individuality, and special identity in relation to others, while simultaneously submerging one's individuality by the acceptance of the idols of the tribe, adopting the fads and mannerisms of one's peers that contribute to generational cohesion. Body piercing is a contemporary example.

The Anxiety of Influence

For adults, the quandaries that follow from the paradoxical nature of the self can be summed up in the term "anxiety of influence." We owe this expression to the literary critic Harold Bloom (1997). Bloom was referring to the problem faced by major poets struggling to preserve their originality while at the same time allowing themselves to be enriched by love and admiration for the works of older poets. Bloom has recognized something of great psychological importance. The anxiety of influence refers not only to the act of creation but to the universal problem that we are influenced by the imagination, values, and beliefs of others while simultaneously needing to preserve a sense of uniqueness of our own thoughts. There is an inner core, the private self, that stubbornly resists influence by others. The anxiety of being able to preserve one's autonomy and one's preferred view of one self while making use of the thoughts of the other is an aspect of the human condition, a fact of life. How can I remain the same in the midst of the other person? How can I maintain my own voice and not be swallowed up by the other? In order to maintain one's own voice in the midst of the other, one needs to be reassured that one is free to have one's own thoughts.

Bloom believed that one device that poets have used to meet the anxiety of influence is a creative misreading of their predecessors. We can take something in from the other if we put our own stamp on it. Winnicott understood this problem when he recognized that there is a need in all of us to preserve aspects of our innermost self; it is essential for all of us that a part of the self remain unfound. In a paper now more than 40 years old, Winnicott (1960) said, "Although healthy persons communicate and can enjoy communicating, the other factor is equally true, that each individual is an isolate, permanently noncommunicating, permanently unknown, in fact unfound."

Winnicott viewed the social self, the face that one extends to the world, not only as a compliance but as a way of protecting the innermost self from exposure. What he called the false self protects the true or private self from exposure. In addition to presenting a false social self, we protect the innermost self, the private self, by noncommunication. This is one of the functions of silence and miscommunication.

The need to remain unfound obviously poses a problem for intimacy. In some marriages, one spouse may be threatened by the partner's need to remain hidden. The partner may complain of being misunderstood while being unaware of a personal need to remain hidden through the use of miscommunication. For some, to love and be loved may mean a blurring of the outlines of the self, the boundaries of individuality, resulting in a merging or fusion with the other. One of the challenges of intimacy then is to experience the sense of merging with the other while maintaining the integrity of the private self. This need to preserve a private self is not sociologically a recent development. As the great 16th-century essayist Montaigne (1935) said, "We must reserve a little back shop, all of our own, entirely free, wherein to establish our true liberty and principal retreat and solitude."

We know that our sense of ourselves may be subtly modified in the presence of another person, but the other's influence is probably greatest in asymmetrical relationships. Psychoanalysis is one such asymmetric relationship. Having a thought of one's own has been a problem for psychoanalysis since its inception. Psychoanalytic technique is confronted with the quandary of fostering the patient's creative spontaneity in the presence of the analyst's authority and influence. One aim of psychoanalysis is to facilitate the emergence of the patient's freedom and autonomy, that is, to facilitate self-actualization. But in order to accomplish this goal, one must first become a patient, which means entrusting oneself to the influence of the analyst. If one does not entrust oneself to the analyst and to the analytic process, this is seen as a resistance. To become more autonomous, one must first become more dependent.

Freud recognized that psychoanalysis's claim to be an empirical science could be justified only if the patient's thoughts were his own. If the patient's thoughts were those suggested by the analyst, the data of psychoanalysis would be corrupted. This would be an illustration of what William James (1890) called the "psychologist's fallacy," which is the confusion of his own standpoint with that of the mental fact about which he is making a report. The analyst's influence on the patient's thoughts reflects the analyst's power of suggestion, a nonspecific aspect of the analyst's authority. Freud believed that the influence attributed to suggestion was present in every doctor–patient relationship so that all physicians, regardless of their calling, are unwitting practitioners of psychotherapy.

But Freud maintained that suggestion played only a minor role in the psychoanalytic cure. Freud (1905) contrasted the role of suggestion with that of interpretation by using the following analogy. He cited Leonardo da Vinci's distinction between painting and sculpture. Suggestion is like painting, where pigment is added to the blank canvas, whereas psychoanalysis is like sculpture, where something is taken away from the initially blank surface of the stone that hides the potential statue contained within. The preferred image of psychoanalysis, according to Freud, would be one in which the analyst chips away, bit by bit, the surface impediments that ultimately release the potentiality of the self. It is therefore an implicit value of psychoanalysis that patients ultimately discover thoughts of their own that were previously hidden. But the paradox for us is that patients discover their own thoughts in the context of the intersubjectivity of the psychoanalytic relationship, that is, in the context of a shared construction of meaning. To return to Freud's sculpture analogy, does the analyst play Pygmalian to the patient's Galatia? Whose creativity is it, whose imagination drives the analysis? Or who places whose thoughts in whom?

This transcendent value of being able to think one's own thoughts was made explicit by Bion, who constructed a theory of thinking. As I find Bion, nearly impossible to understand, I shall quote from a commentary by the Australian psychoanalyst Neville Symington (1990):

> Freedom for Bion is coextensive with the capacity to think a thought, and this capacity is linked to the capacity to be in relation to the sensational world in such a way that what is seen, heard, touched, and smelt is processed and becomes servant to the personal center so that there is a subjective experience. But it is possible for someone to be so screened that all this is by-passed, and there are just injunctions inside the personality, and the personal center is in total subjection to them [p. 103].

Safeguarding patients' rights to have thoughts of their own, although not described in these words, has been the focus of what can be called a reform movement within psychoanalysis. There is now widespread recognition among psychoanalysts that there have been abuses of psychoanalytic technique in earlier decades when psychoanalysts have used their authority to impose their own thoughts, opinions, and values on their patients. There is a story told, perhaps apocryphal, about a well-known analyst, who shall remain nameless. When the patient refused to accept her interpretations, she would say, "Why are you resisting me?"

Merton Gill (1979) was concerned with this issue when he questioned the effect of the analyst's authority in the interpretation of the transference. He questioned the widespread assumption that transference was the patient's distortion of reality. To speak of transference distortion assumes that the analyst and not the patient is in the privileged position to decide what is distorted and what is real. An interpretation by its very nature is an imaginative act. The question that follows is: whose imagination is at work? Is it the analyst's imaginative construction that has been imposed upon the patient? Or is it the patient that is activating the analyst's mind? It is now conventional wisdom to say that it is both. Some observers such as Thomas Ogden (1994), have described this as a shared dialectical process, comprising what he calls an analytic third.

We need to know a great deal more about this process. We need to know more specifically the influence of the thoughts of the other upon the self. We all have the experience in reading a book or listening to a lecture where, in one case, our imagination will be opened up and expanded, while in another it will be constricted and closed down. In the first instance, the self has entered in to what is communicated, and in the second instance the self is excluded. The Russian literary critic and philosopher Bakhtin (Todorov, 1984) has distinguished between speech interactions that interanimate both participants, which can be described as multivoiced, and authoritative communications that have only one voice, analogous to the transmission of a telegraph message that the receiver decodes unchanged. Authoritative discourses are fixed in their meaning, demanding a submission of the self. The self does not transform authoritative communications; they are received only as transmitted.

Finally, we must reaffirm the fact that allowing the other to have a thought of one's own has an ethical dimension, for it is an affirmation of individuality, a respect for the other's unique difference. It is an ethical dimension that respects the privacy and uniqueness of the self. And fortunately for psychoanalysts, it is an ethical dimension that is also good technique.

I have suggested that having one's own thoughts, secure from the intrusion of others, is deeply rooted in our biology. Our brains and minds are uniquely our own and must be safeguarded from invasive influences. Furthermore, we have a need to maintain the coherence and constancy of our sense of self. In this sense, our psychological self, our sense of personhood, reflects a psychological homeostasis that is directly analogous to our body's need to maintain a physiological homeostasis. For all of these reasons, when the private self is breached as a result of involuntary disclosures, that is, by a loss of confidentiality, this is invariably experienced as an assault on the private self. The loss of confidentiality, therefore, is not only an ethical, legal, and psychotherapeutic issue but is also a direct assault on a vital psychological requirement.

References

Beebe, B., Lachmann, F. & Jaffe, J. (1997), Mother-infant interaction structures and presymbolic self and object representations. *Psychoanal. Dial.*, 7:133–182.

Bloom, H. (1997), *The Anxiety of Influence.* New York: Oxford University Press.

Edelman, G. M. (1987), *Neural Darwinism.* New York: Basic Books.

——— (1989), *The Remembered Present.* New York: Basic Books.

——— (1992), *Bright Air, Brilliant Fire.* New York: Basic Books.

Freud, S. (1905), On psychotherapy. Standard Edition, 7:257–268.

Gill, M. (1979), The analysis of the transference. *J. Amer. Psychoanal. Assn.*, 27:263–288.

Hebb, D. O. (1949), *Organization of Behavior.* New York: Wiley.

James, W. (1890), *The Principles of Psychology.* New York: Dover Press.

Llinas, R. R. (2001), *I of the Vortex.* Cambridge: MIT Press.

Modell, A. H. (1965), On having the right to a life: An aspect of the superego's development. *Internat. J. Psychoanal.*, 46:323–331.

——— (1976). The holding environment and the therapeutic action of psychoanalysis. *J. Amer. Psychoanal. Assn.*, 24:285–307.

——— (1993), *The Private Self.* Cambridge MA: Harvard University Press.

——— (2003), *Imagination and the Meaningful Brain.* Cambridge: MIT Press.

Montaigne, M. (1935), *The Essays of Montaigne.* London: Oxford.

Ogden, T. (1994), *Subjects of Analysis.* Northvale: NJ: Aronson.

Sander, L. (1983), Polarity, paradox and the organizing process of development. In: *Frontiers of Infant Psychiatry*, ed. J. Call & R. Tyson. New York: Basic Books, pp. 333–345.

Symington, N. (1990), The possibility of human freedom and its transmission: With particular reference to the thought of Bion. *Internat. J. Psycho-Anal.*, 71:95–106.

Todorov, T. (1984), *Mikhail Bakhtin.* Minneapolis: University of Minnesota Press.

Tronick, E. (1989), Emotions and emotional communication in infants. *Amer. Psychol.*, 44:112–119.

———, Bruschweiler-Stern, H., Harrison, A., Lyons-Ruth, K., Morgan, A., Nahum, J., Sander, L., & Stern, D. (1998), Dyadically expanded states of consciousness and the process of therapeutic change. *Infant Mental Health J.*, 19:290–299.

Winnicott, D. W. (1960), Ego distortions in terms of true and false self. In: *The Maturational Processes and the Facilitating Environment.* New York: International Universities Press, 1965.

Introduction to CHAPTER 4

The Why of Sharing and Not the What: Confidentiality and Analytic Purpose

In a series of papers over the past decade, Allannah Furlong has examined some of the technical stresses inherent in the classical psychoanalytic frame and their clinical and ethical implications. Here she discusses confidentiality as a beleaguered aspect of the analytic frame. In the early 1990s, the legal fallout from the recovered-memory debate brought sharply into focus the dubious probative value of using in court "evidence" from the psychotherapeutic process. Defendants in sexual-assault trials began seeking access to the personal files of complainants. Bioethical conceptions of informed consent threatened to become the standard for all professional work. As a result, the psychoanalytic frame was placed at risk of distortion and collapse. In this chapter, Furlong reasons from the inside out the clinical and theoretical foundation for confidentiality as it is actually practiced in the psychoanalytic situation, the better to distinguish the specific implications for clinical work of sharing it with colleagues and with third parties.

❦

CHAPTER 4

The Why of Sharing and Not the What: Confidentiality and Analytic Purpose

Allannah Furlong

*W*hen analysts speak to each other and the public about confidentiality, contradiction and confusion may ensue. Part of the problem stems from the fact that we have been using terms borrowed from other disciplines, such as law and medicine, which are foreign to our technique and to our theory and which if applied to our domain actually misrepresent, and do violence to, our work. If we are to make any sense of confidentiality in the analytic setting, distinctions need to be drawn with respect to related concepts, such as secrecy, anonymity, privacy, and the privilege of nondisclosure before the courts.[1] None of these related terms, nor even much of our own public discourse on confidentiality, has derived from psychoanalytic thought. Moreover, the exact contours of confidentiality are more meaningfully understood as context-sensitive rather than absolute.

We need to situate our use of the term "confidentiality" with respect to the specifics of psychoanalytic work: the dynamic unconscious, transference and countertransference, and interpretation. What we mean by "confidentiality" needs to derive from these specifics. In fact, it seems that it is not our definition of confidentiality that sets us apart from the practice of other professionals but only our pretense

---

[1] I have tried elsewhere to explain to a nonanalytic reader why a quasi-absolute privilege for psychoanalytic treatment, consistently shielding the integrity of clinical work, is far more likely to promote than to detract from the truth-seeking judicial process (Furlong, 2003).

to a more stringent observance. Is what we espouse simply a super version of the confidentiality offered by other health-care professionals, or does it take on a specialized meaning in the context of psychoanalytic treatment?

Let me pause to address an unwarranted embarrassment about the complexity of the psychoanalytic setting, an exaggerated shame when we compare psychoanalysis to other scientific disciplines. Physicists have known for many years that light behaves like a wave in some circumstances, like a particle in others. Perhaps we should not be astonished by this observation since it is characteristic of all material objects to vary, sometimes radically, under different conditions. The three steady states of matter—solid, liquid, and gas—attest to the dramatic effect on molecular behavior from changes in temperature. Yet we can define an essential "sameness" to the elements of the periodic table by reference to their atomic weight and structure despite significant variations in appearance and behavior under different conditions.

Confidentiality also comes in a number of different sizes and shapes, each one an adaptation to a particular therapeutic context and aim (see for example the Canadian Psychiatric Association's position paper "Shared Mental Health Care in Canada" by Kates et al., 1996). This does not mean that confidentiality needs to be a concept impossible to define or ethically contradictory. I will argue here that much of our current discourse completely misrepresents, to paraphrase Bollas (1987), the "unspoken known" of our practice and of our implicit conceptualization of confidentiality.

The Concretization of Confidentiality

Jean Laplanche (1993) has criticized what he calls the "metaphysical temptation" present in some contemporary psychoanalytic thought, whereby notions that began as adjectives or verbs mutate into nouns, substances. Confidentiality has tended to become conceived of as a thing in itself instead of a qualification of the analytic relationship; this state of affairs is known among philosophers as "reification," and "hypostatization." If we go back to fundamentals, we would be hardpressed to see anything inherently sacred about confidentiality aside from the purpose it serves. It is a technical means, not a moral goal. A protection of the information circulated in the consulting room, the primary rationale for confidentiality in psychoanalytic treatment, promotes the free-association process in the patient and analyst. By reminding ourselves of the function of confidentiality as an essential characteristic and containing property of the framework, we are brought back to its *purpose* in permitting safe and uncontaminated movement from inchoate experience to thought experiment and eventual mentalization by the patient-psychoanalyst dyad.

Analysts have resisted third-party reporting, not so much to safeguard patient privacy as such but because of the insidious effects of outside pressure on the freedom of patients' associations and on the benevolent neutrality of our listening. It is in permitting the suspension of reality claims that confidentiality takes on unique importance to the psychoanalytic relationship and not as a transcendent moral claim. If confidentiality is asserted as an "absolute" value that we must obey without reference to context and function as part of ongoing real psychoanalytic relationships, then it risks becoming a "thing-presentation" rather than a "word-presentation." It will be recalled that for Freud (1915) the unconscious is synonymous with isolation from the network of verbal associations.

Let us examine a typical definition of confidentiality by which analysts try (impossibly) to measure themselves. An exemplary definition appeared in a recent issue of *The Canadian Psychiatric Journal*: "Confidentiality can be defined as the ethical, professional, and legal obligation of a physician not to disclose what is communicated to him or her within the physician-patient relationship" (Chaimowitz, Glancy, and Blackburn, 2000, p. 900).[2]

One has only to scratch the surface of this type of definition to realize that it cannot guide psychoanalytic work. Almost literally a promise of secrecy, confidentiality conceived of in this way is a point of honor more or less identically applicable to a number of health- and nonhealth-professional relationships. Nor can confidentiality, as practiced by psychoanalysts, be viewed as primarily a protection of patient privacy, however crucial privacy is in its own right to individual psychological autonomy and integrity. There are a number of aspects of the practice of confidentiality in our discipline that all

---

[2]A similar definition can be found in the Health Information Privacy Code of the Canadian Medical Association (1998), which states:

> [The] "duty of confidentiality" means the duty of physicians and other health professionals in a fiduciary relationship with patients to ensure that health information is kept secret and not disclosed or made accessible to others unless authorized by patient consent [p. 998].

psychoanalysts basically "know" but that cannot be shoehorned into the ethical categories of other mental-health professions: that psychoanalytic confidentiality is not equivalent to secrecy; that patient privacy is only part of what is at stake in psychoanalytic treatment; that confidentiality in our field serves treatment integrity rather than patients' interests in the lay sense; that in order for confidentiality to be waived, patient consent is a necessary, but not sufficient, condition; and that the boundaries of confidentiality can, and often must, extend beyond the dyad.

I will try to show how we are led to a necessary triangulation of confidentiality among psychoanalysts. For a number of reasons inherent to the psychoanalytic relationship, psychoanalysts must share information about their patients and themselves with other analysts or foreclose entire sectors of their clinical comprehension and interpretive reach. They must share for the sake of the integrity of the treatment in its aim of unraveling unconscious derivatives, whereas automatic disclosure based on patient consent can lead us into unsuitable applications of contemporary ethical principles.

We have all too often reified confidentiality in one corner of our mind as an ethical ideal that has been pulled free from its therapeutic function and then enshrined as a moral precept owed in an absolute fashion to the patient. Yet as students of unconscious communication, we know that context is everything, that meaning can never be divorced from the transference-countertransference field, and that patients and analysts are perfectly capable—by means of the irrepressible inventiveness of primary-process thought—of disguising selfish, and even reprehensible, motives in apparently ethical behavior. We know that patients are often the most eager accomplices in undermining the confidentiality of their treatments, as they attempt to engage us as white knights against the dragons of their imaginary and real universes. It is quite possible to find ourselves asserting confidentiality against the patient's protests, against even what she believes to be her best interests. This is odd behavior if we subscribe to the idea that patients can waive their claim to confidentiality. This apparent contradiction dissipates *if confidentiality is understood as a factor contributing to the integrity of the psychoanalytic relationship, safeguarding the analyst's, as well as the patient's, mental freedom and honesty.*

I propose that we regard confidentiality as a "skin" rather than as a "lock." It must breathe, be flexible to context, and, if need be, stretch to contain therapeutic work in extreme situations. Both skins and locks act as containers, but whereas the former is a porous, dynamic membrane enveloping the entire therapeutic unit, the latter is a mechanical device, impervious to ambiance or relationship, designed exclusively for the protection of the patient in whose hand the "key" allegedly lies. It seems wrongheaded to overemphasize the concrete content of what is divulged outside the therapeutic relationship at the expense of the contextual and relational import of that content.

For example, when a man reveals fantasies of brutally attacking his estranged wife, some contemporary ethicists might view this admission as creating the following dilemma for the clinician: Should I betray his confidence in alerting the authorities or his wife? Yet research has shown that third-party warnings are ineffective in averting violence (Stone, 1988; Dietz, 1990; Slovenko, 1998b). Realistically, this content cannot be judged out of a context, a context that includes the patient's mental status, his accessibility to interpretation and ability to stand back from his aggressive impulses, his depth of commitment to psychological treatment or his capacity to benefit from it (or both), the treatment setting in which the revelation takes place, and the quality of the therapeutic relationship. Most experienced clinicians would not frame the problem as an opposition between the patient's interests and third parties. Most clinicians naturally conceptualize confidentiality as integral to treatment integrity, so they would be more likely to posit the issue raised by a patient's violent fantasies in clinical terms: Is the current treatment plan adequate in the present context to protect the patient from a violent acting out? Violence is not only dangerous to other people; it is equally disastrous to the patient by virtue of concomitant treatment failure, legal repercussions, alienation from family and community, deep despair and regret over the often irreparable consequences of his actions, and potential suicide.

The confidentiality question is best posed uncluttered by secondary legal or social claims: in the present context, should a "third"—professional, family member, or institution—be involved so as to ensure that the patient's aggressive impulses receive optimal treatment? In arguing for fidelity to clinical goals, I am attempting to rehabilitate the traditional backbone of mental health guidelines, which has been vitiated by the antipsychiatric movement of the 1970s and also in the wake of the famous, but much misunderstood, Tarasoff California Supreme Court decision. Slovenko (1998a, 1998b) and Stone

(1988) have shown that this legal decision and a number of academic criticisms of allegedly paternalistic and patriarchal professional attitudes and past psychiatric abuse of civil rights have had unfortunate defensive effects on clinical practice.

The Specific Function of Confidentiality in the Analytic Process

Freud pointed out that the patient's attempt to shield secrets under any guise—altruistic, patriotic, or otherwise—quickly creates a log-jam in the free flow of ideas. Defining confidentiality as a promise to "never tell anything" outside of the relationship could risk the same effect since it doesn't take into account the impact of the outsider's listening on the combined freedom of thought in the analyst and freedom of speech in the analysand. In other words, it does not take into account the *purpose* of the outsider's listening. When we swear our allegiance to "absolute" confidentiality, it makes far more analytic sense to interpret this as faithfulness to an ideal of analytic listening rather than as a concrete question of information passing outside of the dyad. The confidentiality of the process is there to unfetter the patient's discourse and the analyst's reverie. *The circulation of information outside the dyad need not be toxic, may or may not disrupt the analytic couple's openness to new meaning. Key to contamination and inhibition of analytic work is whether or not disclosure continues to serve an analytic end.*

Confidentiality is not so much an ethical matter as a clinical one, the final arbiter of ethical decisions being faithfulness to clinical considerations in the context of our best theoretical understanding. Regarding the narrower issue of patient consent for presentation or publication, Robert Michels (2000) has arrived at a similar conclusion: "The question of autonomy makes clear that consent is as much a clinical as an ethical issue" (p. 369).

Confidentiality in the analytic setting is an inherent part of an offer of a containing space. This containing function should not be mistaken as hermetic. It is not mainly insofar as it "creates an atmosphere of trust" that confidentiality is to be appreciated. Derived from the willingness to treat all confidences with the same benevolent neutrality, a specifically psychoanalytic technical aim, confidentiality's true function is to allow new signification to be generated out of the patient's communications to his analyst. By shielding the relationship from outside pressures, confidentiality adds to the "as if" atmosphere of the session. Encouraged to say anything coming to mind—his trust, yes, but also possibly his hate and his lack of confidence toward us—confidentiality ensures that none of the patient's material will have repercussions on either the relationship with us or on his life outside our office. New suppleness arises in dealing with awkward ethical decisions when we discard the notion of confidentiality as an oath of nondivulgation and recast it as a protective shield for an analytic mode of listening.

Rather than akin to secrecy, is not our promise of confidentiality more properly constituted as a promise to *contain, associate to, and cathect the ongoing generation of meaning within sessions?* It is as a filter against third-party requests to examine clinical material for nonanalytic ends, not as moral code of secrecy, that confidentiality supports the breaking down of old links and the evolution of new ones. The word "secret" comes from *secernere,* which means "to set apart," suggesting hidden, separate, and split-off; whereas "confidentiality" derives from *com* ("together," "with") and *fidere,* meaning to "have confidence in" (Little, Fowler, and Coulson, 1973). We have here a historical reminder that the natural movement of confidentiality is relational sharing, quite the contrary of the blocked communication supposed by secrecy.

When the representational work of the analytic couple is threatened, either on the patient's side by a transferential impasse or pressure to act out or on the analyst's side by a disruption in her capacity to metabolize transferential and counter-transferential affects, the analyst may need the opportunity of relying on other analytic ears for guidance in reinstating the containing and symbolizing function of her "analyzing capacity." Rather than be understood as an inert "setting apart," our notion of confidentiality should allow for an elasticity—at the analyst's discretion—in broadening the containing function beyond the dyad to include analytic listening "with" someone else. As an integral element in the *containing-situation,* a term I employ to distinguish it from the framework understood as the technical parameters of the dyadic relationship, we can expect the boundary of confidentiality to fall most of the time at the limit of the therapeutic couple, though this boundary can, and should be, flexible, *enlarging when needed to permit triangulation of the analytic listening-instrument.*[3] Viewed in this way, *the ethical criterion for disclosure becomes: will it further the analytic listening and thus the treatment, or is it for unrelated purposes which may disrupt this listening?*

A valuable metaphorical adjunct to our usual images of containing environment and framework has been proposed by Donnet (1995). He offers the notion of "analytic site" as a useful "figuration" of the space offered by the analyst for psychic "occupation" by the future patient. Not only is this space temporal and geographical in the way we are used to thinking of the psychoanalytic "frame," but also the notion of site includes the condensation of historical, social, and psychological "local elements" which make up the analyst's mind and personality at the time of meeting the patient. Thus, the analyst's personal metabolization of analytic theory, the conjuncture of socio-cultural representations of psychoanalysis where and when the analysis takes place, and the analyst's parting and ongoing countertransference state all are factors in the virtual-emotional landscape of the analytic site made available to the patient. Besides the heuristic value of explicitly including the individual analyst's mind as part of the therapeutic setup, this notion has the further value of encouraging us to remember that in coming into treatment the patient is hoping to grow and develop psychologically beyond the confines of his or her past. As Donnet explains,

---

[3] The importance of regular consultation for psychoanalysts and psychotherapists has been stressed by two recent contributions on the part of Gabbard (2000) and Pizer (2000). Gabbard offers a very interesting and provocative hypothesis as to one reason why this consultation should be encouraged as part of ongoing analytic identity:

> In my experience as a consultant, supervisor, and analyst, I have become convinced that the wish for specialness and exclusivity is a powerful factor in the choice of a career as an analyst or therapist. . . . We have arranged our lives so that we have a succession of one-to-one exclusive relationships guarded by the mantle of a radical form of privacy. Obviously, there is a quasi-incestuous arrangement inherent in analysis, where the secrecy of the setting can resemble forbidden activity, in reality or fantasy, with one parent or the other. Hence, I am suggesting that at some level the practice of analysis represents an unmentalized enactment of the wish to have a parent exclusively to oneself outside the awareness of the other parent. . . . Although many rationalizations are used for not seeking consultation—including lack of time, lack of money, and high regard for confidentiality—at the core of many such resistances is the wish not to have the privacy shattered by a third party [pp. 211–212].

This [transferential] movement [by the patient] to invest [the site] must be described as a use, as a potentially creative exploitation of it. In effect, as soon as transference is no longer immediately reduced to a fragment of pure repetition, we can conceptualize— and welcome it—as a fragment of [psychic] expansion [p. 39, my translation].

Without the confidential containing-situation of an interanalytic space to expand our own countertransference into, we may not always be able to allow certain patients the unique occupation of the analytic site necessary for the expression and representation of their particular unconscious conflicts.

Conclusion

I have argued that because confidentiality is an integral aspect of the containing function of the psychoanalytic situation, it does not make sense to restrict its meaning to the protection of information circulating exclusively between analyst and patient. Idiosyncratic to the study of the unconscious is the fact that therapist and patient are both, though not symmetrically nor equally, subject to the same primary processes. In a highly unique manner not to be found in the professional culture of other disciplines, the psychoanalyst cannot work continuously alone with patients because, like his patients, it is impossible for him to be always fully aware of "what he knows" unless reflected back from another. Confidentiality for the analyst is more usefully understood as including, rather than as in opposition to, the self-initiated, as needed, expansion of information-sharing into the safety of an interanalytic space, a flexible skin instead of a mechanical lock.

References

Bollas, C. (1987), *In the Shadow of the Object*. New York: Columbia University Press.

Canadian Medical Association (1998), Health Information Privacy Code. *Canad. Med. Assn. J.*, 159:97–1006.

Chaimowitz, G., Glancy, G. & Blackburn, J. (2000), The duty to warn and protect— impact on practice. *Canad. J. Psychiat.*, 45:899–904.

Dietz, P. E. (1990), Defenses against dangerous people when arrest and commitment fail. In: *Review of Clinical Psychiatry and the Law, Vol. 1*, ed. R. Simon. Washington, DC: American Psychiatric Press, pp. 205–219.

Donnet, J.-L. (1995), Le site analytique et la situation analysante. In: *Le Divan bien tempéré.* Paris: Presses Universitaires de France, pp. 7–47.

Freud, S. (1913), On beginning the treatment. (Further recommendations on the technique of psycho-analysis I. *Standard Edition*, 12:122–144. London: Hogarth Press, 1955.

────── (1915), The unconscious. *Standard Edition*, 14:166–215. London: Hogarth Press, 1955.

Furlong, A. (2003), The questionable contribution of psychotherapeutic and psychoanalytic records to the truth-seeking process. In: *Confidential Relationships,* ed. C. Koggel, A. Furlong, & C. Levin. Amsterdam: Editions Rodopi B.V.

Gabbard, G. O. (2000), Consultation from the consultant's perspective. *Psychoanal. Dial.,* 10:209–218.

Kates, N., Craven, M., Bishop, J., Clinton, T., Kraftcheck, D., LeClair, K., Leverette, J., Nash, L. & Turner, T., (1996), Shared mental health care in Canada. Joint position paper by the Canadian Psychiatric Association and the College of Family Physicians in Canada. Available online at: http://www.cpa-apc.org/Publications/Position_Papers/Shared.asp.

Laplanche, J. (1993), Court traité de l'inconscient. Reprinted in *Entre séduction et inspiration: l'homme.* Paris: Presses Universitaires de France, 1999.

Levin, C. (2001), The siege of psychotherapeutic space: Psychoanalysis in the age of transparency. *Canad. J. Psychoanal.,* 9:187–215.

Little, W., Fowler, H. W. & Coulson, J. (1973), *The Shorter Oxford English Dictionary on Historical Principles,* 3rd ed. Oxford: Clarendon Press.

Michels, R. (2000), The case history. *J Amer. Psychoanal. Assn.,* 48:355–375.

Pizer, B. (2000), The therapist's routine consultations: A necessary window in the treatment frame. *Psychoanal. Dial.,* 10:197–207.

Slovenko, R. (1990), The Tarasoff progeny. In: *Review of Clinical Psychiatry and the Law, Vol. 1,* ed. R. Simon. Washington, DC: American Psychiatric Press, pp. 177–190.

────── (1998), *Psychotherapy and Confidentiality.* Springfield, IL: Thomas.

Stone, A. (1988), The *Tarasoff* case and some of its progeny: Suing psychotherapists to safeguard society. In: *Law, Psychiatry, and Morality.* Washington, DC: American Psychiatric Press, pp. 154–190.

Introduction to CHAPTER 5

❧

Civic Confidentiality and Psychoanalytic Confidentiality

Psychoanalytic confidentiality is part of a culture that has developed implicitly over 100 years of practice. Legal conceptions of confidentiality, by contrast, have developed in explicit, rationalized ways appropriate for public discourse and the administration of the law, which have a much longer history. Charles Levin argues that the disparity between these civic contexts of reasoning and the psychoanalytic situation makes otherwise normal procedures, such as informed consent, problematic. The gap between psychoanalytic confidentiality, which has primarily intrapsychic significance, and civic confidentiality, which can be explained rationally in court (e.g., *Jaffee v. Redmond*), needs to be acknowledged and openly discussed.

CHAPTER 5

❦

Civic Confidentiality and Psychoanalytic Confidentiality

Charles Levin

*A*s historical studies show (e.g., Kerr, 1993; Lynn and Vaillant, 1998; Tomlinson, this volume), psychoanalysis did not actually start out as a notably confidential profession. This was probably not because psychoanalysts in Freud's day were somehow less aware or less scrupulous than, say, medical doctors. Of course, the fledgling profession sometimes got a little drunk on its novel status as a radical therapy; some of its pioneers, particularly Jung, were intoxicated by romantic fantasies of discovery and correspondingly ruthless, at least by the standards of today, in their use of clinical material for purposes of self-promotion. Nevertheless, most of the early analysts were medical doctors, and in all probability their ethical practice was roughly comparable to that of the medical profession as a whole. I suspect that it was precisely this sort of average, expectable practice that has until recently served to obscure consciousness of the very different function that confidentiality plays in a psychoanalytic context.

As psychoanalytic thinking has evolved toward fuller appreciation of the grip of unconscious mental life—extending the understanding of its role beyond intrapsychic conflict in the patient to the general and continuous interaction *between* the analyst and the patient—issues related to confidentiality have come to seem much more fundamental to the actual treatment process. We no longer think of confidentiality merely as an adjunct to clinical work derived from ethics; we are beginning to see its role as intrinsic to the therapeutic work itself, and to understand its meaning and effect as largely unconscious. This places psychoanalysis in a somewhat difficult position legally and ethically. It means that many of the standard methods of defining and handling confidentiality issues (such as the issuing of a Miranda-type warning at the beginning of treatment, the practice of obtaining informed consent when professional communication involving the patient is contemplated, and maintenance of a carefully documented, self-protective file of the treatment process) have turned out to be inapplicable or problematic in good analytic practice.

An important recent example of this was discussed by David Tuckett (2000) in an editorial of the *International Journal of Psychoanalysis*. He describes a new policy of the International Committee of Medical Journal Editors (ICMJE) making it mandatory to provide documentation of patient consent for publication and stipulating that "in all cases where patients' clinical records are disclosed in any way, there should be no attempt to disguise or misrepresent details." Of course, a ban on the use of disguise as a means of protecting the patient's anonymity would make ordinary psychoanalytic publishing virtually impossible. In the psychoanalytic context, as in no other, obtaining the patient's consent for disclosure is always a highly problematic and delicate matter. (I will discuss this in more detail later in this chapter.) Informed consent would become even more problematic under the ICMJE rules, which geometrically multiply the chances that the identity of the patient will be discovered.

In the psychoanalytic frame of reference, it is no longer possible to conceptualize confidentiality without object-relations theory and recent developments in the understanding of transference-countertranference dynamics. First, confidentiality obviously serves as a container for the analytic couple in multiple senses (Levin, 2001). On the societal level, it includes and provides the conscious and unconscious cultural underpinnings of social support for the analytic work. Where there is a strong tradition of individual liberty and privacy, in a society that understands the advantages of individual and professional autonomy and respects professional expertise and judgment, confidentiality in this externally containing sense is widely taken for granted—even when the legal infrastructure of confidentiality is undergoing serious erosion for administrative and bureaucratic reasons, as is the case in the Western world at present.

Confidentiality also serves as a container *within* the analytic process. It cushions the holding environment by helping to make the invitation to therapeutic regression unconsciously credible. It is also one of the mainstays of the analytic frame because it suggests and defines most clearly the imaginary boundary separating social space from analytic space, and the conscious and unconscious suspension of the rules and norms of social relationships and conduct.

The Unconscious in Court

In the psychoanalytic frame of reference, then, confidentiality is no longer just a concept or an ethical principle; it has developed into a complex hybrid related to many aspects of the central technical problem of psychoanalysis: how to provide the optimal conditions for the emergence of the "psychic value [of patients' communications], that is, their capacity to carry the contents of unconscious thought" (Bollas and Sundelson, 1995). I borrow the phrase "capacity to carry the contents of unconscious thought" because it emphasizes the fact that unconscious thought is never disclosed or revealed, except perhaps in piecemeal form; it grafts itself silently onto the affective and verbal currents of conscious experience, only gradually forming a recognizable constellation in the mind of the analyst, if he or she is ready and waiting. It is difficult to impart the epistemological ambience of unconscious material, the sense that during the gradual course of analytic treatment the entire mental landscape can seem transformed, as significant sectors of the personality shift newly into view. In certain respects, this may also be true for the analyst, who must deliberately place his mind in a vulnerable position with respect to the unknown and the unconscious. Both analyst and analysand are exposed to the pressures and vicissitudes of an intense emotional relationship whose transformative potential may simply be lost without the interlocking nest of containing functions that confidentiality in the true sense is alone able to provide.

This is not a formulation of confidentiality that will often be heard in a court of law, and that is probably a good thing. The law remains rightly wary of references to the unconscious, which is not something that can be responsibly accessed through cross-examination. Democratic liberal theory wants and needs stable points of reference—in particular, the construct of individual social actors with rational interests, fathomable motives, and conscious intentions who are aware of what they are doing and why. Without this kind of grounding in a commonsense psychology of consciousness, the law risks becoming the handmaiden of political irrationality, unable to adjudicate a potentially infinite regress of ideological claims and counterclaims concerning any number of possible unconscious social and psychological causes of injustice and crime. The bench and the court-room are not at all suitable for carrying the contents of unconscious thought, and any attempt to base legal reasoning on generalized theoretical speculation or "expert testimony" about unconscious motives, ideas, or processes would certainly put the reputation of the law at risk.[1]

Nevertheless, the need for confidentiality in psychotherapy, par-ticularly psychoanalysis, does not seem to be in serious dispute anywhere in contemporary society. The debate is about how confi-dentiality should, or can, be legally protected, if at all: when does the principle obtain, and when does it not? There are many reasons why the law might be sympathetic to the psychotherapeutic profession, but the intellectual basis for it seems to rest on three main pillars:

- The pragmatic requirement that the professional gain access to vital information that would not otherwise be forthcoming;
- Constitutionally based respect for private life; and
- Trust, which the first two imply in different ways.

It seems reasonably safe to say that a public consensus has formed around the idea that psychotherapy requires the patient's "trust." This is part of the popular, bedrock understanding of psychotherapy and how it works. Judges and legislators can listen without embarrass-ment to arguments linking trust to "confidence," not only in the psychotherapist's commitment to maintain confidentiality but also (increasingly, in the present context of professional practice) in the therapist's ability to sustain this commitment under social and political pressure. This is such a basic argument that it has come to seem almost axiomatic. Unfortunately, the trust argument is sometimes stated in a misleading way, which anyone so inclined could easily demol-ish, leaving confidentiality with only the rather precarious right-to-privacy leg to stand on.

The dominant model of psychoanalytic psychotherapy in the public mind is that it is a treatment in which the patient chooses to "disclose" discrete bits of information that have been kept hidden

---

[1] Of course, this natural judicial wariness about building in an active approach to unconscious mental activity is precisely one of the reasons why the courts ought to avoid psychoanalytic case material as inherently unfathomable within a legal con-text of reasoning and investigation.

from others. (Our tendency to add dramatic spice inclines us to assume that this hidden information is of special interest to the law.) On this view, the patient's "trust" in confidentiality is supposed to encourage the patient to "reveal" sensitive facts, things that the doctor should know in the interests of good treatment. Most of the discussion about the legal status of confidentiality turns on this conscious-information model of the therapeutic process. It is assumed that the patient is hiding something, that he knows what it is, and that he will make a conscious decision to go into therapy based on a calculation of the risk of disclosure to the therapist.

It is my impression that psychoanalysts have maintained a kind of discrete silence about the fact that this way of picturing the need for confidentiality is profoundly misleading, if not patently false. First, patients very often do not consciously know what it is they are hiding, if anything, let alone what they want to hide, so there is little likelihood here of a reasonable calculation of "risk." Ordinary human beings are normally ambivalent about whether they would prefer to reveal or conceal those aspects of themselves about which they are aware. One of the most difficult quandaries in psychoanalytic ethics involves the not-uncommon situation in which patients, for unconscious reasons, try to expose themselves in self-destructive ways, notably by using the law to transform the analyst's notes (a focus of intense fantasy activity) into an object of third party or self-scrutiny (see Furlong, 1998; Da Silva, this volume; Garvey, this volume).

A second but also very popular model of the psychotherapeutic process does involve the notion of an exploration of the unconscious. Unfortunately, it is too often conceptualized as the simple inversion of the consciousness model of therapy, particularly under the influence of popular theories of "trauma" and "recovered memory." Dramatic, Hitchcockian notions of what is involved in making the unconscious conscious have encouraged (not caused) an even more misleading view of what it is that psychoanalysts want to be confidential about. As in the conscious-information model, the hidden material in Hitchcockian therapy is still specific, factual, and of great interest to the law. Only it is "in the subconscious." The patient is not aware that this information exists, and the role of the therapist is first to uncover the information (perhaps with the aid of hypnosis) and then to help the patient use the information to bring about justice, which will complete the process of healing.

The reality of psychoanalysis is of course very different from these quaint fantasies. Psychoanalysts are neither accomplices to crime nor detectives in search of it, and the "information" they work with is only superficially factual, usually ambiguous, and changes meaning with time. There is no doubt that when analysands begin treatment they frequently bring all sorts of specific "things" they want to "get off their chests." They are often feeling isolated from family, friends, and colleagues, sometimes because they have managed somehow to get themselves into a "jam"—secret lovers, hidden debts, question-able transactions that may come to light, or shameful impulses that are difficult to conceal from public view. Their conscious motive for coming into treatment may be to find someone they can talk to with-out risk of disclosure—someone who will keep the information secret, give advice, and magically relieve the sense of guilt. What is less well-known is that no matter how much a patient may "believe" in confidentiality, he is just as likely *not* to "disclose" such "secrets," if they exist, until much later in treatment. The fact is that willingness to "disclose" may have more to do with the patient's evolving perception of the analyst, regardless of the state of the law on confidentiality, or the patient's evolving perception of himself, as it develops in treatment. What might have seemed too embarrassing to discuss at the beginning of treatment becomes a year or two later an interesting curiosity to be explored with the analyst.

Patients do not necessarily begin therapy laden with secrets; and even when they do, it is surprising how infrequently they are concerned about confidentiality, or the risks of disclosure, in a con-scious or calculated way. They usually just want to make sense of what they are feeling or not feeling, or to understand a strange mood that is haunting them for reasons they cannot quite grasp. Of course they do not wish to have the details of their private lives revealed to all and sundry. But it would never occur consciously to most patients that a competent analyst would violate the Hippocratic oath for no good reason. Even the reporting laws do not (yet) *consciously* inhibit so many patients because, after all, they believe they have nothing to hide and the analyst will have no reason to report!

The point is that whether or not the patient was thinking in terms of security of secrets at the beginning, the actual unfolding of the treatment will usually not have much to do with hot bits of "con-fidential" information. The latter generally play only a secondary or superficial role in the patient's suffering.

Indeed, there is the strong likelihood that in fact patients ordi-narily do not trust their analysts anyway. They may say they do, but analytic patients will normally raise serious issues of trust as time in the treatment goes on and frequently will betray a very deep-seated lack of trust of everyone, especially the analyst. Successful psychoanalytic treatments are frequently conducted in an atmosphere of suspicion and doubt, which only gradually dispels toward the end of treatment. So the argument that confidentiality is vital to psychotherapeutic treatment because it helps the patient to establish that "all-important" trust in the therapist is less than wholly convincing.

Does this mean that we have to abandon the argument that confidentiality is in a profound sense *constitutive* to the psychoanalytic relationship and process? On the contrary, it means that we have still to make a serious effort to substantiate this claim. In order to begin to do so, we need to distance ourselves somewhat from the standard arguments based on trust, effective as they may be for the moment in the courts. So long as we remain addicted to convenient arguments because they are palatable in the civic arena, we will never bother as a profession really to think through carefully the basis of the claims we are making in this area. Eventually, the flimsiness of the trust arguments will be exposed in legal argumentation or through the inevitably ambiguous results of research surveys. If psychoanalysis is not, at that juncture, prepared to advance a more sophisticated account, legal and public faith in confidentiality may be further undermined.

From a psychoanalytic point of view, trust is both supported and undermined in unconscious mental life and therefore deeply implicated in the transference. It is entirely possible, for example, that an analysand in Hungary after the 1956 Soviet invasion, when confidentiality was for all intents and purposes illegal, might consciously have trusted his analyst because he perceived him as someone willing to break the law to protect his patient. Unconsciously, however, such trust would probably have been fragile. To give a different example, the most scrupulously ethical New York analyst, who would go to jail to protect his analysand's confidentiality, might be experienced transferentially as a liar and a mercenary who would sell his patient down the Hudson River at the first opportunity. No amount of legal protection for confidentiality will convince this patient that he can trust his analyst, yet the analysis continues, and the patient somehow "trusts" his analyst to tolerate and understand his pathological distrust.

It is, I shall contend, absolutely true that this kind of trust in the face of distrust (and even in the face of hostile threats of the reporting laws and managed-care companies) is only possible in an atmosphere of strict confidentiality, but the confidentiality in question is not derived from laws and codes of ethics. It is confidentiality as a *professional ethos*, implied confidentiality, confidentiality as an emergent property of psychoanalytic culture. It is part of the procedural knowledge the patient acquires merely by living in a society where psychoanalysis still enjoys a certain measure of respect. The remarkable thing is that confidentiality in this very deep, preconscious sense is even implicit in the patient's willingness to test the analyst's neutrality, to challenge the reliability of the frame, for example, by provoking, mistreating, and even attacking the analyst. It is not just that the patient believes that the analyst will not do anything to discredit the patient in public or among his family and friends; he senses preconsciously that the analyst will even try to refrain from mobilizing those parts of himself that might react defensively to the patient.

This is a vital aspect of confidentiality in the actual doing of psychoanalytic work. What it amounts to in practice is a sense that the analyst develops, in large measure through profound internalization of the ethos of confidentiality, that he or she must try to avoid "blabbing" about the patient *in the session to the patient*. For example, suppose that the analyst has a superego reaction to the patient's unusual masturbation practice. Bowing to the pressure of his own superego, the analyst appeals in turn to the patient's superego to put a stop to this practice. This is a crude example of an often subtle unconscious process that is impossible for analysts not to fall into sometimes, a kind of distortion of the therapeutic alliance in which the therapist splits the patient into favored and unfavored parts. The temptation then becomes very strong to start "telling on" one side of the patient to the other. This would be "blabbing" about the patient in the session to the patient, and it is precisely where the ethic of confidentiality can sustain the deepest clinical work.

Though seemingly innocuous, blabbing to the patient about him involves an erosion of confidentiality at several levels. First, to put it crudely, within the analyst the superego has failed to keep the working ego's confidence. Second, inside the patient, who is struggling to understand himself, the freed-up parts that are beginning to do analytic work and to free associate must now contend with a reinforced thought police. Not only do the thought police have a new potential ally in the analyst, but also, and worse, the vital sense that experience can be contained has been threatened.[2] Opportunities for internal recognition and integration may give way to more splitting and internal suppression.

The fact that an analytic patient can actually entertain such an impossibly demanding intimacy of his analyst is the stuff of confidentiality. It nourishes the psychological roots of minute, day-to-day technical judgments in analytic therapy. Though related to what we have usually been talking about when we try to make legal arguments for confidentiality, it is really something quite different.

The Very Idea of Confidentiality

These considerations bring us round to an important issue that has been largely overlooked in the current policy debates on confidentiality, namely, that the idea of confidentiality has emerged "internally" from the actualities of professional practice, not from the conceptual instantiation of the law. Law has not (and probably cannot) create confidentiality in any meaningful sense; it can only recognize it where it is already practiced by establishing what in common law is termed a "privilege." This is true even of lawyer-client privilege, which, though considered fundamental to any liberal legal system, does not actually derive from the law itself but from the practice of the law. Realistically speaking, then, we should not expect confidentiality to function well when it is refashioned as a deduction from first principles, or manufactured through the application of a general concept, such as privacy. Functional confidentiality is a kind of procedural knowledge, closer to the understanding that develops in an ongoing relationship, a commitment that asserts itself within the shared performance of a particular task, such as physician care, sacerdotal intercession, or legal advocacy. It is, in other words, the expression of a professional ethos, without which the performance of the task itself would lose all social credibility.

It follows naturally from this argument that confidentiality in a psychoanalytic context involves a unique confluence of cultural evolution (notions of individuality, privacy, and legal precedents for professional secrecy) with the particular, and only recently evolved,

---

[2]This is why when we do feel obliged to set conditions on the patient's behavior, for example with regard to serious suicide threats, we feel that we have lost an important dimension of the therapeutic space, though the patient has given us no choice.

conditions of psychoanalytic practice itself. In other words, confidentiality in the psychoanalytic context is not a self-evident thing that can be inferred from the state of the law, medical or psychiatric precedent, or some ideal definition of the relevant ethical principles. It is something that will have to be explained, and most of the explaining will have to be done by psychoanalysts, in a dialogic process with society.

Moreover, if it is true that confidentiality is the expression of a professional ethos, another very onerous consequence obtains: namely, that when the ethos is ailing, all the privacy laws in the world will not save confidentiality for that profession. What was (or might have become) confidentiality in the true sense for that profession will instead degenerate into an abstract concept, perhaps a "right." The profession may cling desperately to this "right," but its value will be entirely contingent on political and social fashions, to be weighed against all the other rights and duties mandated by the State.

Absolute Confidentiality

The idea of confidentiality arising in the practical context of a relationship as the expression of a professional ethos is a far cry from the mainstream of bioethical discourse, with its administrative functions of codifying, balancing, and applying abstract principles and universal rights in the massive and impersonal domains of funded research and "health-care delivery systems." The contemporary discourse on confidentiality has many points in its favor, but it has also fostered a misleading way of framing certain issues. A good example of the latter is the frequent use, on both sides of the debate, of the phrase "absolute confidentiality." From a point of view internal to psychoanalysis, the idea that confidentiality might ever be "absolute" makes little practical sense. Yet such a position is routinely attributed to those who resist the intrusions of the law on psychoanalytic practice: any attempt to defend the merits of independent professional judgment in situations where the law has intervened to compel disclosure is stigmatized as absolutism. This is a rhetorical gambit that distracts attention from the main object of concern—not the absolute, but confidentiality itself. As Christopher Bollas (2000) has suggested, what is really in dispute is whether there should be confidentiality at all or whether it should be "qualified" into practical nonexistence.

One of the basic assumptions fueling the controversy over the absolute is the notion that confidentiality is actually the patient's right as a citizen, that confidentiality should be conceived as an individual right in all circumstances—or only in certain circumstances, such as those of a woman alleging sexual assault. The inevitable corollary of this argument is that, like all rights, the right will have to be balanced against other rights, such as a defendant's right to a fair trial or the rights of children. Once the definition of confidentiality as a right has been conceded, there is no avoiding the balancing argument, and any attempt to resist this logic will be interpreted as another example of the absurd doctrine of absolute confidentiality, i.e., as holding confidentiality above the law. When confidentiality is a right, rather than a professional practice, then it must *always* (the only alternative is *never*) be balanced, i.e., qualified. In other words, the whole matter is taken out of the clinician's hands. The ethical principle is no longer something that derives from good practice; it is imposed by the State as a universal demand on the profession.

The logical consequences of seeing the situation in this way are twofold. First, the aims of treatment, which can be identified in the present, are subordinated to a kind of generalized legal and political speculation about what might one day be in the greater interests of society; that is, confidentiality is politicized. Second, a solemn professional duty is gradually transformed into an unrealistic pretense of secrecy, i.e., confidentiality is bureaucratized. If things as ordinary as collegial consultations or supervision are required as part of treatment or if the family needs to be told that the patient is very psychotic and must have his medications supervised, absolute confidentiality will require that the patient first be asked permission, which he may not grant. As every practitioner knows, when vital information is withheld and professional communication is blocked for this kind of bureaucratic reason (e.g., the possibility of a lawsuit if the patient's "right" is not respected), entirely avoidable tragedies occur. When this kind of thing happens, what we are in fact witnessing is a bioethically institutionalized form of substandard practice. A kind of looking-glass culture evolves, not very different in principle from one in which surgeons would ask their patients for permission to sterilize the instruments before the operation (Furlong, personal communication, 1997).

The illusion that confidentiality is respected and protected because it is derived from a "right" (i.e., included in the rhetoric of universal bioethics) leads, in actual practice, to a cynical and bureaucratic culture of expediency, in which the loss of professional authority based on expertise invites an erosion of the individual practitioner's sense of responsibility. All sorts of new procedures have to be invented to accommodate the new bureaucratic contingency, and the State naturally intervenes with an ever-lengthening list of exceptions to the legalistic construction of confidentiality in order to deal with all the situations potentially requiring its "breach." According to the logic of the reporting laws, for example, the psychotherapist has no ethical or legal choice but to stand by while his patient commits capital crimes (after all, the patient has a "right" to confidentiality)—*unless* (lo and behold!)—the State obliges the analyst to "breach" confidentiality in the greater interests of society. Any reasonable sense of the reality of actual clinical practice tends to get lost in this kind of shuffle, not the least of which is the fact that no competent psychoanalyst in a real emergency would for reasons of confidentiality simply abandon the discretionary power to modify or override the psychoanalytic stance of nonintervention.

The Professional Use of Clinical Material: The Example of Informed Consent

In the bioethical-legalistic construction of the discourse on confidentiality described previously, society's interest (for example, in preventing murder or child abuse) is mistakenly defined as being in fundamental opposition both to the interest of the patient and the interest of the therapeutic process. Psychoanalysts have usually been aware, at some level, that this is a false opposition; that in a democracy the therapeutic interest normally coincides with the best long-term interests of both the patient and society. We do know that analysis does not go very well when the patient is dead, or in jail, or recruiting the analyst as an accomplice in crime. Yet we have gradually allowed ourselves to become ensnared in this binary discourse, using it to our advantage when we can or when the more technical arguments for confidentiality seem politically inexpedient. The problem is that once we have started to ground confidentiality in the social calculus, we become subject to that calculus, and the public will rightly hold us to it.

It is as if we have been working with two versions of confidentiality. The first, which might be called "civic confidentiality," is adopted for various kinds of public consumption. The second, "psychoanalytic confidentiality," is privately acknowledged in a wise kind of way but never really developed intellectually in our own literature. We have effectively maneuvered ourselves into a kind of doublethink. This is particularly evident in the inclination we have been showing lately to embrace the ethico-bureaucratic device of informed consent, even to argue sometimes for its mandatory use. We say that confidentiality is constitutive to the therapeutic process; but when pressed, we pretend that this is a matter of social pragmatics and consumer trust—or of the civil rights of the patient. Then we proceed to discuss the patient with colleagues and students—worse, to publish articles about him. Critics of psychoanalysis, or of the concept of psychotherapeutic privilege, have quite rightly seized on this opportunity to point out the conflict we are in. Is confidentiality important to us, or is it just a matter of professional convenience? Having tied ourselves to civic confidentiality and not being sure how to explain psychoanalytic confidentiality, we feel morally trapped. So when we want to seek supervision, teach, lecture, or publish, we are tempted to ask the patient to give us permission. In reporting the commitment of this act, some of us positively glow with democratic pride.

The problems with informed consent have already been well argued by others (e.g., Aron, 2000; Gabbard, 2000; Lear, this volume). The main points are the following: asking an analytic patient for consent to "breach" confidentiality for professional reasons such as supervision, teaching, or publication places the analyst in a conflict of interest and the patient in a double bind (though this may be much more difficult for some patients than others). The patient may deeply regret agreeing or not agreeing to grant consent. Moreover, the analyst knows in principle that the patient is not really in a position to answer freely or to predict his later feelings about the decision he takes beforehand. Complicated by the intensity of the transference-countertransference relationship, motivations on both sides in a situation like this are often contradictory and elusive. There is the wish to please the analyst, to be interesting and famous. There is the wish to assert one's independence, to take revenge, to be in control. It is impossible to tell at an early stage what is really going on. The patient knows that the analyst knows this, which makes him wonder what the analyst is really up to. The patient cannot help but ask himself why the analyst has put him in this difficult position. Is it because the analyst is less interested in the analysis than his own advancement? Or is the analyst insecure, guilty, afraid of the patient, or trying to protect himself from the patient?

The last thing that will come to mind is that the analyst is making desperate use of a bureaucratic device in order to wriggle out of an ethical bind that his profession never should have got him into in the first place. The patient may sense that the analyst is in a foolish and awkward position, but he or she will only be able to guess at why and be filled with self-doubt in the process. How long should they analyze these conflicting feelings about the analyst's request before settling on a decision, yes or no? And in the meantime, who should pay for the sessions?

Even if it were possible in this situation to give truly *informed* consent, the informing process might be fatal to analysis, especially in the case of publication (where, paradoxically, the request for consent is actually most justified on ethical grounds). The story here is rather like the one about the operation that was successful, though the patient died. If consent to publish is going to be more than a blanket waiver, then the patient surely has a right to read what the analyst writes in advance of publication. Moreover, the patient, in exercising this right, may legitimately object to certain passages and request changes in others. The analyst will have no choice in this circumstance but to acquiesce, thus compromising his clinical judgment (which the patient will surely note his willingness to do), or else transform the analysis into an editorial bargaining process. The analyst can always decide not to publish, but then he will have to analyze the patient's guilt about this. Or the analyst can apologize to the patient. If consent was what the analyst really wanted from his patient, it might have been better, from both an ethical and clinical point of view, simply to ask in advance for permission to publish as a condition of treatment. Indeed, in comparison to the clinical implications of fully informing the patient once the analytic process is underway, there is a great deal to be said for this procedure, crude as it may be.

Informed consent also has serious implications for the scientific value of our clinical publications, especially if it continues to spread or becomes mandatory. Some authors have argued that submitting clinical reports to the patient for editorial review prior to publication actually enhances the value of the finished product. The patient's vetting of the analytic material not only helps to correct the analyst's blind spots, it liberates the analyst from theoretical prejudices and thus deepens understanding (Stoller, 1988; Gerson, 2000; Pizer, 2000). This may sometimes be true. Indeed, many things might enhance the analyst's understanding of the patient. If this were the issue, we might well consider interviewing the patient's friends and family as well. The question, however, of the greater or lesser subjective accuracy of any given clinical report is secondary to the problem of introducing a systematic, patient-derived slant into *most or all* clinical reports, producing a massive cumulative effect of distortion.

There is no doubt that individual analysts already have strong preconceptions about the clinical process and that the circumstances of the profession make it more or less inevitable that the evidence produced is poorly controlled for "experimenter bias" (Kandel, 1999). Ordinary clinical reports are constructions, as we have become fond of saying, which means that their scientific value does not lie in the finality of the truth of the individual report but in the gathering image of clinical reality that emerges from the interacting cross section of clinical communication at any given time. This is obviously not a precise procedure, and so it might seem reasonable to conclude, on balance, that granting patients subjective editorial control over clinical material would not have a detrimental influence on the growth of psychoanalytic knowledge.

A brief response to this is the following. First, it is important to remember that all science depends on a commitment to let the exchange of views continue, lest we settle prematurely on a closure of investigation. The inconclusiveness of individual research reports is not a unique property of psychoanalytic case studies; it would also apply to Newtonian physics and any number of competent but finally erroneous scientific conclusions. When we say that it is "the gathering image of clinical reality that emerges from the interacting cross section of clinical communication at any given time," we are not really describing some peculiar aberration unique to the psychoanalytic branch of human knowledge. The distinguishing factor is not the competitive and dialogic form through which certain kinds of psychoanalytic evidence accumulates, is compared, and eventually achieves provisional confirmation. What distinguishes psychoanalysis more radically as a form of investigation from much of the rest of the research community is the contingent fact that the primary subjects of investigation have independent wills and desires. And not just this. The conative activity of the research subject is not, as one would expect, neutralized or factored out in some way but actively solicited and engaged as a condition of the first level of the investigative process, which is the psychoanalytic treatment itself. Any attempt to furnish an accurate picture of the psychoanalytic treatment process must therefore be especially careful not to involve the patient in the process of deciding what should be reported, however useful clinically or therapeutically that might turn out to be in individual, isolated instances.

For this reason, the argument that since the analyst is already biased the patient's bias will naturally serve as a corrective, is patently false. Again, the issue is not the alleged perfection of any individual analyst's clinical perception but the reliability of the overall trend in clinical reporting. Once it becomes established that psychoanalytic case studies have all been vetted by the patient, the current sense that such studies represent on the whole a genuine expression of individual analysts' own well-trained capacity for analytic experience dies. In its place will arise a picture of our clinical work that is censored systematically by the narcissistic and cultural demands of the patient population. In other words, to paraphrase a current political cliché, we will have evolved a body of clinical work that is "intersubjectively correct" but of limited use for the transmission and advancement of psychoanalytic knowledge.

There have been some compelling defenses of informed consent in psychoanalysis, but they usually depend on retheorizations of the analytic relationship that either minimize the role of the unconscious or cancel it out by making it so pervasive that only ad hoc clinical intuition can determine appropriate technique at any given time. Stoller, as we have already seen, argued eloquently that involving the patient in the clinical writing process is therapeutically and scientifically beneficial. I am inclined to believe him, though I place his claim in the context of his personal persuasiveness plus the impression that the patients of whom he speaks seem like befriended research subjects. Much of the intersubjectivist- and relational-theory development enters into the same territory when it comes to informed consent. There is a small but significant literature on the therapeutic benefits of asking for informed consent and on the healing effects of inviting the patient to become a coauthor in what is, after all, the account of a clinical cocreation (e.g., Flax, 2000; Gerson, 2000; Pizer, 2000). One senses that certain analysts can "pull it off," either because they are remarkably open and self-confident individuals or because their therapeutic style includes a capacity to sustain consistently a very high degree of emotionally interactive enmeshment with the patient. As Gabbard (2000) has counseled, it would be a mistake to rule out the device of informed consent a priori. Like confidentiality, the meaning and value of informed consent is to a certain extent context-sensitive. Freebury (this volume) has observed of controversial techniques that though they may raise eyebrows, it would be tyrannical and antiexperimental to address them as ethical violations, at least in our present state of knowledge.

The problem posed by arguments for the informed-consent approach is not so much ethical as pedagogical. This or that analyst may be able to make it work; it may be the best approach to take with such and such a patient; or it may even be the best way for certain analysts to work all the time. But how do we teach it to candidates as a standard of practice? Seeking informed consent and then simply dealing with the psychic fallout is very much like self-disclosure. It may do wonders for a particular patient, it may provide all sorts of beneficial "grist for the mill," but how do we know when to use it and the limit on its use? Do we disclose everything all the time? How far do we go when we discuss our reasons for wishing to write about the patient? The usual answer is that it is a matter of intuition, judgment, circumstances, the state of the transference at the time, the personality structure of the patient, the unique dyadic constellation that has emerged in the treatment. All these considerations are important, but what are the generalizable principles that can be taught here? In itself, intersubjective intuition is indeterminate; it provides no background against which the clinical situation can come into view and be assessed, unless we are implicitly presupposing something like standard technique as a point of reference.

It is true that the analyst has not just a countertransference but a *transference* to the patient, which cannot possibly be factored out consciously at all times. It is also true that in principle the analytic situation is constantly in an uproar of mutual enactment. But we need to have some teachable method of helping the psychoanalyst to get a handle on these natural human conditions in order to take advantage of them. This is just what Freud tried to provide by setting some ground rules that help the analyst to distinguish the analytic situation from the welter of everyday events, giving it some continuity and stability so that an essential minimum from the infinity of unconscious activity at play in the consulting room can be flagged, isolated, and analyzed. These are the familiar trilogy of neutrality, anonymity, and abstinence. All that has changed since Freud's day is that we have learned to think of them as approximate "default positions" rather than as immutable rules. The principles themselves help to establish a consistent and reliable experimental stance that serves us well most of the time. They still set the basic contours of the analytic frame and are presupposed implicitly by most methods of working with the unconscious therapeutically, even those that reject the likes of neutrality and anonymity as unnatural, oppressive, or misleading to the patient. So it makes sense to teach that we try to avoid involving the patient directly in the private and personal aspects of our work unless there is very good reason to think otherwise, and our work includes teaching and writing.

The idea that the analytic relationship constitutes an unconscious intersubjective field sometimes gives rise to the suggestion that the patient will already be unconsciously aware of the analyst's intention to widen the circle of interanalytic communication (discuss his case with a supervisor, present his material to a clinical case study group, or write a paper). The thinking here is partly that the analyst has no right to withhold information about something he is doing that may unconsciously affect the patient. It is true that some patients develop an uncanny ability to "read the analyst's mind." But there is a considerable leap from this to the notion that the analyst should preempt the patient's thoughts about the analyst, rather as if the very existence of the analyst as a separate person beyond the patient's control were a toxic iatrogenic irritant to be eliminated for therapeutic reasons.

There is indeed a very common dyadic fantasy, something like what Kurt Vonnegut (1966) called "Das Reich der Zwei," that confidentiality is like a sealed pact of secrecy, the slightest "breach" or "betrayal" of which will deeply wound and harm the patient. The dyadic fantasy has been especially prominent in the listserve discussions of confidentiality I have followed on the Internet. It is often accompanied by a very strong feeling that seems to feed the belief that nothing is worse than running the risk that the patient will later discover a "violation" of confidentiality in print. The intuitive plausibility of this claim seems to come from an understanding of confidentiality as a fusional patient-analyst conspiracy. Indeed, the analyst's sense that publication is fundamentally dishonest, a shameful exploitation and betrayal of the patient, is probably fueled by the unconscious anger, paranoia, and guilt that both patient and analyst have tried to project away from themselves through enactment of the dyadic fantasy or basic assumption group (Caper, 1995).

Many psychotherapists experience feelings of unease about the decision to publish or even merely to present case material. Sometimes they report a sense of relief when the patient's consent is obtained, as if the moral problem is solved. In this case, they seem to be assuming that their uneasiness was caused by the inherent duplicity of the act they were contemplating. This sense of violating the patient may be related to the fact that the analysand's illusion of (or wish for) an exclusive omnipotent relationship with an utterly devoted analyst is to some degree always a necessary development in the therapeutic process and therefore needs to be protected for a certain period of time. It is part of what used to be called the transference neurosis and would normally be resolved eventually, partly through internalization in the "good-object" mode.

If the internal transformation achieved through the dyadic fantasy relationship turns out, however, to be so easily threatened by subsequent encounters with the analyst's separateness, such as his or her publications, the analysis has probably fallen short of enabling the patient to "contain the container" (Levin, 2002). Informed consent would certainly not have solved this problem. On the contrary, the attempt via informed consent to preempt the shattering of the dyadic illusion only guarantees the destruction of the dyadic fantasy, probably too early from a therapeutic point of view. But there is another possibility: that informed consent will simply be used to install the fantasy on a permanent and henceforth virtually unanalyzable footing through the pretense of coconstruction and coauthorship. All that is accomplished in either of these scenarios is an increased risk of aborting the potential space in which the dyadic fantasy can be experienced virtually as both realizable and not realizable, desirable and undesirable, good and bad. The analysand is instead required to make a choice about it, to *decide*, which is tantamount to taking away or "deconstructing" a child's transitional object before he is ready to give it up; forcing the patient to say yes or no and thus to set his own unconscious destiny, and the analyst's as well.

The analyst's negative feelings about the use of clinical material for professional purposes—the demonization of the act as something that needs to be excused and apologized for—may also be a form of scapegoating. In other words, the analyst may be seeking to rationalize internal conflicts and countertransference problems by displacing them not only onto the patient but onto the profession as well. The displacement onto the profession is essentially moral (e.g., "My wish to publish is not a personal issue; it is inherently unethical, and so I am following standard procedures prescribed by my code of ethics"). The displacement onto the patient is of course much more direct and practical ("Let the patient take the responsibility for what I want to do").

Analysts commonly experience feelings of guilt for having more satisfying and successful lives than certain patients who entertain intense wishes for the exclusive attention of the analyst. The analyst's psychopathology may well exacerbate such feelings, and the temptation to externalize the conflict can become very strong. When ordinary professional activities and ambitions become the objects of the analyst's paranoia and guilt, these are surely the analyst's personal problems. There may be an intersubjective dimension that needs to be worked through with the patient in one way or another; but generally speaking, the specific contents of the analyst's personal issues need to be handled internally and privately, perhaps through his own analysis. One of the risks of normalizing the informed-consent procedure is to institutionalize a form of acting out and self-disclosure in which the analyst recruits the patient in the externalization of his own conflicts about being a separate person.

The view that subsequent discovery is so harmful to the patient that it must be preempted at all costs is really a form of the "lesser-of-two-evils" argument. It depends upon a rather dubious quantification, namely, that a deliberately imposed risk to the patient and the therapy in every case (informed consent) causes less harm than a possible risk in a few cases (the chance that a patient may one day recognize himself in a clinical report). The "quantity" that tips the balance in this calculus seems to be the exculpation factor. Something felt to be inherently harmful (breaking the pact of secrecy) is confessed and then mitigated by granting the patient a sort of moral "copyright" over the analytic material. The analyst deliberately places himself in a conflict of interest and the patient into a double bind, but this is felt to be the lesser of two evils because the dread possibility of subsequent injury is averted. How is this actually so? The most obvious answer (which is surely at the root of the whole concept of consent) is that the personal legal risks for the professional seem lighter.[3] Moreover, the therapist need no longer feel that he has "betrayed" his patient or that he is "concealing" something from the patient, because he has "come clean"—confessed his sin (the professional use of clinical material) and received absolution from the patient. Everything is resolved politically and democratically because the patient has been given an opportunity to say no.

Patients who do find themselves in their analyst's publications are likely (but by no means always) to be looking pretty hard to find

---

[3] In fact it seems rather doubtful that this is so. A determined patient could probably still prosecute for breach of confidentiality on the grounds an individual cannot sign away something so basic as a constitutional right to privacy and security of the person.

them, which is an issue for the analysis, not for ethics. One cannot deliberately set out to read something by one's analyst without entertaining at least a faint glimmer of a thought that the analyst might have been influenced in some way by the patient in what he wrote. After all, the entire relationship with the analyst tends to be exclusive of explicit external influences—other people. It is impossible for the question of whether one is alive or dead in the analyst's internal world *not* to be an issue. Frequently, patients will project themselves, imaginatively and sometimes literally, into everything they read by their analyst. (I know I have done this even when I knew the piece was written before my analysis began.) There is also a good chance that what the patient is really looking for is not himself, but precisely the analyst. This leads to consideration of another interesting phenomenon: that even when a patient knows that a case report is not about himself it may be shocking and disorienting to read for all the same reasons; it shows the analyst in a very different light than he or she appears in the context of therapy, thinking in very different ways and doing very different kinds of things.

Of course, it would be absurd to try to obtain consent from every patient who might venture into the sport of the psychoanalytic literature search only to discover that he does not like the way his analyst writes about the analytic process. Again, the problem is clearly the existence of the analyst as a separate person with a separate life, the sense that this reality does not sit comfortably with the dyadic fantasy of an exclusive and fusional relationship. The deeper the sense of betrayal, the more important it is to be dealing with the issue in the analysis itself, but in the form that occurs spontaneously in the transference rather than preemptively, as will occur when the issue of publication is proposed by the analyst.

The Professional Community as a Containing Environment

The experience of reviewing the arguments for and against informed consent in instances of professionally motivated use of clinical material, such as supervision or publication, leaves many readers, I am sure, with an uncomfortable sense of the irreconcilability of the practicing analyst's ethical conflicts. Articles weighing the pros and cons of different approaches to the use of clinical material often conclude in a tone of stoical resignation. They lament the fact that for the purposes of scientific advancement, and so forth, we must live with an unfortunate ethical compromise in which "breaches" and "betrayals" of one of our most fundamental ethical principles will have to be tolerated on a regular basis, for reasons of state, as it were. No wonder our critics have been so scornful. How can a profession base itself on the principle of confidentiality when the very existence of the profession, its teaching and research activities, requires the breaking of that very principle? Is this not an absurd inconsistency, and is not any attempt to get around it through compromise or bureaucratic procedure inherently absurd?

The answer is yes. A profession rooted so fundamentally in flat self-contradiction would be difficult to respect, and any attempt to salvage its reputation by preaching ethical relativism, even in the form of a noble compromise between science and privacy (not to mention securing signatures on pieces of paper) would be worthy of a Kafkaesque satire.

How could such a curious state of affairs have arisen in the first place? This chapter has provided an outline of a possible answer, which will still require a good deal more elaboration. The short version of it is that there is in fact no fundamental inconsistency in the psychoanalytic profession. As argued earlier, the source of the apparent contradiction lies in a misunderstanding or oversimplification, partly condoned by psychoanalysis itself, of the concept of confidentiality. Stated bluntly, anonymous disclosures of clinical material in supervision, teaching, or scientific presentations are not breaches of confidentiality at all. They cannot be considered on the same footing as third-party intrusions on the therapeutic process, mandatory reporting laws, literary self-promotion at the expense of patients, tattle-taling, or idle gossip revealing a patient's identity, the contents of his therapy, or both. Any attempt to equate the professional use of clinical material with unethical breaches of confidentiality or unwarranted intrusions on the privacy of the patient is an exercise in pure political rhetoric, necessarily stripping these incommensurable activities from their defining contexts in order to force a false analogy between them.

The legitimate professional uses of clinical material help to constitute the social context in which psychoanalysis and psychotherapy become possible as organized activities in the first place. They are part of the containing tissue of the confidential relationship, enabling and supporting it in the same way that a social organism is held together by a shared culture. Anonymous professional communication about a patient does not in any way betray the patient or his rights; in fact, it promotes his interests by enriching the scientific and

professional environment that establishes the condition for the psychoanalyst to do consistently good work and to grow as a clinician.
The fact that the psychoanalyst does not and cannot work in isolation is often forgotten. The therapist will not function as well or at all
if he cannot rely on the good faith of the profession as a whole. The
analyst's ability to rely on his supervisors and colleagues to protect
sensitive information is part of the necessary background that en-
ables the patient to trust him unconsciously. It also makes the therapist more, not less, trustworthy in the legal and political sense, because
it removes the therapist from dangerous isolation. All intraprofessional
relationships and forms of communication encompass the therapeutic relationship and are themselves confidential. This does not mean
that they are fetishized secrets, the objects of curiosity and speculation. Rather, it means that they preserve the anonymity of the patient
at all times; that they maintain normal levels of respect for the patient
as a person, regardless of the nature of the information concerning
him; that they only occur within a professional context involving the
aims of therapy or research; and that they are intended for members
of the profession, not produced as exercises in literary self-promotion with the general public in mind.

The importance of respect in all of one's communications with
and about the patient is worth underlining and should probably be
spelled out more explicitly in our official principles of ethics and
guidelines. It is surely an essential component of the culture of confidentiality, of confidentiality as a professional ethos. If respect for
the patient cannot always be felt, it still needs to be demonstrated,
not only to the patient but also to one's colleagues. Lear in this volume has written of confidentiality as a virtue in the Aristotelian sense
of a character trait. Since the method of working in psychoanalysis
does not "come naturally," psychoanalytic training includes the in-
stillation of professional attitudes that usually grow roots in the individual analyst's character. Few educational events are as important
for one's analytic development and self-confidence as the experience of listening to a good clinician speak respectfully of his patient
while protecting his identity. This kind of demonstration *imparts* the
professional ethic of confidentiality in a way that no lecture on the
concept of patients' rights could ever match. We all learn by participating in a good analyst's narrative of an explosive clinical situation.
That analyst's capacity to contain is modeled in his or her way of
describing difficulties with a particular patient in a calm, lucid, sensitive, anonymous, and respectful manner. As we think about this way

of being with a patient, we also share and promote a vigorous supporting and containing professional environment for all. We realize that confidentiality is more than an ethical duty; it is an integral part of the way we try to work and of the culture of psychoanalysis.

References

Aron, L. (2000), Ethical consideration in the writing of psychoanalytic case histories. *Psychoanal. Dial.,* 10:231–246.

Bollas, C. (2000), "The Disclosure Industry." Opening plenary address, conference on *Confidentiality and Society: Psychotherapy, Ethics, and the Law.* Montreal, Quebec, Canada, October 13.

———— & Sundelson, D. (1995), *The New Informants: The Betrayal of Confidentiality in Psychoanalysis and Psychotherapy.* Northvale, NJ: Aronson.

Caper, R. (1995), On the difficulty of making a mutative interpretation. *Internat. J. Psycho-Anal.,* 76:91–101.

Flax, M. (2000), The tapestry of the erotic experience: Weaving the threads. *Canad. J. Psychoanal.,* 8:207–232.

Furlong, A. (1997), Conversation with C. Levin and P. Mosher. Toronto, Canada, May.

———— (1998), Should we or shouldn't we? Some aspects of the confidentiality of clinical reporting and dossier access. *Internat. J. Psycho-Anal.,* 79:727–739.

Gabbard, G. (2000), Disguise or consent: Problems and recommendations regarding the publication and presentation of clinical material. *Internat. J. Psycho-Anal.,* 81:1071–1086.

Gerson, S. (2000), The therapeutic action of writing about patients: Commentary on papers by Lewis Aron and by Stuart A. Pizer. *Psychoanal. Dial.,* 10:261–266.

Kandel, E. R. (1999), Biology and the future of psychoanalysis: A new intellectual framework for psychiatry revisited. *Amer. J. Psychiatr.,* 156:4.

Kerr, J. (1993), *A Most Dangerous Method: The Story of Freud, Jung, and Sabina Spielrein.* New York: Vintage.

Levin, C. (2001), The siege of psychotherapeutic space: Psychoanalysis in the age of transparency. *Canad. J. Psychoanal.,* 9:187–215.

———— (in press), Containing the container: Some experiential aspects of narcissism and the problem of "primary undifferentiation." *Israel J. Psychoanal.,* 1.

Lynn, D. J. & Vaillant, G. E. (1998), Anonymity, neutrality, and confidentiality in the actual methods of Sigmund Freud: A review of 43 cases, 1907–1939. *Amer. J. Psychiat.,* 155:163–171.

Pizer, S. A. (2000), A gift in return: The clinical use of writing about a patient. *Psychoanal. Dial.,* 10:247–260.

Stoller, R. (1988), Patients' responses to their own case reports. *J. Amer. Psychoanal. Assn.,* 36:371–391.

Tuckett, D. (2000), Editorial: Reporting clinical events in the *Journal*: Towards the construction of a special case. *Internat. J. Psychoanal.,* 81:1064–1069.

Vonnegut, K. (1966), *Mother Night.* New York: Dell.

SECTION 2

Dilemmas in Treatment, Research, and Training

Introduction to CHAPTER 6

❧

Some Reflections on Confidentiality in Clinical Practice

There are extreme situations in which it may not be possible to maintain confidentiality for clinical, ethical, social, or political reasons. Otto Kernberg, who over the years has been an astute commentator on the internal organization of psychoanalytic institutions, as well as a noted theoretician, reviews these situations and ventures into larger social issues pertaining to the field. Kernberg argues that whereas confidentiality is a fundamental aspect of the psychoanalytic frame, it may be justifiable in certain circumstances for the analyst to stand "outside an unjust law" in order to maintain the therapeutic commitment to the patient. For the same reason, Kernberg asserts that the profession as a whole is justified in resisting medically inappropriate health-industry intrusions on the patient's privacy. He also points out that confidentiality requires a sharing of basic social values in the analytic partnership; when this is not possible, as in totalitarian societies, psychoanalysis will be difficult or impossible to practice.

❦

CHAPTER 6

Some Reflections on Confidentiality in Clinical Practice

Otto F. Kernberg

*T*he subject of confidentiality is currently of burning interest: the mental health professions have experienced an encroachment by the courts and by third-party payers on the confidential nature of the patient-therapist interaction. The ethical commitments, autonomy, responsibility, and safety of the psychoanalyst are all gravely endangered by the challenge to confidentiality. The serious nature of the ethical dilemma as well as the practical aspects of defending confidentiality raise the question whether the analyst can accept placing himself outside an unfair law that potentially damages patients and runs counter to the analyst's professional and ethical commitments.

Psychoanalysis requires a frame that provides safety and privacy to the patient. The confidentiality of the psychoanalytic situation is a fundamental aspect of this protective frame. Confidentiality may be broken, however, by both internal and external factors—internal in the sense of requirements and challenges derived from the nature of the patient's illness and from the treatment, and external in terms of legal, economic, and even political pressures.

The internal challenges to confidentiality that derive from the patient's psychopathology and potential for acting out can threaten the life of the patient and the life of others, including the psychoanalyst. It may become crucial, in the psychotherapy of patients who are highly suicidal or potentially homicidal, to intervene in the patient's life outside the treatment sessions in order to protect the patient and other people. The usual psychoanalytic treatment in North America seldom has to confront these internal challenges to confidentiality because prospective cases are usually carefully screened for their ability to participate in psychoanalytic treatment. But in countries where psychoanalysis is applied freely to borderline and psychotic states in which severe, chronic suicidal tendencies, an extraordinary potential for transference regression and dangerous acting out, severe paranoia, or antisocial features (or a combination of such states) complicate the treatment, the issue of confidentiality becomes acute.

I question, from an ethical standpoint, the attitude of a psychoanalyst who remains strictly "neutral" while observing a patient's irresistible move to suicidal behavior. In the treatment of patients with borderline personality organization carried out at the Personality Disorders Institute of the Weill Medical College of Cornell University, Department of Psychiatry, we inform our patients that complete confidentiality of the treatment is guaranteed, with the exception of circumstances in which the therapist is convinced that the life of the patient or of someone else is at risk, at which point the therapist would take whatever measures he or she deems necessary to protect the patient and others from such danger.

External interferences with confidentiality are by far the greater challenge to treatment at this time. These external factors include such legal requirements as court-ordered testimony and financial requirements, and I shall explore them briefly. Legal requirements involve reporting child abuse, competence proceedings, court-ordered examinations, civil commitment procedures, and patient-litigant exceptions. In the United States, the Tarasoff principle, requiring a therapist to warn or inform outsiders when they are endangered by the patient, involves child abuse, dangerousness to self and others, and the intent to commit a crime or harmful act. In such cases, internal and external challenges to confidentiality may coincide. The therapist's legal obligation to report child abuse, dangerousness to self and others, or the intent to harm may correspond to a therapist's sense that there exist actual dangers that cannot be reduced by a purely analytic or psychotherapeutic approach and that require abandonment of confidentiality.

In other cases, however, the letter of the law seems clearly contradictory to the well-being of the patient, his family, or both, and the therapist may be ethically and technically justified in ignoring the letter of the legal requirements. Obviously, it is the responsibility of the psychoanalyst and the mental-health profession at large to fight absurd and destructive laws by all legal means available in a democratic society. By definition, a therapist who participates in competency

proceedings, court-ordered examinations, or civil commitment procedures accepts to waive confidentiality under such circumstances;
in the case of legal, particularly litigant, procedures initiated by the
patient, the therapist has to use his judgment as to whether to open
a case, even at the request of his own patient. Often, patients are not
fully aware of what kind of authorization they are giving the therapist to communicate to the court. In general, with the exception of
child-custody cases, court-ordered testimony should be fought off,
as long as it does not involve the Tarasoff principle.

The general implication of what I have said so far is that the
psychoanalyst and the therapist need to have full understanding of
what legal requirements and challenges involve, consult a legal expert to protect themselves and their patients, and exercise judgment,
in each case, as to whether to fight off external intrusions into privacy and challenges to confidentiality or to break confidentiality to
protect the patient and the treatment.

The most prevalent and worrisome external challenge to confidentiality derives from financial requirements of third-party payers,
including state and federal authorities who determine treatment reimbursement in the light of socially established priorities. In the United
States, the ability of the private, managed-care industry to pursue its
primary interest in generating profits by reducing costs regardless of
patients' needs remains unchecked as long as the law continues to
protect the industry from legal liability. The corruption of medical
practice associated with this state of affairs is one of the most disturbing
developments in the delivery of health services in the United States
as well as in other countries influenced by this American model. I
believe that, collectively, the International Psychoanalytic Association
and the component psychoanalytic societies, in consonance with
mental-health professions in general, need to fight this financially
based encroachment on clinical practice and, particularly, the encroachment on confidentiality.

The question of the psychoanalyst's ethical commitment to his
patients and particularly to the privacy and confidentiality of the clinical
situation, however, is affected by other implicit ethical commitments
that also influence the therapist's relationship with his patients. These
are ethical commitments to society at large, to the profession to which
the therapist belongs, and to the law. I have already referred to potential conflicts between the commitments to the patient and to the
law, and there may be conflicts also related to the therapist's commitment to the standards and procedures of his or her profession and to

the ethical principles of society at large that may not necessarily coincide with legal conflicts.

In most treatments, those implicit ethical commitments remain outside concrete areas of conflicts for the therapist. With patients presenting severe psychopathology, a severe degree of regression and acting out, and paranoid, litigious, aggressive, or antisocial behavior, the conflicts between patients' behavior and those ethical commitments may affect the therapist's decision-making process and the therapist's behavior and raise questions about confidentiality that defy any simple general rule.

Perhaps the most extreme case of severe conflicts between the therapist's commitment to the patient and the commitments to his profession, the law, and society at large is presented in totalitarian states where, typically, psychoanalysis cannot be tolerated. Totalitarian states reserve the right to invade the privacy of their citizens, and regard privacy and confidentiality as criminal; psychoanalysis as a profession may be forbidden because it is not subservient to the totalitarian ideology. Technical neutrality becomes impossible because technical neutrality—that is, the analyst not taking sides in the internal conflicts of the patient activated in the transference/countertransference bind—is based on a tacitly assumed commonality of societal beliefs and ethical commitments. In a totalitarian society, sharply split between a dominant class or party and a suppressed and controlled population whose private life is strictly supervised and limited, by definition the psychoanalyst cannot remain in a tacit agreement with a patient adapted to such a society, nor can he join with his patient in underground rebellion against it. The psychoanalytic profession requires a political structure that respects privacy, individuality, and the autonomy of decision-making.

Introduction to CHAPTER 7

❧

Psychoanalytic Research and Confidentiality: Dilemmas

Robert Galatzer-Levy is widely recognized both as a clinician and as a researcher. He has written extensively on scientific theories and methodologies in relation to psychoanalytic theory and practice. This chapter provides an incisive analysis of the reciprocal ethical implications of psychoanalytic research, a growing and diverse field, and confidentiality. Though the ethical dilemmas of clinical research have long been recognized, rapid developments in therapeutic technique, research methods, and communications technology have pushed these dilemmas to the forefront of the ethics debate within psychoanalysis. Galatzer-Levy's contribution questions to what extent the problem of confidentiality itself is amenable to scientific inquiry.

CHAPTER 7

❧

Psychoanalytic Research and Confidentiality: Dilemmas

Robert Galatzer-Levy

> Whereas before I was accused of giving no information about my patients, now I shall be accused of giving information about my patients which ought not to be given? I can only hope that in both cases the critics will be the same, and that they will merely have shifted the pretext for their reproaches; if so, I can resign in advance any possibility of ever removing their objections [Freud, 1905, p. 7].

A century after Freud published the case of Dora, it appears that both anticipated criticisms are legitimate. Freud's self-censorship led to the omission of vital information which, since its revelations, has fundamentally reshaped the understanding of Dora's transferences and treatment (Erikson, 1964; Decker, 1982). His violation of confidentiality negatively impacted his patient. Dora's knowledge that she was a famous patient became a significant element in a poor life adjustment (Deutsch, 1957). That Freud waited five years to publish the Dora manuscript suggests his dilemma in publishing case histories (Jones, 1953).

Both research in psychoanalysis and patient confidentiality are valued ideals, which, unfortunately, can be in conflict. The complexity of the problem has recently emerged in the psychoanalytic literature (Person, 1983; Stein, 1988; Stoller, 1988; Lipton, 1991; Goldberg, 1997; Aron, 2000; Gabbard, 2000).

There are, of course, many types of psychoanalytic research. These include quantitative research on outcome, studies developing psychoanalytic concepts, process and technique research using audio or video tapes of sessions, and published research using case material as data. This chapter focuses primarily on the last—the confidentiality dilemmas that arise in published research based in clinical material and case histories. Publication refers here to any public presentation, including oral presentations to professional audiences. (Issues surrounding educational presentation to supervisors and institute classes are not discussed.)

There are strong arguments for confidentiality in the analytic situation. They are based on principle, anticipated consequences of breaches of privacy, analytic technique, and irrational anxieties. Principled arguments include the right to privacy and the psychoanalytic community's struggle to protect it in the face of ever more intrusive governmental and other powerful institutions. Revelation of private information that harms the analysand's reputation is an example of the consequences of failure to maintain confidentiality. Loss of privacy alters the analytic relationship by introducing new technical problems. Finally, irrational anxieties, shame, or guilt could interfere with a person's use of analysis if confidentiality is not assured.

Each of these concerns must be addressed differently. Some of the arguments include statements about people's behaviors and attitudes and are subject to empirical investigation. Others are outside the empirical realm. It is important to identify questions that can be answered empirically, especially since authoritative statements about the impact of the loss of confidentiality are often confused with demonstrated facts.

There are also strong arguments for making information about analyses public. The value of psychoanalytic ideas rests on their credibility. Francis Bacon (1620) delineated the two major ways ideas are made credible—authority and empiricism. Articulating the new scientific world view, Bacon rejected authority and described features of empirical knowledge. Its central feature for Bacon is that it is public. The empiricist shares his data and describes how he relates data to conclusions. The empiricist claims his statements are true based on information that can be explicitly described and criticized by others. Though analysts sometimes lapse into authority-based arguments, almost all analysts believe that the credibility of our statements rests, as Bacon advocated, in shared and criticizable data.[1]

Almost all analytic evidence comes from the clinical encounter. To achieve the most basic elements of scientific investigation, investigators need publicly accessible materials from actual analyses, of sufficient quality and quantity to allow independent evaluation. Therefore, psychoanalytic data must largely result from a violation of absolute confidentiality.

How to approach this dilemma? The idea of scientific investigation could be abandoned, and, alongside the moral philosophers of old, analysts could discuss the human condition based on personal experience and speculation. This, however, would separate the profession from its ideals, deny any claims to scientific status, destroy all but ad hominem arguments for therapeutic effectiveness, and leave a range of controversies in a state that cannot be satisfactorily resolved.

Some Possible Solutions

Reviewing the literature and more informal discussion I have found eight suggestions for resolving this problem:

1. "What they don't know won't hurt them." As long as the patient does not know of the violation, it does not affect him, so no harm is done. Many psychoanalytic clinical descriptions are implicitly provided on this basis.
2. It is the individual analyst's duty to protect the patient and to ensure no harm comes from publication. The analytic community cannot reasonably formulate a more precise principle. This posi-

---

[1]Of course, like other investigators, especially in the social sciences, analysts sometimes proceed with evidence that appears inadequately empirical, mistake authoritative statements for demonstrated propositions, and fall into errors of believing empirical support for their positions exists when it does not (Galatzer-Levy, 1993). Yet the traditional grounds on which most analyst rest their claims remain empirical. Some philosophers of science (e.g.. Popper, 1965; Grunbaum, 1982, 1984, 1986, 1990, 1994) characterize psychoanalysis as "unscientific" because the empirical methods of the field are not consistent with their philosophical characterization of scientific knowledge. Their arguments concern definitions, and their view of science does not correspond to the realm of inquiry commonly called scientific (Wallerstein, 1988; Wallace, 1989; Meissner, 1990; Galatzer-Levy, 1996). This chapter uses Bacon's view of empiricism because it best reflects the shared ideal of scientific investigators and because it is the most salient for the matters considered here.

tion was adopted by the Committee on Scientific Activities of the American Psychoanalytic Association in the mid-1980s (Klumpner and Frank, 1991; Klumpner and Galatzer-Levy, 1991).

3. The details of the analytic interchange are so difficult to identify that they can be made public without risk. Analytic investigators who believe that small-scale transactions are the heart of analysis have embraced this idea since it simultaneously allows description of the data they believe to be central and protects patients' confidentiality.

4. Patients can give or deny informed consent for their analyst's publication.

5. Omission of identifying information or disguising the subject of the report allows publication and maintains confidentiality.

6. Confidentiality is not as important as moving research in psychoanalysis forward. Much of the concern for confidentiality arises from unproven tradition or is a manifestation of neurosis. From an ethical and reasonable viewpoint, analysts should only limit their publication of patient material when publication would clearly cause harm to the patients or others.

7. "Trust me—I'm an analyst." In this approach, which could also be called "mediated empiricism," data from the psychoanalytic situation are available only to the analyst, who extracts generalizations from it and asserts their validity based on his own observations. This approach is commonly used in psychoanalytic writing.

8. Truth in labeling—the writing analyst should identify the means by which the patient's confidentiality is protected so that the reader has as clear a picture as possible of the relationship between reported events and actual clinical happenings.

1. *What They Don't Know Won't Hurt Them*

This position holds that so long as patients remain unaware of publication they are not hurt by it. It rests on three assumptions: that the analyst can accurately judge whether clinical publications will become known to the analysand or people the analysand knows, that only the analysand whose confidentiality is breached is affected, and that the major impact of publication is revelation of private information.

Each of these assumptions can be mistaken. Experience suggests that analysts' judgments about the extent to which clinical material will be recognized is often faulty. For example, a training analyst presented a candidate's dream in a paper given to a local psychoanalytic society. The analyst believed that only the patient would recognize the dream. In fact, three colleagues easily identified the patient. Another analyst wrote a book about the treatment of a seriously disturbed child, confident the child and his family would never read it. As a young adult, the patient did read it, and, like Freud's Dora, the belief that he was a famous patient became central to his identity, with detrimental effects.

The literary scholar Jeffrey Berman (Berman, 1985) explored an example of such failed judgment. The author Philip Roth's analyst published an article in *The American Imago* (Kleinschmidt, 1967) containing material Roth could easily recognize. Because of the material's similarity to a story Roth published in *The New Yorker*, Roth was identifiable as the patient. To support this contention, Berman compared the *New Yorker* story with the *Imago* article. He points to Roth's fictional account in *My Life as a Man,* in which a young writer discovers his analyst published a scholarly paper that not only mirrors his life but also describes the patient's publication in a national magazine (Roth, 1974). To what extent Roth's account of events, in *My Life as a Man,* corresponds to what transpired between him and his analyst is uncertain. It is even less certain that Roth actually responded with the rage and disillusionment that his fictional protagonist did. However, it is clear that Roth's analyst misjudged the situation. Other clinical reports describe similar distress among analysands who recognized their own case histories (Person, 1983; Stoller, 1988).

Analysands and potential analysands who read *My Life as a Man* (which as Berman observes is among the best literary portrayals of psychoanalysis) are made aware of the possibility that their analyst might write about them. Such awareness can have a range of meanings from horror at real and imagined consequences of such public revelation to exhibitionistic fantasies or longing to contribute to the analyst's fame and fortune. Thus, not only the analysands who are described are affected by analysts' decision to publish. An ethical decision about publishing patient information should therefore include consideration of the impact on other and potential analysands. Awareness that some analysts publish on a "what they don't know won't hurt them" basis can introduce rational and irrational concerns into analyses or make others avoid analytic treatment.

Finally, the "what they don't know won't hurt them" position ignores the impact of writing on the analyst (Stein, 1988; Stoller, 1988; Lipton, 1991; Gabbard, 2000). The anticipation of writing is likely to change the way the analyst listens and interacts with the analysand. For example, the analyst may try harder to transcribe or recall the precise words of the patient and so adopt a different focus of attention than the analyst ordinarily would. Fantasies of the audience's response tempt the analyst to act in ways that anticipate the audience's imagined questions and criticisms. Patients' ideas that their analysts may write about them and their responses to the analyst's altered technique are, of course, subject to analytic scrutiny that may benefit the patient. Other elements that complicate the analytic process might not be addressed or worked through. An analyst's narcissistic investment in writing can interfere with the analyst's recognition of alterations in the analytic technique and the patient's response to such alterations. For example, anticipating writing about the importance of transference interpretations, an analyst might make more such interpretations without being aware of doing so, and the patient might respond to this alteration in the analyst's technique, but none of this would be brought into the analysis for appropriate scrutiny.

2. The Analyst Has the Responsibility to Protect the Patient from Any Harmful Effect of Publication

This standard was first formulated by the Committee on Scientific Activities (1984) of the American Psychoanalytic Association as follows:

> The analyst is ethically free to publish clinical records without the patient's knowledge, provided their publication has no effect on the patient, his relatives, or associates and provided they reveal no confidential material relating to the patient. While absolute certainty is impossible, the analyst can and must know that it is extremely unlikely that the material he reports will be connected to the patient. If it cannot be so connected and if the material contains no secret material of public or business policy that the patient may possess, there is no barrier to the analyst's freedom to publish [p. 440].[2]

The Committee favors this position: "If he does not know of it, the patient and his analysis are spared a complicating set of events.

---

[2] This position was never adopted by the American Psychoanalytic Association but was for many years the only statement generated by an official body within the association regarding the issue of confidentiality and publication. The current ethics code of the association does address these issues and will be discussed later.

Consequently, this is often the optimal procedure to follow. It does, however, require that extremely prudent, careful, and thorough precautions be taken" (p. 441). Vigorous measures to protect the patient's identity are advocated, although not at the cost of introducing misleading information. Informed consent and working through the clinical meaning are recommended in the event that the patient could become aware of the publication. The responsibility to protect confidentiality cannot be placed on others, such as institutional review boards, and, although ethics committees can provide guidelines, the burden of confidentiality rests on the analyst's judgment.

Experience shows that the analyst's judgment, inevitably swayed by the same motives that lead to publication, might not be a good guide. The situation involving Phillip Roth's analysis, discussed previously, is a good example. Roth's analyst, the model for the famous Dr. Spielvogel, was actually Hans J. Kleinschmidt. Kleinschmidt, in his article on creativity, apparently did not realize that he was describing an incident from Roth's analysis that Roth was including in an autobiographical *New Yorker* story (Berman, 1985). The analyst also failed to note that his theory of creativity closely paralleled a theory propounded by one of Roth's characters. While few analysts are likely to blunder so egregiously, opportunities for faulty judgment about protecting confidentiality abound when publishing clinical material. Most clinical material identifies the analyst-author, and many analysands freely identify their analysts. A patient's identity, rather than one among all analytic patients, becomes one among a few. Gabbard (2000) suggests that an analyst other than the treating analyst publish case material to eliminate this identifying factor. However, it seems unlikely that many analysts who write will forgo the rewards of being the identified author of their work.

The analyst cannot assess what information will be recognized in the future, either by the patient or others. Nor can analysts be expected to anticipate future developments in technology or privacy expectations. Until the end of the 1980s, an analyst could anticipate that his contribution would be tucked away in a professional journal, read by professional colleagues, and soon lost to all but the most dedicated searchers. Today, that same analyst's work, published in English-language psychoanalytic journals, can be accessed in minutes using the Psychoanalytic Electronic Publishing Archive, accessible in many libraries. These rapid changes would tax judgment, undistorted by personal motivation, of the most ethical, technically sophisticated analyst.

Analysts can be misled about which information is identifying. An adolescent depreciatingly described a parent's preoccupation with a hobby that seemed to reveal aspects of the parent's personality. Assuming the hobby would be recognized only by family and close friends, the analyst presented case material to a professional audience. He was shocked when two colleagues independently told him that the patient could be easily identified because the parent's hobby received public recognition.

These considerations make it difficult to support the view that the publishing analyst should be the ultimate authority in protecting the patient's confidentiality.

3. Descriptions of Small Clinical Interchanges Protect Confidentiality

In the *Introductory Lectures*, Freud suggests that the details of the analytic interchange are so difficult to identify that they can be made public without risk. For example, it seems improbable that anyone would recognize the following exchange:

> Patient: I . . . er . . . feel kinda . . . I don't know . . . you might say down today.
>
> Analyst: The way you say that suggests you are being cautious and concerned about how I would describe your feeling.
>
> Patient: Yeah. I guess, you've noticed, something like that I always . . . er . . . I guess, I am careful in what I say.

Some analysts believe that much analytic work occurs in such interchanges and that through them analysis can be adequately studied (e.g., Gray, 1973, 1982, 1990). They embrace this mode of publishing case material because it allows description of small transactions that they believe are central to analysis while protecting patient privacy. Researchers have shown that studies even more remote from clinical material, such as investigations of word frequency, can yield significant analytic findings (Bucci, 1985, 1988; Bucci, Kabasakalian-McKay, and RA Research Groups, 1985). Publication of such patient information does not infringe on privacy or breach confidentiality.

The use of microscopic or statistical samples of analytic work, however, has other serious drawbacks. Research methods influence the direction of research and shape not only the answers to questions but also the questions themselves. Researchers can only engage in "doable" research. What cannot be approached using available methods is generally put aside and left unexplored,[3] an occurrence particularly evident in psychology. Because the mind is not subject to direct observation, whole schools of psychology eliminate study of the mind. Similarly, limiting case materials to microscopic events could bias psychoanalytic research. Many analysts believe that the development of analytic theory and technique requires the understanding of large-scale narratives. Limiting detailed case descriptions to small-scale exchanges elevates theories that regard such exchanges as central. For example, the common analytic experience that analytic work may proceed very slowly for months on end to be followed by rapid change has been the subject of interesting investigations based in the theory of nonlinear dynamic systems (Palombo, 1999). Such phenomena can only be studied by exploring the material of several months or years of the analyses. The limitation of research because of methodological considerations can be highly misleading. For example, because brief psychotherapy is easier to study in detail, there is far more published data supporting its effectiveness than there is for psychoanalysis. But the conclusion that brief therapy is more effective than psychoanalysis is misleading (Garfield and Bergin, 1986; Orlinksy, Grawe, and Parks, 1994).

4. Informed Consent

In general, medical-research emphasis has shifted from protecting patient identity to gaining informed consent for potential loss of privacy (Smith, 1995). However, informed consent in biomedical research is often a formal ritual to stave off malpractice litigation. It is often given by desperate patients who can only find treatment as guinea pigs.

Neither analyst nor patient can reasonably foresee the consequences of publishing analytic material. Informing the patient is lim-

---

[3] The mathematician René Thom gives an excellent example. Although the study of water waves is very advanced, until very recently there was no means to study surf mathematically. As a result, even though surf is apparent to the most casual observer of water waves, the phenomenon remained without mention in the study of the physics of water waves. Not even the failure to have an adequate theory of surf was mentioned (Thom, 1975).

ited to stating this uncertainty. Further, the analyst's request for informed consent is likely to disrupt the analysis. If the request is made
before the analysis begins, especially in reduced-fee situations, this
could suggest that the availability of analysis is contingent on giving
consent. To reduce this possibility, some researchers limit their subjects to individuals paying full fees (Offenkranz, and Tobin, personal
communication, 1974). During analysis, such a request could disrupt
the emerging transference. Although examination of the patient's response to the request could enrich the analytic process, the request
is likely to divert attention from more spontaneously emerging issues. Following the analysis, such requests can reawaken transference issues for the patient. Transferences are not fully resolved
at termination, and reengagement with the analyst is likely to reawaken issues for the patient that had been put aside (Schlessinger
and Robbins, 1974, 1975, 1983).

If the patient refuses permission, it takes a strong analyst not to
be influenced in his attitude toward the patient. It is always disap-
pointing for an analyst not to be able to write about noteworthy
clinical situations. When the inability to publish arises from the patient's
refusal, the resulting countertransference could negatively impact the
analytic work.

Some analysts (Schwaber, personal communication, 1990) provide a copy of the material proposed for publication, inviting comments and corrections, as well as asking permission. Such collaboration
provides opportunity for enriched clinical understanding of the material within the psychoanalytic dialogue. At the same time, permission to publish is contingent on the patient's satisfaction with the
analyst's portrayal of the patient. Thus, descriptions not to the patient's
liking are less likely to be published. This could induce the analyst to
write descriptions and interpretations that are designed to please the
patient and invite consent. Such distortions in published reports of
analytic work put the research and the therapeutic venture at risk.
Informed consent for publication, as well as the process of requesting it is fraught with difficulty.

5. Disguise of Patient Identity and Case Material

The term "disguise" has two connotations: the omission of patient-
identifying information and the inclusion of misinformation designed

to veil identification (American Psychological Association, 1992; Aron, 2000; Gabbard, 2000; American Psychoanalytic Association, 2002).[4]

It is argued that confidentiality can be maintained by sufficient disguise, but with the narrative nevertheless remaining true to analytically significant facts and happenings (Gabbard, 2000). Analysts' opinions differ about the extent to which the various forms of disguise achieve this end. It is difficult to judge which information would reveal a patient's identity. It is more difficult to decide which facts are most pertinent and which can be disguised without loss of accuracy. This decision is often contingent on the analyst's theoretical orientation. The common transformation of a physician to a lawyer or vice versa might strike some analysts as a distortion rather than a disguise. Some authors change the gender of patients or describe events from psychotherapy as occurring during analysis. They believe such changes are justifiable since the analytically significant elements are not changed. However, analysts who do not share the same theoretical presuppositions believe such changes introduce misinformation into the clinical report. With regard to the examples of changing gender or treatment arrangements, some analysts argue that they make such a fundamental difference that altering this information inevitably distorts the case report.

Gabbard (2000) argues that analysts are able to judge reliably which facts may be altered. I cannot concur because this opinion presumes that the analyst understands the case material sufficiently to know which facts are pertinent and how the case material will be used by readers.

Adequacy of disguise is also a problem. Phillip Roth's analyst transformed him from a Jewish-American novelist in his late 20s to an Italian-American poet in his early 40s. Still, alert readers were able to identify Roth. It is not uncommon for patients to recognize themselves or to be recognized when the analyst believes the disguise is adequate.

The problem with disguise, however, is more profound. Active disguise distorts, and misinformation is presented as scientific data. If we maintain with Bacon that the core feature of scientific knowledge

---

[4] In his otherwise excellent discussion of these problems, Glen Gabbard (Gabbard, 2000) misquotes the Committee on Scientific Activities, 1984, of the American Psychoanalytic Association (Klumpner and Frank, 1991) as advocating disguise as an appropriate means of protecting patients. In fact, the committee was opposed to disguise because it introduces misinformation into clinical reports, but the committee recommended omission and condensation to protect patient privacy.

is that its data and reasoning can be publicly inspected, the publication of misinformation, whatever the purpose or belief of the author, is unacceptable. Two examples illustrate how disguises thought to be neutral led to significant misinformation appearing in the analytic literature.

In one example, a paper on the impact of traumatic medical intervention in early life included a vignette describing a patient who underwent a common medical procedure: I will call that procedure *A*. The procedure seemed to have a significant impact on the patient's psychological development. Attempting to protect the patient's confidentiality, the analyst substituted another common medical procedure, *B*. The analyst believed the two procedures were equivalent with respect to the central hypothesis. When a study group reviewed the material knowing that procedure *A* rather than procedure *B* was performed, they did not agree that the difference between the two procedures was insignificant with regard to the article's scientific issues. The condition for which procedure *B* was performed involved symptoms that might have contributed to the patient's current personality organization. Consequently, a plausible alternative explanation for several of the findings emerged. The disguise destroyed the clinical report as a useful source of scientific data.

In the second example, Slap and Trunnell (1987) explored the concept of the self-state dream (Kohut, 1971), which includes a self-state representation, not in the form of symbolic disguise but as a vivid concrete representation of this state. Kohut recommends understanding and interpreting these dreams on this basis. Critics suggest that these dreams are best understood in the same manner as other dreams. Whether such dreams are best understood by reading meaning from their manifest content or understanding dreams by traditionally using associations to specific dream elements is near the heart of the controversy about the interpretive methods of self psychologists (Reed, 1987).

Slap and Trunnell (1987) discovered that an analyst apparently used the same dream on three occasions, each time with significant details changed. In an oral presentation the dream was described as follows:

> The patient was in a ghost town. He was surprised to see his parents there. Their house was different and unusual; it had a special room for his [younger] brother, and he [the patient] felt surprised. Then he noticed something had happened to his sports

car—it had become ordinary-looking. It was underpowered, smaller, and he couldn't make it work right [p. 256 n].

In a subsequent published version (Goldberg, 1974), the dream is reported this way:

He had a dream about an empty lake-resort town and how upset he is to discover his parents there. Their own cottage is different and unusual in that it has a special room for his older brother, and he is surprised at this. Moreover, something seems to have happened to his little fishing launch: it has become an ordinary-looking, underpowered rowboat, which he can't make work [quoted in Slap and Trunnel, 1974, p. 257].

In another published version (Tolpin and Kohut, 1980) is the following:

He was in an empty lake resort town. He was surprised to see his parents there. Their house was different and unusual; it had a special room for his [younger] brother, and he [the patient] felt surprised. Then he noticed that something had happened to his fishing launch—it had become an ordinary-looking rowboat. It was underpowered, smaller, and he couldn't make it work right [p. 258].

Assuming the validity of the concept of the self state dream, all three versions of the dream are nearly equivalent. They suggest that the loss of his parents' positive engagement resulting from their attention to his brother left the patient feeling depleted and diminished. In fact, Tolpin (Tolpin and Kohut, 1980) wrote to Slap asking, "Does it matter in essence whether one is lonely in a lake-resort town or in a ghost town? Does it matter in essence if the self is depicted as depleted by the use of an underpowered boat or an underpowered automobile? I think not" (p. 253). For the analyst who does not assume that these dreams refer to self-states and who, for example, focuses on castration anxiety, the various states of wetness and dryness, the choice to represent a car versus a boat as a phallic symbol, the difference between a hand-operated rowboat and a motor-powered launch, as opposed to a less powerful automobile, would likely suggest significantly different meanings for the dream.

In both examples, the author chose to disguise clinical material in a way that hypotheses that differed from the analyst's own were less likely to be given serious consideration. If the reader is informed that the material is disguised, he must rely on the analyst to retain pertinent facts and introduce no new information. The uninformed reader is left with potentially significant misinformation and must remain satisfied with the claim that the analyst knows the meaning of the data that is never directly presented. In either case the possibility of testing the author's hypothesis is lost as a result of the introduction of misinformation.

Having had the opportunity to examine disguises used by colleagues, I am impressed how often analysts fail to see that the clinical material is distorted so as to interfere with the exploration of alternative explanations of data.

After careful consideration, the Committee on Scientific Activities of The American Psychoanalytic Association (1984) recommended against disguise. Instead, it recommended that when information should not be published it should be omitted or accurately described but with less information. Instead of turning doctors into lawyers to protect confidentiality, information about the analysand's work could be omitted or a more general term, like "professional" could be used.

A problem with this recommendation is that it leads to less persuasive writing. It also raises the question of how the data presented in psychoanalytic publications is understood by readers. In all disciplines, authors' capacities to persuade readers of the validity of their viewpoint influence the acceptance of ideas, independent of the quality of data and its support for the hypotheses. Spence (1982, 1983, 1986, 1990, 1994) argues that psychoanalysts have erred far in the direction of adopting persuasive discussion over evidence in reaching analytic formulations. He shows how convincing stories can serve as rhetorical devices in analytic arguments. A narrative typically requires forms and devices that make it convincing and memorable. These include concrete details, which are most convincing if they are manifestly irrelevant while remaining in some sense telling. Such details persuade readers that the narrative is true to life (Ekman, 1992). Proust's sudden flood of recollection on biting into a madeleine is much more persuasive than an announcement that the same recollections had been precipitated by "a gustatory experience."

If, in the foregoing first example, the symptoms of the illnesses were given and medical procedures specified, the vignette would be vivid, memorable, and persuasive, albeit at the cost of further violating the patient's confidentiality but without introducing misinformation into the psychoanalytic literature.

6. Forwarding Research Is More Important than the Maintenance of Confidentiality

This argument is plausible if it is believed that the future of psychoanalysis and its therapeutic benefit is threatened by the paucity of psychoanalytic research. If analysis fails to survive, protecting confidentiality means little. If thousands of people suffer because empirically valid research is impossible, should this not weigh against the risk of damage that could result from violating confidentiality? On one hand, this argument, similar to that used to argue for universally condemned biomedical research makes even the most vigorous research proponents ill at ease. On the other hand, some of the most enthusiastic proponents of confidentiality have largely ignored the impact on the benefits of psychoanalytic research that would result if analysts ceased to describe clinical work publicly.

The tension between private and public information in psychoanalysis has rarely been addressed, so no thoughtful positions have emerged. The research value of a psychoanalytic publication has rarely been raised as a defense against breach of confidentiality. There is a paucity of case opinion, but those that are available are of particular interest because they give the views of disinterested parties.

In *Doe v. Roe and Poe,* a 1977 New York case, Dr. Doe sought the suppression of a book coauthored by her analyst Dr. Roe and the analyst's husband, Dr. Poe. The book included extended descriptions of Doe's analysis. Doe was quickly recognized by several friends. Roe, Poe, and their publisher argued that the book should not be suppressed because of its scientific merit. The case has a complex litigation history, but only the trial judge carefully addressed the science issue. Quoting extensively from psychiatric opinions on the importance of confidentiality he held that the right to confidentiality, is strong but not absolute and asked whether in the current case public interest in the publication of scientific information outweighed this right. Thus, he opened the possibility that if a work has sufficient scientific merit it might be appropriately published despite a consequent violation of confidentiality. In this case, however, the judge found that the defendants "utterly failed" to prove that their work "represented a major contribution to scientific knowledge." The court did not say how it would have determined the level of scientific value needed to overcome the right of confidentiality.

In line with this judge's reasoning, what is needed in other cases, though difficult, is a decision weighing the scientific value of publication against the consequences of violated confidentiality. However, there is a hopeful note here. Weighing public interest against individual interest is the subject of extensive legal and ethical discourse. As a result of this discourse, psychoanalytic discussion can relate to the large body of ideas on these issues.

7. Mediated Empiricism or "Trust Me—I'm an Analyst"

Psychoanalysts put forward their clinical and personal experience as psychoanalytic facts. This generalization is obscured if accompanied by a description of a case. It is often left unclear whether the case is offered as evidence for the clinical generalization or as an illustration designed to clarify that generalization. Information is rarely provided about how the material presented in the case history was selected or how the generalization was reached. The reader must rely heavily on the judgment of the reporting analyst.

The process of this type of generalization is seldom specified in psychoanalytic publications. Issues such as the extent to which the clinician's experience represents a sample of a population or the process by which the analyst settled on the published hypothesis as opposed to others are rarely addressed. To protect confidentiality, Gabbard (2000) suggests condensing clinical material from several patients into a composite. He gives examples of important clinical material that could never have been presented in any other fashion. Unfortunately, such condensation relies heavily on the judgment of the analyst, which the reader has to trust.

It might be thought that reliance on the analyst's judgment parallels the reliance readers in scientific disciplines place on the scientist who presents research findings in summary form. However, researchers in most sciences describe procedures so that they can be inferred from the publication. Analysts are trained neither in the collection nor the reporting of data. Even the sophisticated analytic reader cannot infer how the case material was processed and how the generalizations provided relate to actual clinical happenings. Assuming the scientific integrity of the researcher, readers can relate scientific data to the author's claims. Unfortunately, no such inferences are possible in psychoanalysis because of a lack of agreed-upon scientific methods of interpreting case material as data—that is, ways to move from data to clinical generalization and from clinical experience to public description. The reader of an analytic publication is left taking the generalization from clinical description on faith or treating it as mere collegial opinion to be accepted or rejected to the extent that it fits in with the reader's preexisting views and experiences. Consequently, psychoanalysts are slow to integrate into their knowledge base information developed by colleagues, and psychoanalytic disagreements are difficult to resolve on a satisfactory intellectual basis.

Countertransference and related psychological processes suggest that clinical descriptions can be trusted only as engaging narratives when those descriptions are not carefully and systematically monitored for distortions. There are several ways in which this situation could be improved. Analysts could systematically ask themselves to what extent the information they are providing suggests misinterpretations. A colleague or group of colleagues could be invited to discuss the material prior to presentation to a larger audience. Such consultation could include more information than would be provided in a paper that was to be publicly disseminated, and fellow analysts could suggest how proposed descriptions of the material might be misleading. This would be best achieved if the consultants included individuals with markedly different viewpoints from those of the writing analyst.

8. *Truth in Labeling*

Clearly, there is no entirely satisfactory solution to the conflict between confidentiality and research. However, recognizing and addressing the conflict can diminish its impact. Analysts and editors of analytic publications could diminish the confusion by clarifying the status of the published material. Notes such as the following could accompany clinical publications: "While certain information has been omitted from this report, all statements contained in the report are true to observations." "To protect the privacy of the patient while maintaining narrative coherence, certain facts in this report may have been altered. These facts may include the patient's profession, physical appearance, marital status, and the words used to report his dreams." "The case material presented here is not a record of an actual clinical experience. It is a fictional situation designed to illustrate the author's ideas; the author, however, believes the situation to be clinically plausible." Editors of psychoanalytic publications could require authors either to submit such statements or demand certain standards of veracity for published materials.

It should be noted that truth in labeling does not result in the label being read. Michael Basch carefully indicated in his books on psychotherapy that the clinical vignettes presented were plausible fictions designed to illustrate Basch's ideas (Basch, 1980, 1990, 1992). Despite these warnings, this same clinical material has been reported by others as evidence for some of Basch's concepts as though it represented actual clinical events.

Conclusion

The relationship of confidentiality to the publication of psychoanalytic research is intrinsically difficult. The dilemma is real because both confidentiality and research are necessary for psychoanalysis to survive.

Failure to recognize the dilemma leads to problems. On one hand, many analysts have published case material without thinking through the ethical dilemmas involved. The untoward results can be demonstrated in many particular instances. On the other hand, ethics committees and advocates for confidentiality have formulated regulations and offered opinions that, if enforced, would end psychoanalytic research. Indeed, some leading analysts who have published case material have stopped doing so, whereas others have avoided publication from the beginning of their careers.

Proposed solutions for these problems, in particular the use of disguise to protect patient privacy, have a negative impact on the scientific status of psychoanalysis because of the need for publicly shared data. Unfortunately, apparently reasonable compromises based on seemingly reasonable anticipations of the likely fate of published information do not stand up to close scrutiny. In an age where information is ever more available, reasonable anticipations are extremely difficult to make. Similarly, the seemingly promising informed consent is fraught with difficulty because information is lacking and because the power relationship of analyst and patient is such that consent can hardly be characterized as freely given in the usual sense. Attention must be repeatedly drawn to the complexity of the problem of confidentiality and research in psychoanalysis and to the danger that seeming solutions can create profound difficulties.

References

American Psychoanalytic Association (2002), *Principles and Standards of Ethics for Psychoanalysts*. New York: American Psychoanalytic Association.

American Psychological Association (1992), Ethical principles of psychologists and code of conduct. *Amer. Psychol.,* 47:1597–611.

Appelbaum, P., Uyehara, L. & Elin, M., eds. (1997), *Trauma and Memory*. New York: Oxford University Press.

Aron, L. (2000), Ethical considerations in the writing of case histories. *Psychoanal. Dial.,* 10:231–45.

Bacon, F. (1620), *Novum Organum*, ed. T. Fowler. Oxford: Oxford University Press, 1878.

Basch, M. (1980), *Doing Psychotherapy*. New York: Basic Books.

———— (1990), *Understanding Psychotherapy*. New York: Basic Books.

———— (1992), *Practicing Psychotherapy*. New York: Basic Books.

Berman, J. (1985), *The Talking Cure*. New York: New York University Press.

Bucci, W. (1985), Dual coding: A cognitive model for psychoanalytic research. *J. Amer. Psychoanal. Assn.,* 33:571–607.

———— (1988), Converging evidence for emotional structures: Theory and method. In: *Psychoanalytic Process Research Strategies,* ed. H. Dahl, H. Kächele & H. Thomä. New York: Springer-Verlag, pp. 29–50.

———— Kabasakalian-McKay & RA Research Groups (1985), *Instructions for Scoring Referential Activity (RA) in Transcripts of Spoken Narrative Text*. Garden City: Adelphi University.

Committee on Scientific Activities (1984), Ethical conduct of research in psychoanalysis. *Bull. Amer. Psychoanal. Assn.,* 40:439–445.

Decker, H. (1982), The choice of a name: "Dora" and Freud's relationship with Breuer. *J. Amer. Psychoanal. Assn.,* 30:113–136.

Deutsch, F. (1957), A footnote to Freud's "Fragment of an analysis of a case of hysteria." *Psychoanal. Quart.,* 26:159–167.

Ekman, P. (1992), *Telling Lies*. New York: Norton.

Erikson, E. (1964), *Insight and Responsibility*. New York: Norton.

Freud, S. (1905), Fragment of an analysis of a case of hysteria, *Standard Edition,* 7:1–122. London: Hogarth Press, 1953.

Gabbard, G. (2000), Disguise or consent: Problems and recommendation concerning the publication and presentation of clinical material. *Internat. J. Psycho-Anal.,* 81:1071–1086.

Galatzer-Levy, R. (1993), The rewards of research. *J. Amer. Psychoanal. Assn.,* 41:393–409.

———— (1996), Review of validation in the clinical theory of psychoanalysis: A study in the philosophy of psychoanalysis by Adolf Grünbaum. *J. Amer. Psychoanal. Assn.,* 44:594–598.

Garfield, S. & Bergin, A. (1994), Introduction and historical overview. In *Handbook of Psychotherapy and Behavior Change,* ed. S. Garfield & A. Bergin. New York: Wiley, pp. 3–18.

Goldberg, A. (1974), On the prognosis and treatment of narcissism. *J. Amer. Psychanal. Assn.,* 22:243–254.

———— (1997), Writing case histories. *Internat. J. Psycho-Anal.,* 78:435–438.

Goldstein, J., Freud, A. & Solnit, A. (1979), *Before the Best Interest of the Child*. New York: Free Press.

Gray, P. (1973), Psychoanalytic technique and the ego's capacity for viewing intrapsychic activity. *J. Amer. Psychoanal. Assn.,* 21:474–94,

—— (1982), "Developmental lag" in the evolution of technique for psychoanalysis of neurotic conflict. *J. Amer. Psychoanal. Assn.,* 30:621–655.

—— (1990), The nature of therapeutic action in psychoanalysis. *J. Amer. Psychoanal. Assn.,* 38:1083–1097.

Grunbaum, A. (1982), Can psychoanalytic theory be cogently tested "on the couch"? Part 2. *Psychoanal. Contemp. Thought.,* 5:311–436.

—— (1984), *The Foundations of Psychoanalysis*. Berkeley: University of California Press.

—— (1986), Precis of the foundations of psychoanalysis: A philosophical critique. *Behav. & Brain Sci.,* 9:217–284.

—— (1990), "Meaning" connections and causal connections in the human sciences: The poverty of hermeneutic philosophy. *J. Amer. Psychoanal. Assn.,* 38:559–577.

—— (1994), *Validation in the Clinical Theory of Psychoanalysis*. Madison, CT: International Universities Press.

Jones, E. (1953), *The Life and Work of Sigmund Freud*. New York: Basic Books.

Kleinschmidt, H. (1967), The angry act: The role of aggression in creativity. *Amer. Imago,* 24:98–128.

Klumpner, G. & Frank, A. (1991), On methods of reporting clinical material. *J. Amer. Psychoanal. Assn.,* 39:537–551.

—— & Galatzer-Levy, R. (1991), Panel reports, presentation of clinical experience. *J. Amer. Psychoanal. Assn.,* 39:727–740.

Kohut, H. (1971), *The Analysis of the Self*. New York: International Universities Press.

Lipton, E. (1991), The analyst's use of clinical data and other issues of confidentiality. *J. Amer. Psychoanal. Assn.,* 39:967–985.

Meissner, W. W. (1990), Foundations of psychoanalysis reconsidered. *J. Amer. Psychoanal. Assn.,* 38:523–557.

Orlinksy, D., Grawe, K. & Parks, B. (1994), Process and outcome in psychotherapy—Noch Einmal. In: *Handbook of Psychotherapy and Behavior Change,* 4th ed., ed. A. Bergin & S. Garfield. New York: Wiley, pp. 270-376.

Palombo, S. (1999). *The Emergent Ego*. Madison CT: International Universities Press.

Person, E. (1983), Women in therapy: Therapist gender as a variable. *Internat. Rev. Psychoanal.,* 10:193–204.

Popper, K. (1965), *Conjecture and Refutations*. 2d ed., New York: Basic Books.

Reed, G. S. (1987), Rules of clinical understanding in classical psychoanalysis and in self psychology: A comparison. *J. Amer. Psychoanal. Assn.,* 35:421–446.

Roth, P. (1974), *My Life as a Man*. New York: Holt, Rhinehart & Winston.

Schlessinger, N. & Robbins, F. (1974), Assessment and follow-up in psychoanalysis. *J. Amer. Psychoanal. Assn.,* 22:542–567.

—— & —— (1975), The psychoanalytic process: Recurrent patterns of conflict and change in ego functions. *J. Amer. Psychoanal. Assn.,* 23:761–782.

—— & —— (1983), *A Developmental View of the Psychoanalytic Process*. New York: International Universities Press.

Slap, J. W. & Trunnell, E. E. (1987), Reflections on the self state dream. *Psychoanal. Quart.,* 56:251–62.

Smith, R. (1995), Publishing information about patients: Time to change from guarding anonymity to getting consent. *Brit. Med. J.,* 311:1240–1241.

Spence, D. (1982), Narrative truth and theoretical truth. *Psychoanal. Quart.,* 51:43–69.

―――― (1983), Narrative persuasion. *Psychoanal. Contemp. Thought,* 6:457–481.

―――― (1986), When interpretation masquerades as explanation. *J. Amer. Psychoanal. Assn.,* 34:3–22.

―――― (1990), The rhetorical voice of psychoanalysis. *J. Amer. Psychoanal. Assn.,* 38:579–603.

―――― (1994), *The Rhetorical Voice of Psychoanalysis.* Cambridge, MA: Harvard University Press.

Stein, M. H. (1988), Writing about psychoanalysis part 2: Analysts who write, patients who read. *J. Amer. Psychoanal. Assn.,* 36:393–408.

Stoller, R. (1988), Patients' responses to their own case reports. *J. Amer. Psychoanal. Assn.,* 36:371–91.

Thom, R. (1975), *Structural Stability and Morphogenesis.* Reading: Benjamin.

Tolpin, M. & Kohut, H. (1980), The disorders of the self: The psychopathology of the first years of life. In: *The Course of Life, Vol. 2.* Madison, CT: International Universities Press, pp. 229–253.

Wallace, E. R. (1989), Pitfalls of a one-sided image of science: Adolf Grunbaum's "Foundations of psychoanalysis." *J. Amer. Psychoanal. Assn.,* 37:234–240.

Wallerstein, R. S. (1988), Psychoanalysis, psychoanalytic science, and psychoanalytic research—1986. *J. Amer. Psychoanal. Assn.,* 36:3-30.

Introduction to CHAPTER 8

❧

Confidentiality and Training Analyses

Ronald Britton and Robert Michels, both eminent psychoanalytic educators and clinicians, were invited separately to present their views on the confidentiality of the training analysis. Each emphasizes that a training analysis is inherently a personal analysis that prepares the candidate for the emotional challenges of analytic work. Although a consensus appears to have been building in favor of nonreporting training analysts, the controversy over this issue has by no means subsided, as recent articles in *International Psychoanalysis,* volumes 9 and 10, indicate (Gampel, 2000; Johns, 2000). A consideration is the kind of situation that developed in Brazil, where a training analyst in a Rio institute, SPRJ (Rio 1), remained silent about a candidate who was acting as a consulting psychiatrist in the torture of political prisoners (Gampel et al., 2000).

Commenting on the impossibility of a perfect containing function in any area of life, Ronald Britton (1992) stated, "If we are to live within ourselves or in our families or institutions, a degree of mutual recrimination between container and contained seems inevitable." In this chapter, Britton maintains that training analysts, institutes, and psychoanalytic societies face conflicting responsibilities to the candidate, the profession, and the public, responsibilities that single ethical codes cannot resolve. To deal with these inherent tensions and dilemmas, he proposes that simple flexible arrangements based on ethical principles rather than rigid procedures can and should allow for limited communications between training analysts and institutes.

CHAPTER 8

Confidentiality and Training Analyses

Ronald Britton

*I*n this chapter, I discuss the compromises in absolute confidentiality regarded as necessary by some training organizations, those that I believe are inevitable in a training analysis. What I mean by a training analysis is one that has the purpose of equipping a candidate to practice analysis. I believe that a training analysis should be no different from any other analysis. Along with supervision and seminars a personal analysis is a required component of psychoanalytic education. Before discussing the question of confidentiality, I put forward reasons why I think a candidate's analysis is an essential part of training.

First, the candidate experiences the benefits of a personal analysis, including self-understanding, increased permeability to his or her own unconscious, increased capacity to contain emotional reactions and impulses to action and familiarity with personal transference reactions.

Second, the "would be" analyst develops the ability to use oneself as an instrument in the analysis of another person. This development involves an increased access to unconscious communications and the undeclared internal emotional states of other people. Such enhanced capacity can be destabilizing for the candidate and can make the emotional proximity of others more threatening and uncomfortable. This disturbance needs to be worked through in the candidate's personal analysis.

Third, the analyst needs to develop the ability not only to contain the projections of his patients but also to reflect on his interaction with patients and to monitor the inevitable tendency to enact his particular unconscious object relationships with his patients.

Essentially, two situations exist with regard to the confidentiality of training analyses—that is, the confidentiality obligation of the training analyst to candidates in personal analysis. In certain institutes, there is some communication, however limited, between the training analyst and the organization. In most others, the analysis is regarded as independent of the training organization and there is no communication about it. Whether the analysis is concurrent with the training or, as in France, precedes it, in my opinion, makes no real difference to the question of compromising the confidentiality of a *required* analysis. In most systems, confidentiality is not breached *beyond* the knowledge somewhere in the organization that a candidate is, or was, in analysis with a particular analyst. A training organization may require nothing more from their candidates than their agreement to undergo this analysis and from the analysts their agreement to undertake it.

My experience of supervising analysts working in such a system has made me acutely aware that the analyst's ethical problems do not end with the protection of confidentiality, whether or not the particular institute has a no-reporting policy. The problem is that the candidate is not only a patient to the analyst. The analyst has, in addition to the well being of his or her patient, *implicit responsibilities*. Because the analysis is a core component of the training, the candidate's analyst plays a part in the training and hence in the eventual *attestation* of the candidate's suitability to be an analyst. There is also a responsibility to psychoanalysis in that the quality and integrity of an institute's graduates reflects on the profession as a whole. The training organization attests that a candidate has an acceptable degree of professional competence, ethical values, and emotional stability. The analyst may be the only person in the training institute to seriously doubt a candidate's possession of emotional stability and ethical integrity.

In the following case, these responsibilities are in conflict and presented a confidentiality dilemma to the training analyst. A candidate was apparently proceeding through the training with no adverse opinions from her teachers or supervisors and was progressing without interruption. In the analysis, however, nothing resembling an ordinary analysis had ever gotten underway. The candidate was extremely phobic of the analytic situation, had never used the couch, could not tolerate interpretations, and was nevertheless clinging and dependent on the analyst, reacting to weekends and breaks with suicidal feelings. The analyst worked with the patient sensitively but was concerned. The candidate now had a patient with whom she completely identified, and was secretly at odds with her supervisor. She saw her role as protecting the patient from "that sort of analysis." It was fairly clear "that sort of analysis" was *any* sort of analysis. Her control case was not particularly unusual nor did it pose great problems for analysis, but this was a serious and very ambitious candidate who was about to qualify as an analyst. In defense of complete separation of training analyst and training organization, it is often said that the analyst can refuse to continue the analysis if, after expressing misgivings to the candidate, the candidate nevertheless insists on completing the training. In practice, however, in the sort of case such as the one here, the last thing an analyst can do is abandon the patient. If the analyst did so, the decision would have to be communicated to the institute and would thus breach the shield of confidentiality.

One way or another, whether the analysis is concurrent with the training or precedes it, the absolute degree of confidentiality that we would like to offer our patients is to some extent compromised in the training analysis of a candidate. How then can this breach of confidentiality be minimized? I have reached the conclusion that *overt and strictly limited contact* between training analyst and the institute leads to less leakage than the various informal aberrations that otherwise are likely to arise. The conflicts between maintaining confidentiality and attestation of suitability arise at those points in the training where a new step is being taken. Should the analyst have any part in the decision about a candidate's readiness to take the next step, for example, at the time of registration, beginning work with patients, completion of the supervision of training cases, and graduation? One possibility is that the training organization could inform the analyst of its intention to allow the candidate to take the next step unless they hear from the analyst that there are analytic reasons for not doing so. The silence of the analyst attests to the candidate's readiness in that it is an indirect communication that the analyst does not have grave concerns about the candidate progressing, concerns that cannot be worked out in the analysis. I think that it is not necessary or desirable for the analyst to give reasons and certainly not to discuss the candidate with the institute.

And here there is another difficulty. The wish to protect the patient's confidentiality is in conflict with safeguarding natural justice. Clearly, the training organization needs to trust the training analyst and so does the patient. The patient is more likely to do that if she feels that she has chosen the analyst herself and has the freedom to leave that analyst and go to another without prejudice. I realize that local circumstances can make that impossible, and that is one of the general difficulties that arise in small and isolated institutes.

The training analyst has certain responsibilities that present confidentiality dilemmas, namely maintaining patient confidentiality, while participating in the training of candidates who will be ethical and competent analysts (thereby protecting the public from incompetent treatment, upholding the reputation of the profession, and protecting the rights of individuals). These responsibilities are inevitably in conflict at times. No legislation or ethical code can eliminate these dilemmas faced by training analysts, institutes, and psychoanalytic societies. Principles seem to be better guides than procedures in these matters, and the simplest arrangements allow for the greatest flexibility.

References

Britton, R. (1992), Keeping things in mind. In: *Clinical Lectures on Klein and Bion.* London: Tavistock/Routledge, pp. 102–113.

Gampel, Y. et al. (2000), Comments on the IPA Executive Council's decision at the meeting in December 1999, in New York, in relation to Rio 1. *Internat. Psychoanal.,* 9:5–6.

Johns, J. (2000), The status of training analyst. *Internat. Psychoanal.,* 9:20–22.

Introduction to Chapter 9

❦

Confidentiality, Reporting, and Training Analyses

In a recent article, Robert Michels (2000) says of case reports that "all of them are stories told in one relationship about what has transpired in another. . . . The context in which a story is told may become even more important than the story itself." In this chapter, Michels argues in effect that this is especially true of the practice of the analyses of candidates in psychoanalytic training. He maintains that even minimal reporting by a training analyst deprives the candidate of a real analysis, thereby disadvantaging candidates, their institute, and the profession as a whole. His argument in support of the shift away from reporting in training institutes "is based on the principles of clinical practice rather than the ethics of confidentiality."

CHAPTER 9

&

Confidentiality, Reporting, and Training Analyses

Robert Michels

*T*here was a time when many training analysts felt a conflict between their responsibility to their candidate-patients and their responsibility to their institute and profession, a conflict reflected in the
quandary between the confidentiality that is an essential component
of clinical analysis and the evaluating and reporting function that is
part of all professional education. Today, at least in North America,
this time has passed, and the great majority of training analysts are
happy that this is so.

The fundamental reason for this change is based on the principles of clinical practice rather than the ethics of confidentiality.
There is a growing recognition that a training analysis is, first and
foremost, a clinical psychoanalysis and that true psychoanalysis is
impossible if the analyst has a reporting responsibility. The old reporting system was based on a fundamental paradox. The formative
analytic experience of candidate-analysts that was to serve as the
basic prototype for their future clinical work was a sham, a pretend
analysis that was contaminated by a major conflict of interest, conducted by an analyst who was listening in part with a concern that
was not related, and at times even contradictory, to analyzing the
patient and involving a patient who had an adaptive, rational, and
therefore unanalyzable motivation for massive resistance.

Of course, all analyses are conducted by analysts with conflicting interests, and all resistances have adaptive motives. There is a
difference, however, in the case of the reporting training analyst in
that these are not unavoidable unconscious or inevitable contami-

nants. They are purposefully and intentionally structured into the situation by the analyst's choice, and particularly because most training analysts do not do this it is apparent that it need not be so. Analyses can tolerate a great many potential intrusions and interferences, as long as patient and analyst can maintain a basic contract to explore, understand, and work them through. What analyses cannot tolerate is an explicit, conscious intentional decision to conduct some other business that is contradictory to the analysis and will interfere with it. It may not make much difference whether that other business is financial, sexual, or educational evaluative—each violates a boundary and exploits a potential analytic relationship for a nonanalytic motive.

In spite of this rather strong statement, a great many presumably successful training analyses have been conducted under reporting conditions. Concerns about reporting may not have been central, or critical, to many analysts and many candidates, and the reporting that did occur may have been trivial or pro forma. One might suspect that major interference was most likely when the reporting was potentially significant—that is, that only candidates who might have been in greatest need were deprived of the possibility of analysis. Of course, the reporting arrangement would still have a negative effect on all analyses in that it offered an educational model at odds with the profession's core beliefs, and not all candidates would be good judges as to whether their reporting analyst might actually feel compelled to report.

As long as the candidate is aware of the reporting arrangement, the issue is not one of the ethics of confidentiality so much as the ethics of professional practice. The patient-candidate who knows that the analyst is reporting has at least been alerted to the potential risk of exposing him or herself. By contemporary clinical standards, the candidate should also be alerted that the great majority of the profession believes that this is the wrong way to conduct an analysis and that the value of the procedure is likely to be compromised as a result. The patient will not share thoughts and feelings that he or she wants to keep confidential, while the analyst who is preparing a report will shift from the mental state of doing analysis to that of grading and evaluating. The candidate may pretend to be in analysis, while the training analyst pretends to conduct one, but this only adds an additional note of inauthenticity. They are both involved in a mutually negotiated contract to pretend to do analysis. Many have noted the frequent result that after graduation, analysts view their training analyses as having been conducted "for the institute" and embark on a postcandidacy analysis "for themselves." This can also occur in the absence of reporting but when there is reporting, the chances of an institute analysis being "for the candidate" are greatly reduced.

The essence of psychoanalysis is an analyst who tries to be there, with and for the patient, listening in order to understand and to share that understanding. Other motives intrude, and when the analyst recognizes them they are treated as countertransference signals, potentially valuable in understanding the relationship. If the analyst embraces another motive rather than attempting to analyze it, he or she is regarded at worst as unethical and at best as unanalytic. It is appropriate, and ethical, to interrupt an analysis in order to prevent great evil or danger—murder, mass destruction, or child abuse. There may be times when candidate analyses might be interrupted for such reasons, but certainly they would be few and far between and would raise serious questions about the institute's selection processes. The reporting function was not designed for such purposes, but rather to guide educational decisions. It suggests that analysts view their own profession as more vital, or perhaps more fragile, than the social roles of their other patients, that it is more important to report on candidate analysts than on airline pilot analyses, or surgeon analyses, or psychotherapist analyses. It also suggests that a problematic candidate may perform in a way that is evaluated as competent by his or her instructors, supervisors, and colleagues but is actually defective and can only be detected by the training analyst. Many have found the opposite to be more common; training analysts attempt to convoy candidates who are seen as problematic by others on the faculty.

In sum, a reporting analyst is doing something other than analysis. A reporting situation is not really an analytic situation. The breach of confidentiality may be unethical not because it violates an analyst-patient contract (in a reporting institute, there is no such contract) but because it leads to substandard professional practice. Reporting deprives the candidate of a real analysis and hurts the candidate, the institute, and the profession.

References

Michels, R. (2000), The case history. *J Amer. Psychoanal. Assn.*, 48:355–375.

Introduction to CHAPTER 10

◦◦

Confidentiality, Privacy, and the Psychoanalytic Career

Patient confidentiality inevitably overlaps with concerns about the analyst's own privacy throughout the analytic career. Mary Kay O'Neil argues that absolute confidentiality potentially complicates privacy, thereby affecting the analyst's professional development, self-expression, reputation, and legacy. A preliminary report of a survey of current North American and British Societies' and Institutes' policies and practices provides the basis for discussion of this inherent tension in the analyst's experience surrounding confidentiality. Consideration is given to how the profession can assist analysts in maintaining patient confidentiality while protecting their own privacy.

CHAPTER 10

❧

Confidentiality, Privacy, and the Psychoanalytic Career

Mary Kay O'Neil

*C*onfidentiality and privacy are of concern to both analyst and patient in varying, overlapping ways. Initially confidentiality was not part of the analytic vocabulary but was implicitly understood. Contemporary psychoanalytic theory and codes of ethics explicitly articulate confidentiality as fundamental to ethical practice. Privacy is not usually stated as a professional requirement; yet it is the privacy of the analytic couple and the analytic space that confidentiality protects.

Understandably, much attention is given to confidentiality as the patient's right and the analyst's professional obligation. Little systematic consideration, however, has been given to the impact on the analyst of maintaining patient confidentiality or to the privacy dilemmas that psychoanalysts encounter at each phase of their professional lives. Although the analyst must keep the patient's confidence, the patient has no such obligation to the analyst or to the analytic situation, nor is there formal protection of the analyst's privacy. Furthermore, there are ways in which the maintenance of *absolute* confidentiality can potentially impinge on the analyst's own privacy, professional development, self-expression, reputation, and even right to practice.

This chapter will examine the predicaments faced by analysts as candidates, as practitioners, and at retirement and posthumously with regard to patient confidentiality as it relates to their own needs for privacy. In general, I will argue that the analyst's experience at different stages in his or her career tends to foster a more relativistic and potentially more flexible attitude toward confidentiality than the often cut-and-dried strictures that appear in the literature and in ethics codes, and that are taught in ethics courses. I will suggest, moreover, that central to how analysts tacitly experience issues of confidentiality is an overlapping area of concern for their own sense of privacy.

Confidentiality and the Psychoanalytic Candidate

Candidates are taught through the modeling of personal analysts, through supervision, and through ethics courses that patient confidentiality is based on respect for the privilege of entering another person's inner world. They soon become aware, however, that confidentiality is far from absolute. Paradoxically, just as they realize that confidentiality is integral to good analytic practice, they are confronted with certain breaches taken for granted throughout training.

From the first, the patient's confidentiality and the analyst's privacy are intertwined. Supervision of control cases, essential to learning analytic technique, depends on candid discussion of the interchange between candidate and patient. Just as patients struggle with resistance to say whatever comes to mind, so too candidates struggle to reveal in supervision what they do with patients. The struggle is twofold and revolves not only around revealing patients' confidences but also around revealing their groping attempts to analyze. Candidates no less than patients have to trust that supervisors will protect their confidences. Certainly, discussions of confidentiality are part of the learning process, but a supervisor's attitude toward the privilege of entering a candidate's inner world as well as the patient's teaches more about respect for a person's privacy than didactic talk about confidentiality. Perceived attitudes teach values and reinforce the basic principles that become an ingrained sense of confidentiality boundaries.

Patients are also discussed, in principle anonymously, with faculty members and other candidates in continuous case seminars as an integral part of the curriculum. This practice has long been considered indispensable as a teaching tool and, to paraphrase one institute's handbook, greatly adds to the responsibility that each candidate assumes. Morally and ethically, candidates and faculty who are privy to illustrative case examples are expected to treat these with the same respect given to their own patients. The task, however, of maintaining patient confidentiality and the felt necessity of protecting one's own sense of privacy overlap readily for the candidate vis-à-vis their own cases. And this sense of a dual reticence, which may not be articulated, informs how the candidate hears senior practitioners as they describe their own work. In point of fact, what the candidate readily grasps is that discussions of patients are the seeming lifeblood of the institute and that concern for confidentiality, although always presumably present, is a second-tier concern most of the time. This exposure to wide-ranging discussions of patients, moreover, comes at a time in the candidate's professional development when anxieties about his or her own privacy are likely at a maximum.

Candidates' own confidentiality is most threatened during their training analyses. The longstanding controversy over reporting or nonreporting training analysts has never been fully resolved. Based on decades of experience, most intitutes have adopted a nonreporting policy and seek to maintain separation between progress in training and personal analyses. Yet questions remain. If a training analyst is active on institute progress committees, it is hard to believe that some leakage does not occur, when a candidate is discussed, if only through a look or perhaps through silence. It is interesting to note that a few institutes openly continue to involve the training analyst in the decision to allow a candidate to begin a training case. In support of such minimal reporting, it has been argued that the analyst might be the only one to know that a candidate is not suitable for analytic work. Obviously, even minimal reporting, with potentially grave consequences, represents an incursion on the candidate's confidentiality. Joan Fleming (1973) suggests that constructive use can be made of the analyst's opinion about a candidate's progress within the training analysis itself:

> An honest "I don't know if you are ready to start with a patient," or "I don't think you are ready," or "Yes, I think so," followed by, "And what is your reaction to what I say?" provides more productive analytic work than a dead silence or an interpretation which does not include the realistic elements of current professional ambition, or a statement such as, "You know I have nothing to do with your training" [p. 76].

Her comment recognizes that candidates sense the hypocrisy of pseudoneutrality just as patients are cognisant of the limits of absolute confidentiality. Candidates also sense when "nonreporting" does not quite mean *no* reporting. Cabaniss et al. (2003) report that vague criteria for candidate progress, even in nonreporting institutes, induce paranoia and potentially exacerbate threats to their confidentiality and sense of privacy.

It can be argued that, unlike patients, candidates forfeit privacy in that those aspects of their "private self" related to the development of their "analytic self" necessarily must become known to many institute members. During the application process, suitability for training is assessed through intrusive personal interviews and reports. Dossiers are kept on accepted applicants, and minutes of institute meetings record progress decisions made by the training committee. Only members of the institute directly involved can access candidates' files; one would assume that candidates have access to their own files. Such access is not always institute policy and even when it is, few candidates dare to ask. What protects candidates' privacy are commonly understood ethical guidelines; for example, the British Psycho-Analytical Society's Ethical Code and Guidelines (2000) reads: "Reports and other personal communications on students must be treated as strictly confidential and for use of only those immediately responsible in the training organization."

In essence, candidates need to know that it is safe to reveal their self-doubts, mistakes, unacceptable feelings, and impulses aroused by the emotional intensity of their work, and that their learning will be assessed and discussed purposefully to facilitate their growth as analysts. Their concerns about their privacy frequently give rise to untoward anxiety. Institutes do try to alleviate such anxiety by facilitating access either to the director, another designated institute member, or, for issues that cannot be discussed with assigned advisers, to faculty not involved in progress decisions. Yet there remains a paucity of literature or formal consideration of this issue.

Evaluations regarding candidates' progress also involve other privacy issues. For the most part, training-committee decisions are communicated on an individual basis, and problems are discussed with supervisors or advisors. Providing a protected learning frame, however, does not mean avoidance of confronting candidates who have problems. As Kernberg (2000) points out, however, direct discussion with the candidate is all too often avoided:

> Supervisors as well as seminar leaders tend to be reluctant to express their criticism to candidates and often do it only indirectly, in communication to other members of the faculty, so there develops a less than totally honest atmosphere surrounding candidates who have problems in the course of their education [p. 109].

Such an atmosphere, obviously, feeds back into the training milieu and affects candidates' willingness to share more sensitive information about themselves and their work. Thus, the goal of confidentiality can become associated with avoiding the worst, as the patient's right becomes contaminated with the beleaguered candidate's fear. Dismissal of a candidate when lack of suitability becomes evident is a difficult and often-avoided decision. Aside from brief statements in student handbooks to the effect that the training committee reserves the right to suspend an unsuitable candidate, there is also a paucity of discussion on this topic.

Then there is the matter of records. Despite privacy considerations, there may be cogent reasons for preserving candidate training records beyond graduation, the primary one being learning from experience to improve selection criteria and training programs. Anna Freud (1971) urged that training analysts, when assessing candidates, "look not only into the future of the candidates but into the past of the psychoanalytic movement" (p. 78). The importance of examining the selection and progress of candidates was recognized almost 40 years ago with the Columbia University project, "Psychoanalysts in Training: Selection and Evaluation" (Klein, 1965). This study, of two decades' duration, had available rather unique data: each candidate's complete dossier. It is doubtful whether such a study of candidates is feasible today. Most institutes keep minimal information (training and graduation dates, hours of supervision, name of training analyst) beyond a candidate's graduation. Those that do maintain full files do not have a systematic method for defining the nature of the data and standards for ethical use. In some APsaA institutes, such records are used for membership certification. Since the Columbia project, no further studies of candidates' training experience seem to have been undertaken nor has there been a study comparing accepted versus rejected applicants. Selection criteria have changed due more to external factors than to internal evaluation of optimal selection methods to predict a "good fit" between applicant and institute.

More recently, attention has turned to comparing successful and unsuccessful control cases. In the report of Glick et al. (1996), candidates' and patients' confidentiality was protected by anonymity, and it fell to the candidates/analysts to explore reasons for premature termination of their control cases. Might such a study not be enriched if the candidates' case reports and supervisory evaluations were additional data to be considered? The onus is on institutes to find ethical ways of collecting, interpreting, and utilizing data on candidates' progress and their control cases to improve case selection, supervision, and teaching methods. A format for collecting such data in which candidate privacy and patient confidentiality is protected would be of value, not only in studying the efficacy of control analyses but also in studying candidate learning patterns and the effectiveness of training programs.

Policies and practices of psychoanalytic societies, under the guise of confidentiality, have long been cloaked in mystery for all, including candidates, who are not members. Fortunately, candidates are no longer excluded from scientific meetings, and now most institutes encourage their participation on various educational committees. It remains a challenge for societies and institutes to provide an atmosphere in which unnecessary secrecy has no place, where respect for privacy and patient confidentiality can accommodate appropriate sharing of knowledge.

Privacy and confidentiality take on different meaning at graduation, as candidates make the transition from analysands to colleagues of their training analysts. Certainly, the ethic of confidentiality for what transpired within the analytic relationship remains unchanged; there are shifts, however, to aspects of privacy. Negotiation of the posttermination relationship has more possibilities and pitfalls for new analysts than for former analysands not in the mental-health field who have fewer opportunities for professional or social contacts with their former analysts. Joseph Schachter (2002), in questioning the traditional analytic attitude toward termination ("no further contact except for therapeutic purposes"), opens the possibility of subsequent collegial and friendship relationships. He notes that when this "occurs it requires major changes of both patient and analyst. The patient must abandon the comforting investiture of the analyst with benign authority and omniscience, and the analyst must relinquish the gratification of this investiture and become much more self-disclosing" (p. 219). Such private posttermination relationships, though rare even for graduate analysts, as Schachter cautions, "will probably always mean traversing a rocky path" (p. 219). The attitudes regarding their training analysts' posttermination contacts will influence how they deal with posttermination relationships in their own practices.

Privacy for the Practicing Psychoanalyst

The "private self" (Modell, 1993) is an integral part of the expression of the "analytic self." The analyst's "private self" in relation to the patient's inner self is the sine qua non to the "analytic self." Herein lies the paradox: analysts need privacy to integrate their private self with the analytic self. At the same time, they feel called upon, and even need, to risk purposeful self-revelation, not only in relation to patients but also in professional communications to colleagues. A daunting tension arises from the reality that analysts' professional development utilizes that which they are obliged to protect—their clinical experience.

Apart from publications, the analyst must also decide what sort of records to keep. Psychoanalytic data is cocreated. Impingements on records from the outside create confidentiality dilemmas that intrude not only into the analytic relationship but also on the analyst's own professional privacy.

These external challenges most often involve giving evidence in court, subpoenas of records, third-party requests for information, and patients' requests for their own records. Currently, there is legislation in progress that distinguishes the formal record from the analyst's private working notes. Recent judgments and minority opinions further protect the privacy of records and restrict their use as evidence in court. This does not, however, protect the analyst from being subpoenaed to give evidence and sometimes having to identify a person as a patient.

Requests for information by insurers and other third-parties, albeit with patient permission, also intrude on the analytic relationship, even when limited to treatment demographics. That the patient is being treated is no longer private; the analyst enters the patient's external world, and outsiders are brought into the analytic communication. The privacy of an analyst's practice can be further intruded on by third-party audits and quality-control agents. Some professional associations, to maintain standards, also randomly monitor record-keeping practices.

Patients may ask to see their own dossiers. To share the clinical record with a patient is not a breach of confidentiality, as it is commonly now accepted that health-care records belong to the patient. Indeed, some analysts propose that discussion of their notes can be therapeutic (Stoller, 1988). Patient access to the analyst's notes, however, might not advance and can potentially harm the analysis and its outcome. More specifically, working notes usually contain thoughts, feelings, fantasies, and countertransference experiences. Does the analyst have a right to keep private those notations that normally are shared with the patient only selectively and purposefully through verbal interpretations? As Furlong (1998) suggests, the "analytic mental space, symbolized by the dossier, is viewed as neither uniquely the analyst's nor the patient's [but as] a complex dialectical chamber, the privacy of which must be respected, even by the patient whose discourse contributes to it, in order for it to function effectively" (p. 727).

Protection of the Analyst's and the Profession's Reputation

Psychoanalytic ethics committees have the tasks of protecting the public against unethical treatment, the psychoanalyst against false complaints, and the reputation of the profession. The degree to which privacy and confidentiality are compromised in this process varies with the seriousness of the complaint and the way in which the ethics committee handles it. When a complaint of unethical behavior is made, an analyst must respond to the Society's ethics committee to defend himself. Although the confidentiality obligation would then rest with the ethics committee, the analyst inevitably struggles with breaking confidentiality beyond what is revealed in the complaint as well as the intrusion into his professional privacy.

How much clinical material is needed for the analyst to present a defense, for the patient to be satisfied of a fair hearing, and for the ethics committee to reach a just decision? The evaluation of clinical material (the analyst's records and testimony) presents dilemmas for the committee and the analyst. An analyst's commitment to not disclose a patient's secrets, even at personal expense, is weighed against the need for self-defense. This is particularly painful because the analyst is confronting both colleagues and a patient with whom there has been a therapeutic relationship. The wrongly accused analyst may have to reveal very sensitive aspects of interaction with the patient to demonstrate that his practice was ethical. An innocent analyst's records may contain the analyst's self-observations that can be misconstrued by others, including the patient and the ethics committee. On one hand, careful clinical notes, especially of the treatment of suicidal, paranoid, and borderline patients, can provide useful protective evidence. On the other hand, there is potential for harm when a patient prematurely learns about diagnosis, dynamics, and transference. With or without records, the accused analyst must decide whether to remain silent or reveal what he knows to protect himself. Obviously, the guilty analyst will want to avoid revealing anything that could provide evidence of wrongdoing and will not record incriminating behavior. The ironic twist to the goal of protecting both analysts' privacy and patients' confidentiality is that, under the guise of confidentiality, a realm of secrecy and a cover for unethical practice can be created.

Confidentiality, Privacy, and Professional Self-Expression

To learn, teach, write, and express their own thinking, analysts draw on their clinical experience. Without access to patients' inner worlds, advances in psychoanalysis would not have occurred. In no other profession is this raw data so integral to the essence of the theory, the technique, and the work itself. And in no other profession is there such a commitment to restricting the communication of these very findings.

Analysts' need to communicate their experience has to be weighed against the yet little-understood effect on the analytic self of not communicating. The challenge consists in distinguishing between what constitutes patient information and what belongs to the analyst, given that there is a permeable boundary between the patient material and the analyst's thinking. The maintenance of a standard of absolute confidentiality can detrimentally inhibit analysts' communication. Analysts with an extreme view of their confidentiality obligation refuse to write or present professionally because of discomfort with revealing any patient material whatsoever. (Of course, for some this masks a writing inhibition or inability rather than a true confidentiality concern.) If in the interests of confidentiality, however, boundaries become too impermeable, if the profession's collective superego is too rigid, or if it seems impossible to separate whose thoughts are whose, the inhibition is as much a professional as a personal concern.

In practice, the usual manner of maintaining relative confidentiality for the patient's benefit allows analysts to reveal what occurs in the consulting room during personal analysis, teaching, supervision, and consultations, provided due discretion to protect patient identity is used. Unquestionably, confidentiality is unethically breached if carelessness about notes or appointment books results in disclosure of patient information, if patient identity is otherwise revealed without consent, if consultation with colleagues is casual and discussion verges on gossip or carelessly takes place in a public venue, or if insufficient attention is paid to what information is disclosed how, where, and to whom.

Does a practicing analyst's revealed confidences about self in relation to patients also conflict with patient confidentiality? Yes, in the sense that what derives from the analytic dyad is taken outside the consulting room. Patients are not always told specifically that the analyst confides in a personal analyst or a consultant or makes clinical presentations at professional meetings. Although patient identity is rarely revealed deliberately, the patient can sometimes be recognized. This is especially a risk when the patient is a member of the therapeutic community. Personal analysts, consultants, and supervisors, however, are equally bound to confidentiality.

Are patients aware that confidentiality is circumscribed, that the confidentiality promised implicitly or explicitly has its limits? Most, preconsciously at least, realize that their analysts might discuss their treatment with a colleague and trust this is done anonymously and for their benefit. The unconscious meaning of such awareness obviously varies and is of differential concern. Is the analyst's need to communicate thoughts about patients made explicit and the patient's reaction subsequently analyzed as it arises? Does the analyst say nothing unless questions are raised by the patient? Again, the meaning of these alternatives to the analytic dyad has to be weighed in each situation. Further discussion is required in the interest of greater openness regarding such impingements on confidentiality in analytic practice.

The importance of the case history to the development of psychoanalytic theory, technique, research, and teaching is of current relevance. David Tuckett (1991, 1993, 1995, 2000), as editor of the *International Journal of Psychoanalysis,* called attention to the paucity of published clinical accounts of analyses, encouraging ethical and creative use of case histories in the literature. *The Journal of the American Psychoanalytic Association* (2000) devoted most of its Spring issue to discussions of Robert Michels' plenary address, "The Case History" (Michels, 2000). Michels proposes that the scarcity of clinical material "reflects not only the methodological problems in describing cases but also the complex intentions of psychoanalysts who want both to present and to conceal aspects of their work."

Psychoanalysis is at least as much an art as it is a science. Clinical data is not the same as objective scientific data. Whether in a case presentation, consultative discussion, or published accounts, what is presented is always filtered through the psyche of the analyst. As important as facts are to the reporting of a case, possibly more is learned from the analyst's conceptualizations of the material presented. This does not solve the dilemmas of using conventional methods to protect confidentiality while attempting to provide accurate data from which others can draw conclusions. Nor does it address the relative value of strictly accurate versus disguised, fictitious, or amalgamated data. The clinical communications of a presenter or author generate thoughts not so much about the particular case presented as about the listener's or reader's own work. Is it really known which aspect of published case material stimulates thinking and increases others' understanding of their psychoanalytic work with patients? How reports of clinical material are processed and applied to work with other patients has rarely been addressed. From Freud to the current generation, however, analysts' reports about their patients have inspired the analytic work of others.

Privacy at Retirement

Most analysts are in private practice, many without secretaries; their patient lists are known only to themselves. There are accepted ways to deal with planned absences, but analysts are also vulnerable to human crises—accidents happen, and illnesses or death can occur unexpectedly. Although leaving a sealed patient list with a trusted colleague or a Society representative might be considered a breach of confidentiality, the obligation to provide the best patient care is primary.

What about an unanticipated inability to practice at all? How can an analyst assure confidentiality in the event of life-threatening illness, infirmity, premature aging and retirement, or sudden death? These uncontrollable eventualities deserve timely consideration, and professional wills can be useful here. What of the analyst who is unaware of, or in denial of, incompetence and has made no provisions for patient care? Often, concerned colleagues assist. In addition, psychoanalytic societies can lend support by defining a process, respectful of patient confidentiality, analyst privacy, and the public good, to handle not only unethical behavior but also unexpected or unacknowledged incompetence.

Posthumous Privacy

Analysts want to ensure that patient confidence will not be breached posthumously and that their own privacy will not be invaded. Ideally, they plan ahead for closing their practices and leaving a psychoanalytic legacy. Unless otherwise specified in a professional will, it is assumed that a close colleague or the family will destroy patient files or seek guidance from the local Society. What actually transpires, however, will depend not only on the analyst's directives but also on the perceived importance of the analyst's contribution, the local availability of psychoanalytic archives, and archival policies.

The histories of individual analysts, of analytic organizations, and of the contributions of their founders and members are essential for the preservation of the history of psychoanalytic ideas. Biographies, autobiographies, memoirs, historical documentation, published papers, and commentaries all contribute to the continuity, growth, and relevance of the profession. Without archival records, it is difficult to track the origins, development, and vagaries of psychoanalytic concepts. Without some personal record, accurate biographical histories of analysts and their careers cannot be written. An example of professional "deception" came to light when it was revealed that the case of Mr. Z was autobiographical and that Heinz Kohut was referring to his first analysis with Ruth Eisler and, in Mr. Z's second analysis, to his self-analysis (Strozier, 2001; Gedo, 2002).

Anna Freud (1971) links the first phase of an analyst's life, as a candidate, with a predicament in the last phase, that of analysts writing their own history:

> Thus candidates are guided how to extract the maximum of information from transference, resistance, dreams, other id derivatives, or ego mechanisms; how to time their interpretations; in short how to cure their patients. They receive no guidance in such important matters as how to record their material or shift and summarize it or verify their findings or pool them with others; how to trace the history of psychoanalytic concepts, to inquire into their definitions, and to clarify and unify their technical terms; how to select specific areas for their research interests or to become alerted to the gaps in our knowledge [p. 57].

There are, of course, confidentiality pitfalls in writing psychoanalytic history. As Michels (2000) notes, the true identities of all of Freud's patients are known today, despite Freud's assurance that "every case history which I may have occasion to publish in the future will be secured against their perspicacity by similar guarantees of secrecy."

The potential conflict between the writing of a biography based on accurate information and respecting the analyst's privacy is illustrated in recent biographies of Karen Horney (Quinn, 1987) and Karl Menninger (Friedman, 1990). Out of respect for the privacy of Horney's daughter on whom she depended for information, Susan Quinn, Horney's first biographer (1987), decided that Horney's relationship with a younger ex-patient was not relevant to the story of her life. Such protection of Horney has since been questioned, however, on the grounds that her boundary crossings were too serious not to be discussed. Seven years later, Bernard Paris (1994), another biographer, who did not have the same involvement with Horney's family and whose attitude perhaps reflected the change in social attitudes toward privacy, was less hesitant to write about that same relationship. Notably, he attempts to connect the "messy details" of Horney's life with her mature theory. Arguably, Menninger and his family were personally harmed by the publication of his previously secret love affairs while no important historical purpose was served. The Horney episode is more complex.

Scrutiny of the private self is a risk of the profession if the analytic self is to be communicated. Even Freud, the first such communicator, was aware of this risk and destroyed many of his personal papers. As Gay (1988) observes, "He reported and closely analyzed some of his most revealing dreams; he recorded some embarrassing memories of his early years. On the other hand, he dammed the stream of self-disclosure the moment he felt it threatening to wash away his cherished secrets."

Being an analyst involves a privacy paradox; the work requires both the space for private reflection and the ability to let others into one's inner space. As Kohut remarked, "The good analyst will have a personality characterized by central firmness and peripheral looseness" (Gabbard and Lester, 1995, p. 24). The analyst's privacy is always relative given that much of the inner self is revealed whenever an analyst communicates his way of thinking and working. Most analysts, it seems, are content to adapt a variant of Kohut's maxim vis-à-vis their willingness to reveal themselves, maintaining a private core and a loose periphery. The point here is that this same attitude informs the preconscious orientation of most analysts to patient confidentiality; without thinking things though necessarily, they feel that some "central" aspects of the patients' material must be protected with unshakeable "firmness" but that other aspects are peripheral and may be shared more or less readily with appropriate others. This attitude toward confidentiality, which remains only tacit, has been in place since the analysts' days as candidates, has endured during the course of their career as they communicated with colleagues, and may survive them, with all its ambiguities, in the form of records that will be disposed of at the discretion of family or colleagues or the local archivists.

Epilogue
Current Practice: Preliminary Findings

A research project, *Confidentiality and the Role of Psychoanalytic Societies and Institutes* (O'Neil, 2001), approved by the International Psychoanalytical Association's Research Committee, surveyed by questionnaire all American, British, and Canadian psychoanalytic societies and institutes. The purpose was to obtain information about policies and practices with regard to confidentiality in psychoanalytic education, ethical codes, ethics committees, guidelines for publication, and archives.

Preliminary results give evidence of increasing attention to confidentiality issues. Societies in all three countries include in their national and local codes of ethics principles of confidentiality for candidates, analytic practitioners, teachers, and consultants. Almost all institutes now have courses, or at least a seminar, on Ethics, which include confidentiality issues. Coinciding with an emphasis on the development of ethical codes specific to psychoanalysis, candidates are now explicitly expected to abide by these, and in some institutes by signed agreement. At the local, national, and international levels, programs of annual meetings increasingly include sessions on confidentiality. The majority of Societies surveyed reported that formal mechanisms have been set up to facilitate members' consultation with colleagues who have expertise in ethics or with chairs of ethics committees. The American Psychoanalytic Association's Practice Bulletins on record keeping, informed consent, and other confidentiality issues provide guidelines specific to psychoanalytic dossiers and are readily available on the Internet to psychoanalysts from all three countries. Most societies do not yet have professional wills, and the model suggested by the APsaA is not widely used, although there is an increasing awareness of the value of such psychoanalytic documents.

A somewhat surprising finding is that most Societies reported that they had never had a complaint regarding breaches of confidentiality on the part of analysts, in sharp contrast to the unfortunately larger number of other, primarily sexual violation, complaints. This could be interpreted several ways. Either analysts are doing a good job in maintaining confidentiality and patients have no cause for complaint, or patients are accepting of relative confidentiality (for example, candidates and clinic patients are often aware their analyst is being supervised, which may complicate the transference but does not preclude effective analysis). Or alternately, patients could be too intimidated by the psychological power of the analyst to complain or too ashamed to go to court.

With regard to all types of complaints, the majority of Societies take care to separate the functions of ethics committees from the governing role of the Society executive. In most Societies, there are guidelines to ensure that information about both the patient and analyst remains with the committee until a complaint has been resolved. Usually, only in the case of a serious ethical breach warranting suspension or expulsion is the identity of the offending analyst made public. Such policies do not prevent the gossip leaks, which commonly occur. Protecting privacy is particularly difficult in small Societies where it is rarely feasible to have local ethics committees or to hold hearings. The responsibility of the national association in relation to local Societies with regard to ethics hearings remains under discussion. Increasingly, local Societies that have experienced the trauma of members found guilty of ethical violations turn to psychoanalytic consultants or provide opportunities for members to communicate their reactions (Gabbard and Peltz, 2001).

With regard to guidelines for psychoanalysts having to testify in court, it seems that little reliable information is available. Societies report not knowing how many of their members have testified about their analytic cases or how many refused to do so. Few Societies offer formal advice. This is unfortunate because a case book of analysts' struggles in coming to a decision about what to do and the consequences of their decisions could be useful to others faced with similar dilemmas. Similarly, financial aid for legal advice is rarely available, and professional insurance often does not provide adequate coverage.

Few psychoanalytic organizations have official archives, and even fewer have an archivist. Most analysts are not aware of options for preserving their own material or for delving into psychoanalytic history. Often enlightening historical material is discovered by chance. Some local Societies struggle to find space and funds for the preservation of archival material. Most depend on members with an interest in the local history to maintain the story of their organizations' development and of their members' contributions.

The larger psychoanalytic societies, such as the New York Psychoanalytic, do have archivists who develop and maintain policies appropriate to psychoanalytic material. In addition to the New York Archives, which comprise the official papers of the Society and the Institute, the Special Collection of the A. A. Brill Library contains information received from the outside, primarily from the bequests of individual analyst papers. What is kept depends on what is given. Often, families do not know what is in an analyst's papers, and the archivist has to decide what to keep. Patient material is always destroyed. The New York Institute's general restriction and access statement reads as follows:

> It is the responsibility of the A. A. Brill Archives and Special Collections to balance the researcher's need for access with the needs for confidentiality of persons and institutions whose activities are documented in the material. Consequently, the use of some materials is subject to restrictions by the donor or by the Curator.

National associations have begun to consider ways to lend support to local societies in the preservation of psychoanalytic history. For example, the American Psychoanalytic Association's History and Archives Committee has discussed providing assistance on a consultative basis.

References

The British Psycho-Analytical Society. Ethical Code and Guidelines. December 1, 2000.

Cabaniss, D. L., Schein, J. W., Rosen, P. & Roose, P. (2003), Candidates' progression in Analytic Institutes. *Internat. J. Psycho-Anal.*, 84:77–94.

Fleming, J. (1973), The training analyst as an educator. *The Annual of Psychoanalysis*, 1:280–295. New York: International Universities Press. Reprinted in *The Teaching and Learning of Psychoanalysis*, ed. S. S. Weiss.

Freud, A. (1971), *The Writings of Anna Freud*. New York: International Universities Press.

Furlong, A. (1998), Should we or shouldn't we? Some aspects of the confidentiality of clinical reporting and dossier access. *Internat. J. Psycho-Anal.*, 79:727–739.

Gabbard, G. O. & Lester, E. P. (1995), *Boundaries and Boundary Violations in Psychoanalysis*. New York: Basic Books.

———— & Peltz, M. L. (2001), Speaking the unspeakable: Institutional reactions to boundary violations by training analysts. *J. Amer. Psychoanal. Assn.*, 49:659-673.

Gay, P. (1988), *Freud, A Life of Our Time.* New York: Norton.

Gedo, J. E. (2002), Book review: *"Heinz Kohut: The Making of a Psychoanalyst."* *American Imago,* 59:91–111.

Glick, R., Eagle, P., Luber, B. & Roose, S. (1996), The fate of training cases. *Internat. J. Psycho-Anal.,* 77:803-812.

Kernberg, O. F. (2000), A concerned critique of psychoanalytic education. *Internat. J. Psycho-Anal.,* 81:97–120.

Klein, H. R. (1965), *Psychoanalysts in Training.* New York: Psychoanalytic Clinic for Training and Research, Department of Psychiatry, Columbia University, College of Physicians and Surgeons.

Michels, R. (2000), The case history. *J. Amer. Psychoanal. Assn.,* 48:354–420.

Modell, A. H. (1993), *The Private Self.* Cambridge: Harvard University Press.

O'Neil, M. K. (2001), Confidentiality and the Role of Psychoanalytic Societies and Institutes. Final results of this research project to be reported at IPA Congress, 2003.

Paris, B. J. (1994), *Karen Horney: A Psychoanalyst's Search for Self-Understanding.* New Haven: Yale University Press.

Quinn, S. (1987), *A Mind of Her Own: The Life of Karen Horney.* New York: Summit Books.

Schachter, J. (2002) *Transference: Shibboleth or Albatross?* Hillsdale, NJ: The Analytic Press.

Strozier, C. B. (2001), *Heinz Kohut: The Making of a Psychoanalyst.* New York: Farrar, Straus & Giroux.

Tuckett, D. (1991), Fifteen clinical accounts of psychoanalysis—A further invitation. *Internat. J. Psycho-Anal.,* 74:377–381.

———— (1993), Some thoughts on the presentation and discussion of clinical material of psychoanalysis. *Internat. J. Psycho-Anal.,* 74:1175–1190.

———— (1995), The conceptualisation and communication of clinical facts in psychoanalysis. *Internat. J. Psycho-Anal.,* 76:653–662.

———— (2000), Reporting Clinical events in the Journal: Towards the construction of a special case. *Internat. J. Psycho-Anal.,* 81:1065–1069.

SECTION 3

❦

Clinical Practice
Introduction to Section Three

*C*ase material providing evidence of the effects on treatment of threats to confidentiality is extremely rare. There is no officially recognized need for published reports in this area, and the clinician who dares to describe the damaging effects of compromised confidentiality risks the accusation of self-contradiction. In fact, the ethical dilemma in publishing case reports of confidentiality conflicts is no different in principle from that of any case presentation. Though inherently problematic as evidence, case narratives, even when heavily disguised or fictionalized, are an essential component of clinical research and scientific justification. They could play an equally important role in the development of psychoanalytic ethics.

With respect to confidentiality, psychoanalysis is just entering the data-gathering stage of ethical inquiry. The IPA Interregional Conference, "Confidentiality and Society"[1] (2000), brought together researchers from law, ethics, social science, and mental health. A similar conference, "Confidentiality and Mental Health," was held in Sheffield, England (Cordess, 2000). Following up on the Montreal conference and in preparation for this volume, Mary Kay O'Neil surveyed all Canadian, American, and British societies and institutes with regard to current confidentiality policies and practices. In January 2002, the IPA funded a research project to be undertaken by the British Institute of International and Comparative Law.[2]

---

[1] Confidentiality and Society: Psychotherapy, Ethics and the Law: Social, Philosophical and Psychoanalytic Perspectives, October 13–15, 2000, Montreal, Quebec, Canada. In addition to I.P.A. funding, the conference also received financial support from the Social Science and Humanities Research Council of Canada, Justice Canada, the Law Commission of Canada, Heritage Canada, Government of Quebec, Concordia University, McGill Faculty of Law, and the Canadian Psychoanalytic Society.
[2] According to Penelope Garvey, Chair of the Steering Group of this Project, "The aim of the study is to examine and compare the stand taken on confidentiality by

Although external legal threats are growing alarmingly more common, it is significant that most case material involving confidentiality issues features not so much an intrusion from outside the analytic space as the desire, on the part of at least one member of the psychoanalytic dyad, to invite such an intrusion. Philip Roth's *My Life as a Man* (Roth, 1974), though fictionalized, is a good firsthand account, from a patient's point of view, of what might happen when the analyst publishes case material without the patient's permission (Gabbard, 2000). Recently, there have been a number of interesting case reports presenting the experience of psychoanalytic "coconstruction" and authorship, in which the therapeutic drama of the analyst's request for permission from the patient to publish is described (Aron, 2000; Flax, 2000; Gerson, 2000; Pizer, 2000).

Less common are accounts of the analyst's way of handling the patient's wish to disclose the "file" to a third party or to read the file himself. From a certain perspective, the latter circumstance may seem unproblematic because the patient is seen merely to be exercising his option to waive confidentiality, to gain access to *his* "file" or both. In the analytic situation, however, the problem is not nearly so clear cut. The file may be idiosyncratic in nature, and the patient's ethical options and rights are not easy to separate from the clinical issues of transference and countertransference. We hope that the cases of this type presented in this section by Guy Da Silva and Penelope Garvey will be joining what proves to be an expanding genre.

The issue of confidentiality in psychoanalytic societies and training institutes has been the focus of careful ethical scrutiny for some time now and still remains controversial. It is difficult, however, to find narrative reports of the circumstances surrounding breaches of confidentiality in psychoanalytic institutes. One instructive example may be found in Shevrin (1981), involving an institute study of supervision in which supervisees were not informed of their participation (or their patients' unknowing participation) in the study. David Sundelson's chapter provides an uncommonly detailed description of the kinds of things that can go wrong when the psychoanalytic community is not attentive to the handling of conflicts and breaches of confidentiality in its own administrative procedures.

---

different psychoanalytic societies and to compare the status of the confidentiality privilege and its application within the various jurisdictions" (personal communication to C. Levin, September 9, 2002).

To provide the background for these unusual case reports, the Clinical Practice section begins with Craig Tomlinson's thoughtful historical review of the practice of confidentiality since the early days of the Vienna Society meetings, among the first generation of analysts. It is hoped that these four chapters will provide a useful perspective on the difficulty in gathering reliable information on the range of actual ethical practice and the concomitant problem of establishing clear and acceptable principles and guidelines.

References

Aron, L. (2000), Ethical considerations in the writing of psychoanalytic case histories. *Psychoanal. Dial.,* 10:231–246.

Cordess, C., ed. (2000), *Confidentiality and Mental Health.* London: Jessica Kingsley.

Flax, M. (2000), The tapestry of erotic experience: Weaving the threads. *Canad. J. Psychoanal.,* 8:207–231.

Gabbard, G. (2000), Disguise or consent: Problems and recommendations concerning the publication of clinical material. *Internat. J. Psycho-Anal.,* 81:1071–1086.

Gerson, S. (2000), The therapeutic action of writing about patients: Commentary on papers by Lewis Aron and Stuart A. Pizer. *Psychoanal. Dial.,* 10:261–266.

Pizer, S. A. (2000). A gift in return: The clinical use of writing about a patient. *Psychoanal. Dial.,* 10:247–260.

Roth, P.. (1974), *My Life as a Man.* New York: Vintage.

Shevrin, H. (1981), On being the analyst supervised: Return to a troubled beginning. In: *Becoming an Analyst,* ed. R. Wallerstein. Monograph of the Study Group on Supervision of the Committee on Psychoanalytic Education. New York: International Universities Press.

Introduction to Chapter 11

❦

The Early History of the Concept of Confidentiality in Psychoanalysis

The social and professional conditions in which the practice of psychoanalytic confidentiality first emerged and developed were quite different than from our own. Clinician and historian Craig Tomlinson traces the influences that shaped the evolution of confidentiality, subtly identifying precursors of current ethical dilemmas. Of particular interest is the early emergence of varying standards of confidentiality depending on context and often without clear rationale and justification. The leakiness of the professional atmosphere in Freud's day is striking, though Tomlinson rightly notes that historical research can provide little evidence of the observance of confidentiality, as only its breaches are documented, mostly in letters. A historically informed view suggests that the damaging legacy of inconsistent or casual standards of confidentiality has been confined mainly to psychoanalytic organizations.

CHAPTER 11

The Early History of the Concept
of Confidentiality in Psychoanalysis

Craig Tomlinson

*E*arly psychoanalysts inherited a basic notion of confidentiality that is of course at least as old as Hippocrates. This tenet—that clinical discretion is a prerequisite and basis for all patient care—was a part of the medical and psychiatric world in which Freud was trained and that he shared with all European physicians in the nineteenth century. Thus, whereas any discussion of confidentiality in the early decades of psychoanalysis must necessarily begin with Freud, medical and psychiatric notions of confidentiality certainly did not.

How did these concepts of medical discretion evolve along with the specific development of psychoanalysis, with its revolutionary demands for unprecedented and total candor on the part of the patient and complete discretion on the part of the physician? This is harder to answer.

According to Clinton Dewitt's authoritative 1958 survey, *Privileged Communications Between Physician and Patient*, throughout the late nineteenth century the confidentiality of communications between physician and patient was generally left to the ethics of the profession or the dictates of the physician's conscience. Such confidential communication was not protected from disclosure in courts of law, a legal tradition dating to an eighteenth-century English common law ruling (Dewitt, 1958). Contemporary medical encyclopedic references appear to offer little information on how late-nineteenth-century physicians and psychiatrists dealt with the issue. There seems to be no discussion whatsoever, for example, of confidentiality in such compendia as Foster's (1888–1894) *Illustrated Encyclopedic*

Medical Dictionary, Villaret's (1889) *Handwörterbuch der Gesamten Medizin,* the *Real-Encyclopadie der Gesamten Heilkunde* (1907–1914), or the Edinburgh (1899–1910) *Encylopedia Medica.*

Freud's concern for confidentiality in presenting case material begins of course with himself. Numerous accounts of his own dreams appear in "Interpretation of Dreams" (1900) either anonymously or thinly disguised; other early works, such as the "Screen Memories" paper of 1899, also contain thinly veiled autobiographical material. This kind of circumspection is of some interest to ponder with respect to Freud's writings about patients in general, for not only did Freud eschew identifying the patients in his case histories, he chose to focus on clinical discoveries primarily as a way of illustrating developments in theory. It is reasonable to wonder how much his relative distance from narrated case material was a matter of medical discretion and how much it was the natural course of cultural sensibility of a nineteenth-century bourgeois.

This question raises one frequently overlooked point about Freud's attention to confidentiality: considering the total output of his writing and the enormous number of patients he treated over a span of five decades, he wrote relatively little about his own clinical work. The fame of Freud's case histories tends to obscure the fact that compared to his total output, Freud's clinical case histories are actually few in number and are written in a style and with a focus that tends to emphasize theory over immediate clinical experience. After the "Studies on Hysteria," Freud (1895) wrote only six longer case histories, and the last of these was published in 1920 ("The Psychogenesis of a Case of Homosexuality in a Woman"). The development and elaboration of structural theory in the 1920s and 1930s, for example, were all based on his clinical work, yet he completely avoided direct presentation of that clinical work.

Explanations given for this eschewal have typically disparaged Freud's interest in clinical work while stressing his interest in developing a theory of the mind and of human behavior. One need not deny this general tendency in Freud to acknowledge that his clinical experience, and his interest in it, was bedrock for him. Freud's theories were not developed in a library, and it is not unreasonable to assume that concerns about privacy—particularly as he was analyzing so many in his own movement by that time—played at least some role in Freud's preference.

Freud's choices in terms of what to present in public reflect a basic dilemma of psychoanalysis: Although clinical experience constitutes the basic data from which theory and treatment are developed, that same raw data cannot be freely revealed for evaluation and assessment by others. The more mimetic the case discussion, the more psychoanalysis may be criticized for breaching the very confidentiality on which it fundamentally depends; yet the more distance or disguise there is in the presentation of clinical material, by definition, the greater the liability of theorizing without data or with corrupted data.

Some of the basic principles of medical discretion, as well as some of the profession's unspoken compromises in dealing with them, were already apparent in the early meetings of Freud's followers. The *Minutes of the Vienna Psychoanalytic Society*, at least, record frequent presentations of clinical case material almost from the beginning. In 1906 and 1907, for example, cases were presented by Freud, Adler, Sadger and Stekel (*Minutes of the Vienna Psychoanalytic Society*, vol. 1: pp. 57–61, 138–145, 154–158, 172–174, 227–237, 248–253). The most frequent and lively contributor of case material in the early days, besides Freud himself, appears to have been Adler, but Freud's entire circle contributed case material either overtly or in the discussions. Although of course we do not know in full what was actually said, only what was recorded in the *Minutes*, the record at least was set down in such a way as to preserve the anonymity of cases discussed. Freud himself presents substantial patient case material as early as 1907. Patient names are not mentioned, and in fact even the actual case material presented is often omitted altogether, with only the fact of its presentation recorded (often one can glean what the case was about only from the ensuing discussion). Contributions to the meetings were not predominantly case presentations, however, but dealt with theoretical and "applied" topics (the term "applied analysis" was not used at the time).

It is important to take note, however, that some fundamental principles of professional social organization were thus already established in the earliest meetings of Freud's followers: While efforts were made to preserve anonymity, confidential clinical material could be shared freely among colleagues at meetings and even recorded in writing (whether for publication or not), for purposes of therapeutic and theory development. Furthermore, a fundamental distinction was already made in practice between the privacy of the patient and that of the analyst, whose name is readily recorded. Yet in keeping perhaps with Victorian and medical sensibilities and the contemporary lack of understanding of the importance of the role of the analyst, analysts revealed virtually nothing whatsoever about themselves or their own conduct during treatments (although they frequently recorded their names). Little was then understood about the importance of the analyst's actions or of countertransference; intersubjectivity as a theoretical construct remained, after all, almost a century in the future. Thus, early analysts often managed to protect their own privacy, if not their anonymity, in some ways more securely than that of their patients. It is worth imagining that it might have been otherwise: The attendees at the Wednesday meetings at Berggasse 19 might have adopted altogether different standards as to what could or could not be spoken out loud or what levels of privacy were appropriate to maintain for both patient and analyst.

Perusal of the *Minutes* also reminds us that in determining anything about the early history of confidentiality in psychoanalysis we are of course faced with a basic historiographic conundrum: namely, that those historical documents on the subject by their very existence bias the discussion. For in an absolute sense, it is precisely only infringements of confidentiality that can be documented; where confidentiality is entirely preserved there *is* no documentation. In this regard, the tact as well as the concept of open but anonymous case discussion shown in the *Minutes* suggests that some of the aforementioned principles had already become established, not just in Freud's own investigations but also in the social and organizational forums of professional discourse. It is also of interest to the present discussion that these *Minutes,* although preserved by Freud and entrusted to his close colleague Paul Federn when he fled Vienna in 1938, were not published until the 1960s. This fact suggests another precedent was being established: that written records of clinical material for internal educational purposes were already regarded as a more permissible infringement of privacy than published case histories.

Freud's explicit published recommendations concerning confidentiality are interesting to read closely. In "On Beginning the Treatment" he not only takes the physician's need to preserve it for granted but advocates advising the *patient* to keep his treatment in confidence in order to preserve the treatment from disruption (Freud, 1913):

> One will soon find that the patient devises yet other means by which what is required may be withheld from the treatment. He may talk over the treatment every day with some intimate friend and bring into this discussion all the thoughts which should come

forward in the presence of the doctor. The treatment thus has a
leak which lets through precisely what is most valuable. When
this happens, the patient must, without much delay, be advised
to treat his analysis as a matter between himself and his doctor
and to exclude everyone else from sharing in the knowledge of
it, no matter how close to him they may be, or how inquisitive. . . .

Certain patients want their treatment to be kept secret, often
because they have kept their neurosis secret; and I put no obstacle in their way. That in consequence the world hears nothing
of some of the most successful cures is, of course, a consideration
that cannot be taken into account. It is obvious that a patient's
decision in favor of secrecy already reveals a feature of his secret
history. In advising the patient at the beginning of the treatment
to tell as few people as possible about it, we also protect him to
some extent from the many hostile influences that will seek to
entice him away from analysis [pp. 136–137].

That the patient's wish for secrecy is itself eminently interpret-
able did nothing to alter its need for respect; Freud is here equally
prepared to interpret his patient's *non*secrecy and to recommend
discretion on the part of the patient, as well as the analyst, as essential to the treatment.

The extent to which Freud followed his own recommendations
on confidentiality, abstinence, and neutrality—or rather, did not follow them—has, however, been an issue of considerable interest in
recent years. Several studies offer evidence of significant infringements of all three. Most definitively, Lynn and Vaillant (1998) established that Freud communicated with others who were known to the
patient in 23 of 43 cases between 1907 and 1939 for which substantial information about the actual conduct of the analysis was available. These communications also identified the patient, and the
recipients were not consultants or referring practitioners. Though it
cannot always be established, in many cases such communications
were clearly without the consent of Freud's analysands.

Vaillant and Lynn also note that in nearly half (47%) of these
cases, it could be shown that Freud's analysands received information about Freud's other analysands during their analyses. Some of
the details are arresting: With Albert Hirst, Freud discussed two of his
patient's family members in some detail—his sister Ada and his aunt,
none other than Emma Eckstein. With Sandor Ferenczi, Freud communicated extensively about his analysis of Elma Palos in 1912—and
astonishingly, given his correspondent's emotional and sexual en-

tanglements with both the patient and her mother (Lynn and Vaillant, 1998). With Ernest Jones, Freud discussed in detail his analysis of Jones's common-law wife Loe Kann, not only during their affair but after Kann broke it off (Lynn and Vaillant, 1998). In fact, Freud and Jones regularly discussed patients with complex and intricate relationships to themselves and to their own circle in their correspondence, including Joan Riviere and Horace Frink as well as Loe Kann. Joan Riviere had been analyzed by Jones before he sent her to Freud for analysis. Riviere was developing a complex relationship with Jones based on plans for the English translations of Freud. The Freud/Jones correspondence about such patients would today be regarded as highly problematic (Kris, 1994).

With Edith Jackson, Freud both discussed other analysands and violated confidentiality by discussing her with others, including his son Martin. Freud kept the secret of his analysis of his own daughter Anna much more intact within his own circle, despite publishing two papers derived in part from clinical material that developed from it (Lynn and Vaillant, 1998).

Freud's motives for making the technical recommendations that he did, as well as his violations of them, have been the object of much reflection and speculation. Anton Kris (1994) has the following thought:

> I believe that Freud's failure to acknowledge his breaking of the rules should be understood not only as the result of egotism, countertransference, and fear of the unethical misuse of technical freedom but [also] as the result of a divided allegiance between his sense of what was needed by his patients and his determination to promote and preserve the scientific standing of psychoanalysis [p. 661].

It is likely, also, that in at least some cases Freud believed his communications about patients to family members and colleagues, even those with personal entanglements with the same patients, to have been actually useful to their treatments. In other cases, though it would seem hard to understand by today's standards, he may have sincerely (perhaps naively) believed that those same personal entanglements could simply be separated from professional collegial relationships. Charges that Freud sometimes knowingly put the perceived welfare of the institution of psychoanalysis above that of his patients, as has been alleged with respect to his handling of the Frink case, have also been made.

The aforementioned pioneering studies of early psychoanalytic practices remind us mostly, however, of how little we in fact know. In assessing how confidentiality was handled in the first half century of psychoanalysis, we face one enormous problem of psychoanalytic historiography: An adequate and comprehensive history of clinical practice and technique during the first decades of psychoanalysis remains to be written. In addition, much of the relevant information may be presumed to have been orally transmitted, yet our knowledge and records of this oral history are thin. It is of note that essentially all of the many violations of confidentiality cited here do not refer to publications but to letters; of what transpired orally but was not written down we know even less.

When we turn to written records, we remain at a relative loss, as these are few. Interestingly, one of the first descriptions of psychoanalytic case records in the literature discusses various problems connected with record-keeping by analysts but not the effect on the patient (Saul, 1939). Saul noted that extensive record-keeping had been introduced at the Chicago Psychoanalytic Institute six years prior and that the use of records for teaching purposes and analyst study was advocated. Nothing about the confidentiality of such record-keeping, or consent, is indicated in the paper.

Written confidential records of clinical cases for purposes of teaching and education bear a fundamentally different relation to confidentiality from case histories that are written to be openly published. It is important, however, to remember that by definition case histories for both education and publication are a rupture of the absolute privacy of an analytic session.

There appear to have been no court cases involving confidentiality until 1952, more than a half century since the beginning of psychoanalysis. This fact is itself of interest and suggests that, given the enormous numbers of patients treated up to that point, confidentiality was by and large well-maintained. It appears that the first legal challenge in any country was to the *principle* of confidentiality and occurred in the United States in the case of *Binder v. Ruvell* in 1952, in which one side in an Illinois court case sought to *compel* the testimony of Dr. Roy Grinker about a patient (Mosher, 1999).

Though a comprehensive history remains to be written, another notable source of material, letters of the early psychoanalysts, suggest some early problems that developed. During the 1920s, the circular letters of Freud's first "secret committee" of seven, established in 1912, appear by and large to have been more concerned with organizational politics than patient treatment (Grosskurth, 1991). These letters were of course intended as confidential in any case. However, discussions of Rank, including his own confessional circular letter of 1924 based on his "analytical interviews with the professor" again appear to blur the boundaries of confidentiality where Freud's own inner circle was concerned (Grosskurth, 1991). It is of interest to note here that there is a clear parallel to issues of patient confidentiality in the developing precedents being set about *analysts'* confidentiality and privacy. These discussions of colleagues among a select group of analysts have also had a long legacy in the organizational politics of psychoanalysis and the different standards of confidentiality that have often been applied by analysts to their fellow analysts, most notoriously in the convention of the reported training analysis.

One may well ask whether the exceptions to the rule, the over-stepping of the boundaries of confidentiality in the early history of analysis, had far-reaching effects. One likely consequence of the failure to acknowledge the rule-breaking was that this lack of candor contributed to a reification of strict standards of technical procedure that were not followed. This problem, by no means limited to issues of confidentiality, plagued psychoanalysis throughout the latter half of the twentieth century. Furthermore, one of the most important exceptions, as previously noted, was that confidentiality seems to have been *least* strictly maintained within and for those with connec-tions to the psychoanalytic movement. It seems quite possible that this is the single most important legacy of the early history of confi-dentiality boundary violations. For the failure to maintain confidenti-ality boundaries within psychoanalytic training organizations has arguably had far-reaching effects on the culture of organized psycho-analysis, by contributing to authoritarianism and a culture of para-noia within psychoanalytic organizations (Kernberg, 1986, 1996). The concomitant belief that some were privileged to hold such informa-tion by virtue of a special status of being Freud's anointed heirs has been extensively documented by Kirsner (2000) and provides a so-bering tale of the misuse of authority and power in psychoanalytic organizations. In many psychoanalytic organizations within the United States, the practice of reporting analyses—the direct descendant of Freud's breaking of his own rules of discretion in a number of the analyses he conducted with analysts he trained—continued well into the 1970s, with considerable costs.

During the early decades of psychoanalysis, the available record dealing with confidentiality suggests that in the main, anonymity was respected along the medical guidelines of strict confidence between doctors and patients. It also suggests, however, that the issues that arose regarding privacy and confidentiality were already far more complex for this developing science and treatment method than anyone had considered. These issues included differing levels of privacy among patients and among analysts, for written versus oral records, and for publications versus written records. Furthermore, a pattern developed of outright violations, particularly with analytic colleagues. Such exceptions are of course more understandable in the historical context of a fledgling science and psychoanalytic movement, groping to establish precedents and guidelines in a pioneering treatment method, than they would be today.

References

Dewitt, C. (1958), *Privileged Communications Between Physician and Patient*. Springfield, IL: Thomas.

Eulenberg, A., ed. (1907–1914), *Real-Encyclopadie der gesamten Heilkunde; medizinisch-chirurgisches Handworterbuch fur praktische Aerzte, 4. ganzlich umgearb. Aufl.* Berlin: Urban & Schwarzenberg.

Foster, F., ed. (1888–1894), *An Illustrated Encyclopedic Medical Dictionary. Being a Dictionary of the Technical Terms Used by Writers on Medicine and the Collateral Sciences, in the Latin, English, French and German Languages.* New York: D. Appleton.

Freud, S. & Breuer, J. (1895), Studies on hysteria. *Standard Edition*, 2:1–309. London: Hogarth Press, 1955.

——— (1899), Screen memories. *Standard Edition*, 3:301–322. London: Hogarth Press, 1962.

——— (1900), The interpretation of dreams. *Standard Edition*, 4 & 5. London: Hogarth Press, 1953.

——— (1913), On beginning the treatment. *Standard Edition*, 12:121–144. London: Hogarth Press, 1958.

——— (1920), The psychogenesis of a case of homosexuality in a woman. *Standard Edition*, 18:145–172. London: Hogarth Press, 1955.

Grosskurth, P. (1991), *The Secret Ring*. Reading, MA: Addison-Wesley.

Kernberg, O. (1986), Institutional problems of psychoanalytic education. *J. Amer. Psychoanal. Assn.*, 34:799–834.

——— (1996), Thirty methods to destroy the creativity of psychoanalytic candidates. *Internat. J. Psycho-Anal.*, 77:1031–1040.

Kirsner, D. (2000), *Unfree Associations*. London: Process Press.

Kris, A. (1994), Freud's treatment of a narcissistic patient. *Internat. J. Psycho-Anal.*, 75:649–664.

Lynn, D. & Vaillant, G. (1998), Anonymity, neutrality, and confidentiality in the actual methods of Sigmund Freud: A review of 43 cases, 1907–1939. *Amer. J. Psychiat.*, 155:163–171.

Mosher, P. (1999), Psychotherapist-patient privilege: The history and significance of the U.S. Supreme Court's decision in the case of Jaffee v. Redmond. Available at http://psa-uny.org/jr/articles/mosher.htm.

Nunberg, H. & Federn, E., eds. (1962–1975), *Minutes of the Vienna Psychoanalytic Society.* New York: International Universities Press.

Saul, L. J. (1939), Psychoanalytic case records. *Psychoanal. Quart.,* 8:186–190.

Villaret, A., eds. (1888, 1891), *Handwörterbuch der gesamten Medizin.* Stuttgart: Enke Verlag.

Watson, C., ed. (1899–1910), *Encyclopaedia Medica.* Edinburgh: William Green.

Introduction to CHAPTER 12

⚬❧⚬

Confidentiality in Psychoanalysis: A Private Space for Creative Thinking and the Work of Transformation

Case reports detailing quandaries about confidentiality are surprisingly rare in the literature. In the following contribution, Guy Da Silva summarizes two analytic cases, one involving the analysand's conscious desire for disclosure of the analytic work, the other an unconscious desire for "exposure." Each case, in different ways, illustrates how the desire for disclosure can intertwine with the patient's psychopathology. Like Penelope Garvey in the chapter that follows, Da Silva found that his psychoanalytic community had accumulated very little reliable experience or capacity for professional support at the time of his quandary. Drawing on the clinical ideas of Bion, he details how the analyst's ethical dilemma and his personal struggle to maintain confidentiality further the clinical "work of transformation" in which the analysand's internal difficulties can evolve through the analytic relationship.

❦

CHAPTER 12

Confidentiality in Psychoanalysis: A Private Space for Creative Thinking and the Work of Transformation

Guy Da Silva

Some years ago, I had an analytic patient to whom I gave the fictive name of Pandora because of her propensity to invite complications into her life and to walk on the brink of personal disaster. At the time she came to analysis with me, she had been refused by a few colleagues, in her words "because of my predicament." Her "predicament" was indeed rather unusual. She had been in analysis for a few years with an analyst who, due to major difficulties with the patient and also to a painful situation in his own life, decided to terminate abruptly with no other explanation than that the patient "should continue with a more experienced analyst." The patient told me that the analyst had "failed her" and that she wanted to denounce him; indeed, she considered it necessary for her psychic survival to do so. The alternative, she felt, was either to kill herself or to go mad. She had already addressed a complaint to her analyst's professional association, but the recommendation had been the same: to find another analyst. This response had only increased her sense of crisis. She decided to take the further step of suing her ex-analyst in civil court. Perhaps there she could enlist some support in her need to condemn the analyst who had so badly let her down.

When I learned that Pandora had already been refused by several colleagues (in some instances with the advice that she should first resolve her court battle before reentering analysis), I realized I was faced with a daunting task. But I also felt moved by her distress and encouraged by my impression that her need to denounce was related to her early history with a psychotic father and a melancholic mother who failed to "denounce" his crazy and abusive treatment of the child. All the mother had been able to say to the children was, "Ignore him, act as if nothing has happened." I felt that there was room for analytic work here and that Pandora's "need to denounce" the "failing" object might be resolved by working through her transference to me.

After a few months of analysis with me, however, the court appearance was already approaching. Would it be necessary for me to appear as a witness, as the patient wished? I felt it would place me between two very conflicting moral obligations. I would have to decide whether to obey the law or to abide by the rules of professional conduct. My strong preference was to protect my work as a psychoanalyst, which requires that all my patients feel free to discuss everything that concerns them, including matters of great intimacy that they would not be able to reveal if there were any doubt about my trustworthiness. I consulted widely, but the consultations only increased my perplexity. Most said that I had no choice but to testify, and they warned me to be careful about what I said! Others felt that it was up to the patient to relieve me from my duty to maintain confidentiality. One colleague in a somewhat similar situation informed me that he had followed the professional liability insurance recommendation that all his notes belong to the patient; they should be given to the patient and the patient should decide whether to use them in court. According to this colleague, acting otherwise on principle would be masochistic, because it risked going to jail! None of these alternatives made me happy.

I thought that confidentiality was a core issue here. The patient's attempts to draw me into her external battle and therefore away from her internal conflicts dramatized the untenable situation of her childhood, which she reexperienced in the silence and "failure" of her previous analyst and the "failure" of the ethics committee. As a child, she had been forced to submit to her mother's abusive injunction "to turn a blind eye and do nothing." Now I felt that because of the threat of a subpoena I had become the depository of her untenable childhood situation. On one hand, to maintain confidentiality and silence would be experienced as "failing" her. It would also expose me to the risk of being held in contempt of court. On the other hand, my testimony would also be experienced as "failing" her in my analytic promise of confidentiality (which I felt was necessary for the resolution of her internal conflicts). The worst part of this alternative was the prospect of self-contempt for having destroyed my ethos as a psychoanalyst. Moreover, I had been presented to her as a "more experienced analyst"! For weeks, I struggled in confusion, unsure what to do or say. Perhaps I was being presumptuous in accepting to see her, and the colleagues who had refused her were wiser than I? I felt sympathy for her previous analyst. I was angry at the patient and felt guilty about this. I feared going to jail for contempt of court. Should I consult a lawyer or my insurance company? Yet I knew that I was in the midst of a confusion similar to the one my patient had been unable to resolve. It fell to me, and to the work of analysis, to contain and to tolerate her impossible demands and her accusations in the hope of doing the work of transformation[1] needed to resolve this confusion. I was finally able to reach a state in which the idea of going to jail no longer seemed so terrifying, only repugnant. I knew then that I could interpret something to her.

I informed my patient that it would be impossible for me to focus on her internal conflicts if I agreed to play a role in her external life. She replied that it was not only she who wished to call me as a witness; the adverse party in court might also want me to testify. I suggested that it would be important for her to distinguish between the adverse party in the legal battle and the adverse part within herself, a part that might be adverse to the painful psychoanalytic work we were doing together. She became very angry; if I was afraid to go to court, then she would free me from my analytic responsibility immediately by stopping analysis. After all, she had committed no crime and had killed no one. I told her that if I was called as a witness, I would be under the obligation to go, but I would ask the judge to exempt me from testifying because it might compromise the analytic treatment. If, however, the judge upheld my obligation to testify, then I would be forced to choose between going to jail for contempt of court or testifying in the knowledge that I would be betraying my pledge of confidentiality to her, as well as the ethics of my profession. In either case, I would have to stop the analysis. I

---

[1] In his teaching, Henry Rey (1994) was adamant on the subject of transformation; for him, it was the essence of psychoanalysis and one of its universals. *Transformations* (1965) is one of Bion's major works. The word "transformation" and its variants (immediately after the variants of the word "dream") is one of the words most often used (577 times) in Freud's work, according to the 1980 Freud Concordance. I believe that if it were possible to sum up psychoanalysis with just one word, it would be "transformation."

would explain my dilemma to the judge, and my decision to interrupt the treatment.

Her first reaction was one of anger. It was as if I were telling her to stop the legal suit, just as in the past her mother had refused to protect her by denouncing the craziness of her father. For my patient it seemed an imperative duty and a matter of life or death, physical and psychical, to denounce her previous therapist, in contrast to her mother who had always turned a blind eye. So now I, too, was failing her deeply.

Later, she tried to reassure me that "even if you do receive a subpoena, you are still tied by confidentiality, and if I do not authorize you to speak, you cannot speak." She added that "this is the Charter of Rights and the judges are obliged to go along with the Charter." I felt that the patient's permission to speak or not to speak was missing the essential point, that is, the unconscious motives impelling her to give or not to give permission. Moreover, I told her that the issue of confidentiality was at the center of her dilemma. Indeed, not only was she asking me to break confidentiality by getting involved in her external life, she was asking me to betray her motives for coming to me in the first place! She had come to me convinced that her previous analyst had "failed" her. Now she was placing herself and me in a no-win situation. If I didn't go to court, I was "failing" her in her external life, but if I served as a witness I would also be "failing" her as a patient in analysis by not keeping my promise to ensure confidentiality! In order not to fail her as an analyst and not fail myself in my ethos as an analyst, I was prepared to risk going to jail!

As it turned out, she asked her lawyer not to send me a subpoena. Fortunately, the case was settled out of court at the suggestion of a very sensitive judge who begged the two lawyers to come to some arrangement because he felt that if the case was heard, the two contestants would be very psychologically damaged. I was relieved indeed.

Once this bone of contention had been set aside, a more trusting relationship could be established, and the analysis continued in a less tempestuous manner. It became more evident for Pandora and for me that the constant threat of external interference had prevented the deepening of our work together and served as a resistance to facing her internal conflicts. Behind her desperate insistence that no one should ever fail her was the conviction that *she* must never fail anyone for fear of rejection. Some work could be done on the persecutory aspect of the wish for self-perfection that she had projected into others. She came to the painful realization that no one and no analysis is "perfect" and was able to develop some compassion for her parents, her previous analyst, and me. Most importantly, she realized that her wish for perfection in herself and in others was a cruel persecutor that had prevented her from ever being at peace with herself or with anyone else.

The Analytic Situation

Psychoanalysis is in a paradoxical position: it exists within the law and yet by asking for a confidentiality privilege (in Latin, *privus* and *lex*, a private law), it is also asking to exist in some sense outside the law. Psychoanalysis makes the claim that its work cannot be accomplished if there is a threat that the intensely private partnership of the analytic couple can be exposed to the interference of an outside third. This position is not unlike that of Roman law, as Shuman (1985) relates:

> The earliest reference to any relational privilege or professional secret in contemporary literature is the refusal of Roman law to compel the testimony of an attorney against a client . . . [which] seems to relate to the attorney's role as a servant, obliged to keep his master's secrets. Just as a slave could not testify against a master because the slave was a part of the family and, therefore, a party to its mutual fidelity, so the attorney had a similar moral duty. . . . The rationale for this relational privilege appears to be deontological: for society to compel a citizen to divulge a secret and therefore breach a moral duty is wrong [p. 667].

As an analyst, in my "state of servitude," I feel bound by a duty to defend the principles of treatment that allow me to render a unique service to my patients. In this, I follow the distinction proposed by Bollas and Sundelson (1995) between social therapies, including aspects of psychiatry, with their focus on direct adaptation to society, and analytic psychotherapy, which is concerned with the patient's internal world. I would feel guilty of treason if I did not do everything in my power to shelter that internal world.

Both law and psychoanalysis, each in its own way, may be seen as undertaking complementary tasks. Whereas the law attempts to regulate the opposing forces within a group of individuals, the work of psychoanalysis integrates the conflictual parts *within* the personality of an individual. To achieve its work properly, psychoanalysis needs to center its service solely on the individual. Even though a societal concern cannot be the aim of psychoanalysis, it is through the ability of the psychoanalytic frame to bracket out the societal point of view that some benefit accrues to society indirectly, through the resulting internal growth of the individual, as I demonstrate in a second clinical example at the end of this chapter.

The Search for Personal Truth: Dreams and Reverie

Psychoanalysis may be understood as a process of transformational development achieved through the exploration of internal truth. During this process, irrational, even "unborn," parts of the personality benefit from the opportunity to make emotional contact with a "transformational object" (Bollas, 1979).

What patients bring to analysis is often beyond words: their somatic and emotional distress in a confusional state. These troublesome, nonintegrated parts of their personalities have not yet been transformed into thinking and meaning. Bion (1963) was the first analyst to propose a systematic apparatus for thinking about thinking and to offer a description of the progressive transformation of experience as well as its failings. For him, thinking was not a given but a progressive evolution from concrete somatic sensations to more and more abstract processes. It seems reasonable to assume that during the emotional experience of the early postnatal relationship with the mother, who "thinks" for the baby, a thinking apparatus, that is, a capacity for thinking thoughts, gradually emerges in the mind of the growing child. This idea is closely related to a very special state of mind that Bion ascribed to the mother and termed "reverie" (Bion, 1962, p. 36). The way that the mother "thinks" for the baby will have a great deal to do with the way the thinking apparatus will develop. Thinking commences with the observation of an emotional experience, and the emotional experience is right there in the body. It is apprehended first as a bodily event that may then be processed through symbol formation and dreams, and thus become available for transformation into thought. We see this in the clinical situation all the time: people first experience a somatic state and then begin to apprehend it as a conscious emotional experience. Bion describes this mysterious function of transformation from body sensations into the sphere of the mind as alpha function. What alpha function works upon is in the body, suggesting a monistic view of body mind, not a dualistic theory of body as separate from mind.

Thus, one way to understand the analytic response to the problem of truth is to think of the patient as bringing the failures of his thinking apparatus, failures due to "undigested," unthinkable emotional experiences. At a concrete level, there is such a striking parallel with the digestion of food[2] that often, as emotional experiences are being worked over and transformed into thoughts, some borborygmi or gurgling sounds from the patient and from the analyst occur during important sessions (Da Silva, 1990, 1998).

Indeed, one of the findings of psychoanalysis is that emotional growth requires psychic truth as much as the growth of the body requires food. Yet if truth is necessary for the growth of the mind, human beings nevertheless have a great reluctance to learn about themselves. This reluctance is the delicate crux of the analytic situation, what makes it so sensitive and vulnerable to disruptions of all kinds, and most especially the inhibitory effects of exposure and external intrusions on the analytic process. This is why it is so important to establish a *confident* analytical situation—confident in the emotional sense of basic trust and also confident in the ethical sense of commitment to maintain the patient's confidences, not to act upon them or to "spread them abroad" in the social sphere.

It is precisely this confidential relationship, in the full *relational* sense of that term that makes it possible for the analysand to get beyond his or her reluctance and to uncover fragments of truth. The analytic situation facilitates the pursuit of Socrates' recommendation: know thyself. But we have to be constantly aware of the risk inherent in self-revelation and to remind ourselves of Oedipus' misfortune, his attempt to blind himself to the unbearable truth. We are caught between the necessity to know in order to survive and the terror of having to know. Coming to terms with dream life is an

---

[2] Bion (1962) writes:

> I am assuming that an apparatus existed and had to undergo . . . adaptation to the new tasks involved in meeting the demands of reality by developing a capacity for thought. The apparatus that has to undergo this adaptation is that which dealt originally with sense impressions relating to the alimentary canal [p. 57].

important aspect of this process of internalizing confidence. Dreams may in some ways be the most authentic expressions of individual or internal truth. They provide deep insight into the process of transformation from action into thinking. Indeed, dreams *are* the cornerstone for this process of transformation.

But what of the psychoanalyst's mental space? The analytic situation favors the meeting of *two* states of mind, both closely related to a dreamlike state: the patient in free association and the analyst in the free-floating attention of what Bion called *reverie*. In reverie, attention is directed to feelings, phantasies, ruminations, and, in fact, anything that goes on in the body and the mind of the analyst, whether or not it seems related to what is being expressed by the patient at the moment. This "dreaming" or reverie of the analyst cannot take place if there is an undue interference or (as in the case of Pandora) the threat of it. As Bion (1992) expressed it, "The analyst . . . must be able to dream the analysis as it is taking place, but of course he must not go to sleep" (p. 216). In many ways, these two states of mind are close to an "altered state of consciousness" for both partners in the confidential relationship. We might say that the analytic situation allows the dreaming process we associate with sleep to continue and to expand in the session by favoring a relaxation of the censorship. This confidence is enhanced by the presence of the analyst, which provides the necessary mental assistance in the form of a transformative medium.

Bion's view is that the baby and the patient are essentially impelled to evacuate the contents of their experience into the mother, or into the therapist, and that the essential function of the mother, or therapist, is to receive and contain this massive projection. Bion (1970, p. 125) borrows the term "negative capability" to describe this stance, i.e., "the ability to remain in uncertainty without irritably reaching after facts and reasons" (Keats, 1817). During analysis, this ability means the capacity to receive the patient's confusion, which includes all of the pain implicit in it, and to contain it. The analyst must wait for something to happen in his mind that may help to put order and meaning into what is received. Then he must try to return it in partially detoxified form. The essential thing is to hold the projections long enough to allow something to happen in the mind. As in the mother's reverie, the "unthinkable" in the patient's mind needs at first to be thought about and contained in his mind of the analyst. This is an important part of the process, related to Bion's alpha function, in which meaning emerges in the analytic space. With the analyst's help, bodily and mental contents become "thinkable" and integrated in the patient's thinking apparatus.[3]

This "unthinkable" in the patient's mind, which used to be expelled in action or projected into the various persons of his life, becomes progressively gathered in the transference toward the analyst, the context in which they can be transformed. We can see this progressive transformation towards humanization of representation in dreams, and Meltzer (1967, p. 49) has expanded on this subject: what was projected into inanimate machines becomes projected into animals and then into members of the family and finally is recognized as parts of the self for integration into the personality. As Freud (1900) stated, "each person in a dream represents a part of the personality of the dreamer" (p. 232). Our work, as analysts, is to help the patient to become the author of his own dreams, of his own mind, and of his own life. In so doing, fragmented parts of the personality of the patient become progressively integrated and therefore more authentic. As we say in French: *une personne mieux intégrée devient plus intègre.* And yet we never become fully the master in our own house, and the struggle for integration is a lifelong task.

The Legitimacy of a Private Space

It should now be more evident that a private space[4] safeguarded by confidentiality is vital to carry the work of transformation. Indeed, the invitation to "tell whatever comes to mind and body" would make no sense if it were not linked to the requirement of strict confidenti-

---

[3] To summarize Bion's view (1962): "I shall abstract for use as a model the idea of a container into which an object is projected and the object that can be projected into the container; the latter I shall designate by the term 'contained'" (p. 90). The whole sequence then is the following in an abstract form: bad feelings (beta elements) are projected into the good breast container (♀). They are cóntained (o) and transformed there by the alpha function (T∝) of the receptive understanding (reverie) of the analyst and reintrojected in the modified (alpha element produced by reverie and alpha function) and hence detoxified form, so the product of container-contained relation is meaning.

[4] The necessity of a private space does not preclude the fact that this is very hard work, impossible to carry always in solitude. Analysts do need a facilitating environment for collective containment and collective reverie. Therefore, consultations with colleagues, supervision for beginning analysts, seminars, and publications for enhancing knowledge are a necessity for analysts and consequently a benefit for our patients. These activities can be done and must be done in a milieu of privacy and in observing the rules of shared confidentiality.

ality on the part of the analyst, not only to protect the patient but also to ensure for the analyst his capacity to listen without judgment, oriented only toward the discovery of meaning. It is this free space of mind, wandering into the senseless until something begins to make sense, which is threatened by the outside party demanding action, whether to give a report or to express an opinion to an insurance company or to a professional order or to appear in court as a witness. Such interference obstructs the fragile dreamlike state necessary for the emergence of new thoughts in the analytic process. The effect may be compared to the way dreams frequently vanish from memory immediately upon waking. The analysand's permission to break confidentiality is of no help at all here because it invites the analyst to play a part in the patient's life, thus compromising the usefulness of the analyst as a transference object and therefore also as an agent of transformation. Bion recommended that analysts should try to reach a state of mind "without memory and without desire," a state of mind in the "here and now," not preoccupied with memory of the past and desire for the future. This attempt at immersion in the "present" is necessary because the present being enacted in the transference toward the analyst is really a still-active past, a past that has never been able to become a past.

Sometimes, therapists or psychoanalysts are requested by their corporations or by the court to submit the records of their treatment of a patient or analysand. This is usually done with the signature of the patient authorizing the analyst to do so. I believe that this loophole in confidentiality constitutes a violation of the private mental space necessary for creative thinking. Most of the time, such an authorization, whether or not it is presented as the debatable concept of "informed consent," represents a resistance to pursuing the work of analysis, to avoid psychic pain, and even an attempt to stop analysis (which is often the effective outcome of such a request). In fact, many analysts keep no records, or only very sketchy ones. Note-taking during the session may prevent the necessary immersion into the state of reverie.

Freud recommended that analysts not take notes during sessions because the practice interferes with good listening. Even if notes are taken after the session, they contain as many of the analyst's fantasies and thoughts as those of the patient. These thoughts and fantasies will help formulate an appropriate interpretation only once they have been "mentally digested." These notes can never be a record of objective facts about the patient. They are an extemporaneous reflection of the analyst's own mental work, as private as our own dreams at night. They help the analyst to emerge from his mental perplexity as he is trying to contain and to sort out the mental states of the patient. There is a parallel here between the perplexity of the analyst and the perplexity of the mother trying to make sense of her infant's distress. If submitted to a court, an insurance company, or a professional corporation, such notes[5] would be largely indecipherable and inherently misleading due to the impossibility of reconstructing their context outside the analytic situation.

The Transformation of an Exhibitionistic Symptom

The argument for the confidentiality of the analytic space has an important obverse dimension. The analysand is of course under no obligation to respect his own privacy, let alone the confidentiality of the analytic space. Yet for many patients suffering from what we now sometimes call "boundary issues," the main problem of the analysis may be summed up in terms of the patient's inability to understand the psychological significance of privacy or the meaning of confidentiality. In such cases, much of the work will revolve around the need to grasp the meaning of confidentiality and to acquire, through the analysis, his own self-containing function. In so doing, the work of analysis may be seen indirectly as complementary to the societal concern of the law.

A patient came into analysis with intense suicidal ideas after being arrested in a male toilet for indecent exposure. Since he was a public figure of some notoriety, his fear of humiliation and dishonor was intense; the expectation of having to appear in court led him to disguised suicidal behavior in the form of crossing streets in very dangerous ways. It became evident that his exhibitionistic behavior was motivated by a need to be reassured he was still a man after a defeat in an electoral vote that he had experienced not only as a humiliating castration but also, in the deeper layers of his mind, as a punishment for being male.

After he was born, his mother had suffered a severe postpartum depression related to her disappointment over having a son instead

---

[5] Here there is an interesting comparison to be made with judges' deliberative notes, which do remain confidential (Bollas, 2000). My own description of the analyst's notes may correspond partly to this notion of "deliberative notes" though the analyst would include the deeper mental processes of reverie.

of the wished-for daughter, who represented for the mother a "new beginning." All his life, the patient felt inwardly somewhat feminine, in accordance with the mother's wish; yet he needed outwardly "to stand as a man" and be "elected as a man." After the electoral defeat, exposing his penis expressed a desperate attempt to assert his entitlement to be alive as a male. His arrest achieved contradictory aims. On one hand, it reinforced his prohibitive conscience into limiting his misbehavior, while at the same time it also reassured him that he still had a penis (in view of all the fuss it created). On the other hand, going to court magnified the impending threat of feminization and of castration and, in so doing, increased his impulse to repeat the acting out as a form of infantile reassurance. He was tortured by the idea of appearing in a criminal court for gross indecency.

If he were killed by a car, would the life-insurance money be granted to his wife and children, or would the insurance company refuse to pay on the grounds that his death had been a masked suicide? Would I betray my pledge of confidentiality and testify about his disguised suicide, thereby preventing the sacrifice of his life for his loved ones from succeeding? The fact that I would not have been present at the scene of this imaginary accident and would therefore be useless as a witness did not seem to appease him.

It was not until three months after the police report that he realized, to his great relief, that he was only charged with a misdemeanor and could avoid a court appearance simply by pleading guilty and paying a $200 fine. It was never clear whether his lawyer had misinformed him or he had simply misunderstood the whole situation from the beginning.

Analysis revealed that he had partially identified with his mother, adopting female attitudes, to do some mothering for her in her depression, and for the other women of his life, in a desperate attempt to rescue them from their woes. During the months following his arrest, we learned how he felt deeply responsible for the lasting unhappiness of his depressed mother and how desperate were his futile attempts at changing her mood. He was miserable watching her be so miserable. He could not be the master of his own life and of his own mind as long as she remained depressed.

The analytic sessions became a sanctuary where he could progressively construct a mind of his own within the containing structure of the analysis. His depressive mood eventually lifted. He dreamed of "a computer brain functioning by being fed a diet of *topinambour.*" He realized that this vegetable, seen previously in a market place, was shaped like many nipples on a breast and had been imported from Brazil, perhaps the country of my origin because of my name. A mind-brain and a thinking apparatus were being constructed.

One day, he reported the following dream: "I am walking with an attractive woman, very early in the morning, while going to work. I meet a colleague on the street who, noticing that I have a huge erection under my pants, says jokingly, 'I can see you have had an enjoyable night!'" After recounting his dream, he had the following associations: He was reminded of the incident that brought him to analysis years ago; but contrary to what had occurred then, this time he was not accused of misdemeanor. Rather, the joking and slightly envious remark of the colleague about his night with the attractive woman was a recognition that he had regained his masculinity. I agreed with his interpretation of the dream but pointed out also the remarkable psychic change involved. He had moved from acting out the conflict over his sexual identity in public to asserting his masculinity in a dream. Indeed, we can say that he had, through his dream, made use of new mental equipment (dreaming and thinking instead of acting) to express a wish for an enjoyable night with an attractive woman. The confidentiality of the psychoanalytic process had provided him with the possibility of a private experience of his own mental activity, something that he had not previously been able to tolerate; this had enabled him to contain his sexual impulses, reducing the need to express them in conflictual action.

The dream also indicated relinquishment of the impossible "mission" that had characterized his whole life: treating depressed women as substitutes for the depressed mother. Abandoning this mission and being with an attractive woman was no longer interpreted as a betrayal of his mother. So perhaps he had then acquired not only a mind of his own, and a sex of his own, but also "the right to a life of his own" (Modell, 1965).

Conclusion

As Anne Hayman (1965) wrote: "In principle, there may be less conflict between our moral obligations to the law and to the rules of professional conduct than would appear at first sight. Justice as well as our ethic is likely to be served best by silence" (p. 785).

The emotional experience of the patient with the analyst as a transformational object helps to increase self-knowledge and therefore self-containment. But it depends on confidentiality. While psychoanalysis renders a service centered on the individual, some benefit to society flows from it; its work may therefore be seen as complementary to the work of the law.

References

Bion, W. (1962), *Learning from Experience.* New York: Basic Books.

———— (1963), *Elements of Psychoanalysis.* London: William Heineman.

———— (1965), *Transformations.* London: William Heineman.

———— (1970), *Attention and Interpretation.* London: Tavistock Publications.

———— (1992), *Cogitations.* London: Karnac

Bollas, C. (1979), The transformational object. *Internat. J. Psycho-Anal.*, 60:97–107.

———— (2000), The Disclosure Industry Keynote address—International Conferences on "Confidentiality and Society: Psychotherapy, Ethics and the Law." Montreal, October 13–15.

———— & Sundelson, D. (1995), *The New Informants.* Northvale, NJ: Aronson.

Da Silva, G. (1990), Borborygmi as markers of psychic work during the analytic session. *Internat. J. Psycho-Anal.*, 71:641–659.

———— (1998), The emergence of thinking: Bion as a link between Freud and the neurosciences. In: *Psychoanalysis and the Zest for Living—Writings in Memory of W. C. M. Scott,* ed. M. Grignon. Binghamton, NY: E. S. F. Publishers, pp. 189–202).

Freud, S. (1900), The interpretation of dreams. *Standard Edition,* 4 & 5. London: Hogarth Press, 1953.

Guttman, S., ed. (1980), *Concordance to the Standard Edition of the Complete Psychological Works of Sigmund Freud, Vol. 6.* Boston: G. K. Hall, pp. 219–222.

Hayman, A. (1965), Psychoanalyst subpoenaed. *The Lancet,* October 16:785–786.

Keats, J. (1817), Letter to George and Thomas Keats, December 21. In: *Letters,* ed. M. B. Forman, 4th ed. London: Oxford University Press, 1952.

Meltzer, D. (1967), *The Psychoanalytical Process.* Perthshire: Clunie Press.

Modell, A. (1965), On having a right to a life of one's own. *Internat. J. Psycho-Anal.*, 46:323–331.

Rey, H. (1994), *Universals of Psychoanalysis in the Treatment of Psychotic and Borderline States.* London: Free Association Books.

Shuman, D. (1985), The origins of the physician-patient privilege and professional secret. *South Western Law J.*, 39:661–687.

Introduction to CHAPTER 13

❦

Whose Notes Are They Anyway?

Penelope Garvey's chapter provides a gripping account of an unfolding web of legal entanglements that threatened to engulf her work with a confused and disturbed patient. Her generosity in making this sensitive material available is intended, the editors believe, not only as "a cautionary tale" but as an appeal to the analytic community. Psychoanalysts who find themselves in the position Garvey describes are often isolated and shamed through the experience, as Christopher Bollas (2000) pointed out at the Confidentiality and Society conference in Montreal. The professional situation is the same here as with clinical difficulties and impasses. Psychoanalysts can always seek private supervision or consult colleagues on ethical matters, but there is clearly a lack of more general opportunities to exchange firsthand experiences in a context where colleagues can speak freely without fear of judgment. The absence of such forums hinders progress within the psychoanalytic community toward provision of a more organized method of learning and professional development in this area.

CHAPTER 13

❧

Whose Notes Are They Anyway?

Penelope Garvey

*C*onfidentiality is the cornerstone of the psychoanalyst's ethical code. The successful stand of a British psychoanalyst, Anne Hayman, when subpoenaed to appear in Court in the 1960s, was described in the *Lancet* and is enshrined in the *Handbook of the British Psychoanalytical Society* (Hayman, 1965). In July 2000, the International Psychoanalytical Association Executive Council altered the statement "Psychoanalysts shall respect the confidentiality of their patients' information and documents" by deleting the clause "within the contours of applicable legal and professional standards." This means that it is now possible for the IPA to support members who choose to resist when ordered by law to disclose information on their patients. Unless some thought is given to the extent and nature of the support by the IPA and its member Societies and to the complex question of whether we believe confidentiality to be an absolute principle, psychoanalysts may find themselves vulnerable when up against the law and unprepared for the questions of how far they are prepared to go to defend confidentiality and in which situations they should consider disclosure.

The following account is a disguised version of an actual legal conflict. The patient's character structure and motivation are a composite of several cases reported by psychoanalysts and psychotherapists who have been involved in legal proceedings concerning disclosure. The account is not presented as a clinical report for scientific purposes; it is an illustrative example intended to provoke a discussion of professional ethics. For this reason, details of the patient's identity and circumstances have been removed or altered to the point where the material is useless for clinical discussion. In order to evoke the flavor of the circumstances and to give some sense of the connection between the legal situation and the clinical situation, some broad characterizations of the transference and some generalized nonspecific interpretations of the patient's actions are described. These bear only an analogous relationship to the actual circumstances and details of the case.

A Cautionary Tale

Quite a few years ago, a patient was referred to me for psycho-therapy by a colleague who had seen him for a medical legal report regarding the psychological effects of an accident in which he was hit by something falling from a building. The patient had left his home country and come to live in London to get away from journal-ists who were intruding into his life and at times lying in wait for him outside his house. He was not a well-known man, but aspects of his behavior, which were contrary to the ethical stand of his profession, had captured the interest of members of the press, who were felt to take pleasure in exposing him and describing his downfall. For these and other reasons, he had resigned from his position. The accident, which was not held to be his fault, occurred just as he was trying to regain some equilibrium after his move. He recovered from the physi-cal damage caused by the accident but not from its psychological effects: nightmares, panic attacks, and depression with occasional suicidal thoughts.

The patient sued for compensation for the psychological dam-age that he had sustained. The builder's insurance company awarded him an interim sum. The full amount of the damages remained to be agreed. At the time that I took the patient on, I did not appreciate, as it would later be argued, that the interim sum of money had been given to him specifically and solely for psychological help. The focus of my concern was whether the patient would be able and willing to continue in psychotherapy if no further money were forthcoming from the insurance company. I did not want to involve a vulnerable and disturbed patient in a psychotherapy that would have to end prematurely. When I went into this with the patient, he told me that he was able and prepared to pay for future psychotherapy himself.

I had, in hindsight naively, no fears of being dragged into court. The referrer and I had made an arrangement for a similar case; that he would deal with the court, seeing the patient for court reports, and I would see the patient for psychotherapy. I had no reason to believe that the same arrangement, one that is commonly used to protect treatment from intrusion, would not apply in this case. I did not go in any detail into the arguments that had been advanced to secure the money from the insurance company.

Some months after the start of the treatment, the patient told me that his solicitor wanted me to provide a report for the court. The solicitor would be getting in contact with me. I explored what it would mean to my patient were I to become involved with the Court case. There were three main themes.

First, I was someone to whom he could talk, who had no contact with anyone else in his life. Our relationship was quite unique in being well-defined, something particularly unusual for my patient, whose present and past relationships were confusing because they were lacking in boundaries. It seemed clear that if I were to provide a report to the courts, a similar kind of confusion would arise in the analytic relationship, as my role would become ambiguous and the treatment would be subject to invasion by the external interference of a nonclinical agenda. For this reason alone, I thought it very important that I stand firm.

Second, there was the question of the rights of his case and his wish to pull me into taking a position. A potential minefield: What did I really think? Would I support the argument that provided funds for his therapy, that is, that the accident had penetrated his defenses and activated a dormant disturbance? Was this how he saw it? However he saw things, could he stand up for what he felt to be the truth?

Third, the holidays were approaching, and it seemed to me that my patient had found the chance of a way to gain control over me. He both wished to protect and wished to destroy the possibility of treatment; I thought if we could work on this he would be better able to deal with the legal issues. We came to the holidays with my feeling that some progress was being made and that the patient was protecting the therapy.

I was wrong. On the first day of my holiday, I received a fax from the patient's solicitor in which he said that he had referred the patient to my colleague, that my colleague had recommended treatment, that he believed the patient had been referred to me, and that, as the case was due in court in four weeks, he wanted me to send him my notes and a report on the patient's progress. He reassured me that he appreciated it was a "sensitive" case. He also faxed a form, signed by the patient consenting to the release of his notes. My notes, such as they were, consisted of one full process recording of the initial consultation, which was typed; a few partial accounts of sessions; and a number of notes in shorthand. They contained information about events in my patient's life as yet unexposed in the press; I did not wish to see these enter the public sphere.

During the time that I was on holiday, the patient's solicitor left a number of phone messages. When I first returned to work, I avoided answering the phone as the solicitor rang frequently, with increasing insistence that I contact him. I did not want to talk to him at all; certainly not before speaking to the patient. At this point, I considered all this to be an extension of my patient's acting out, connected to the holiday break. I put this to the patient on his return. He told me that he wanted me to protect my notes and said that he had been told that he had to sign the form. He seemed to feel unable to stand up to his solicitor. I felt reasonably confident that the situation would be contained.

The patient's solicitor rang several times a day, leaving messages saying that, as the interim payment had been obtained purely on the basis that the patient would have treatment, effectively the insurance company had paid for the treatment and so the notes belonged to them. He said that in order to make decisions for the future, everyone—the patient's solicitor and their expert witness psychiatrist (my referrer), the solicitor for the insurance company and its expert witness psychiatrist—needed to know how the treatment was proceeding. They no longer wanted a report, just my notes. Court proceedings were threatened.

The referrer was away, and so I could not ask him to deal with the patient's solicitor on my behalf. I replied by letter, with the patient's agreement, explaining that I did not divulge information about patients unless I had taken them on with the specific purpose of making an assessment for a report. I explained that it was important for patients to feel that nothing they said would be repeated outside the consulting room and that breaching confidentiality would jeopardize psychotherapeutic work. I stated that a report from me would add nothing to the assessments of the two expert witnesses in the case. I also explained that the patient had contacted me on the recommendation of the referrer and that, on the basis of a consultation, I had taken him on purely for treatment. I emphasized that this was the basis of our relationship. He was not under my treatment on the basis of a court referral.

The patient's solicitor replied by return fax reiterating all the points that he had already made, once again reassuring me that he understood the "sensitive" nature of the case, and he said that his request was quite normal. He said he would be happy to discuss this with me on the telephone but had so far been unable to get through to me. With reluctance, I returned his call. He was, not surprisingly, quite hostile; he repeated the points he had made in his letter, and he emphasized that my referring colleague wanted to see my notes. He told me that the psychiatrist for the insurance company thought the accident to be a red herring. He tried to persuade me by arguing that it was in the patient's interest for the case to be dealt with as soon as possible. Hoping to reassure me that I would not be exposing my patient to further publicity, he told me that he appreciated that it was a sensitive if not sensational case and there would be no press in court.

I told him that I was certain that his expert, my referrer, did not want my notes. I asked him to discuss the matter fully with him to confirm that this was correct. By the end of our conversation the solicitor seemed to understand my points; that is, that it was nothing to do with the sensitive nature of the case, the content of the notes, and whether or not the patient consented to disclosure. Rather, it was my professional conviction that psychotherapy could not proceed without confidentiality and that I wanted to stick to the task I had undertaken. He gave the impression of being sympathetic to the patient and of wanting to protect the therapy. He was well aware of how unusual it was for the patient to have a relationship with clear boundaries. He asked, would I consider coming to a meeting of solicitors once this was all over to explain the reasons for confidentiality? I said I would be delighted. He said that he thought the insurance company would settle for a modest further payment. I felt pleased that a hostile situation had been turned into a cooperative one.

Four days later, I received a fax from the patient's solicitor letting me know that the solicitors for the insurance company had asked for a postponement of the court case because they had not seen my notes. He mentioned that there had been an earlier court judgment that the case could not proceed without disclosure of all medical records. I did not, at the time, appreciate how seriously this earlier judgment undermined my position; I felt I would be able to argue that my notes were substantially different from medical notes. The patient's solicitor also wanted (that afternoon) a fax in which I stated my qualifications, the date of my first meeting with the patient, and my arguments in favor of confidentiality.

I telephoned him next day. He told me that the solicitors for the insurance company were really "gunning for" my notes and that I would need a "Rotweiler" on my side if I wanted to fight them. He said they were seeking to have the hearing adjourned, this would be costly, and my patient would pay the costs; this would be my fault. (He later told me that the costs would be covered by my patient's insurance.) He added that the press would be in court.

I wrote the letter stating my qualifications and so on. I was relieved that the costs would be covered by the insurance and that I would not be responsible for running my patient into debt. I was, however, disturbed that the press would be in court. I thought the press would make the most out of the new revelations that would inevitably come out in court. I did not think such exposure was in any way advantageous for my patient; the last thing he needed was the exposure of highly personal information. I also considered that, even if I divulged nothing, my involvement with the court could lead the press to attribute the revelations to me: "Psychoanalyst reveals . . . in Court proceedings." I feared the impact of this on potential future patients as well as those currently in treatment.

Prior to these events, it had not occurred to me that my notes were anyone's property other than my own. I had given little thought to the fact that, under new legislation, patients and others had the right of access to notes. I immediately stopped taking notes on all my patients. I telephoned my Psychoanalytical Society and my Psychological Society for advice. I was told by both that I probably would have to hand over my notes but that if I thought this would not be in my patient's best interest I should explain my position. The chairman of the Ethics Committee of the Psychoanalytical Society said that the Society would support me if I stood against disclosure.

Soon after, I received a fax from the solicitors for the insurance company. They claimed that they were entitled to my notes and enclosed another and different signed consent form from my patient and a copy of an application to the court for a court order that I disclose my "notes, correspondence, documentation, or memoranda" within seven days of the date of their letter. They said they would be seeking costs against me—things had moved into a different gear. By now, the patient's complicity in the intrusion into the treatment was only too evident; for the time being, he was cut off from his vulnerability and any need for the treatment to be protected. All this and other aspects of his situation were projected into me leaving him excitedly watching to see how I coped. I too might be brought down and might have contravened my profession's ethical code.

I again contacted my professional bodies and spoke to my solicitor. All agreed that I would be required by law to produce my notes unless I could show a good reason for not doing so; there was little optimism that I would win. I enquired about the nature and extent of the support I could expect from the Psychoanalytical Society; I was told that no money would be forthcoming. The case was not one on which the Society itself would take a stand. If a stand was to be taken, it was up to me to do so. I was told that it would be unwise of me to refuse to hand over my notes if ordered to do so by a judge; there was a chance I would be sent to prison. I was given a very useful piece of advice, however, one that I was able to use later: that I could argue for a restriction. This meant that if I had to hand over my notes, I could ask to do so to restricted individuals only. I felt let down by the lack of financial backing but pleased to know that I had the option of a compromise. I was urged by my Solicitor to try to get my patient to revoke his agreement to the release of the notes.

I spoke to my insurers; I was insured via a group scheme arranged by the Society. The spontaneous response from the spokeswoman for the insurance company was one of incomprehension. "Why don't you hand over your notes?" I discovered that our insurance covered neither for fighting a confidentiality case nor even for the costs of legal advice. I was disappointed and surprised. I spoke to my previous insurers, who were well informed because they had fought a number of confidentiality cases. They said that they would now rarely fight such a case, as they had always lost. They thought the best thing to do would be to negotiate at an early stage; I had no power to hold back. They told me that they would not fight a case if the patient had signed a consent form. As I shall explain later, I felt that I too had been hit unexpectedly by something which penetrated through to the underlying disorder.

I would not have contacted either Society again had I not had an informal conversation with a friend who happened to be on the Executive of the Psychoanalytical Society. I told her what was going on. She was horrified and advised me to let the president know about the insurance position. She felt the Society should back me, as it was the Society that had organized the insurance. She was sure that Council would support me. I rang the president, who suggested various people I might speak to for advice, and requested the Executive to consider providing funds for costs or at least for a legal consultation. A senior barrister friend advised that I must find a solicitor; I should be legally represented if I wanted to be taken seriously by lawyers.

He thought I was in danger of being viewed as a crank or at least as thoroughly unprofessional; my credibility would be seriously damaged by visible lack of support from my professional bodies.

I spent a considerable amount of time on the telephone trying to find a lawyer who knew something about the issues involved. Eventually, I was driven to trying just to find someone interested in taking the case. I had not appreciated how difficult this would be. For example, I spoke to a solicitor who is also a county court judge, and he said, "Doctors always say the patient will commit suicide if they see their notes. I take no notice; I always order that the notes be seen." I became increasingly disheartened. I had a full caseload, some NHS sessions, and a family—I was busy. My evenings and every gap between patients were spent dealing with correspondence and making phone calls to do with this case.

I informed the solicitors for the insurance company that I was taking legal advice. I told them to take no action for seven days from the date of my letter to them and threatened counter costs. They wrote back in under a week enclosing their notice of application from the court, with a court date fixed for the following week. By now, I knew that I was not required to produce any notes until the insurance company provided a documented reasoned argument to the court (an affidavit). The solicitor threatened that their costs would be greatly increased if I insisted on their writing this document. I insisted.

Around this time, the chairman of the Executive Council phoned me to let me know that the Psychoanalytic Institute would give me some money. I felt heartened by the support, although I knew it would not go far in legal fees (about four hours). My barrister friend found and briefed a solicitor who was willing to fight my case. I faxed him all the correspondence, and we met the following day, the one on which I was meant to have replied to the court order. After initial pessimism, the solicitor began to think that I might have a case. Nonetheless, he thought that coming to an arrangement out of court would be safest. He advised me to meet the insurance company's psychiatrist/expert witness. I felt reluctant. I did not want to become engaged with my patient's adversary.

On reflection, I thought that I might be able to persuade the insurance company psychiatrist, a consultant psychotherapist, that he did not need my notes. I hoped that he in turn would argue on my behalf with the insurance company. I felt this was probably my best chance of averting the impending court proceedings. My solicitor set up a time for us to talk on the phone. The psychiatrist told me that he was not asking for my notes, that he did not need them, nor would they add anything to his opinion. He was, however, not prepared to respond to my request to inform the solicitors that he was not asking for my notes and that they would not add to his opinion; nor would he tell them that he thought disclosure would damage the patient's relationship with me. He said that he had already told the insurers that, as I was a psychoanalyst, I would be asserting the importance of confidentiality. He said that he would tell them he did not need my notes, but he would not say that he did not want them.

My solicitor sent a letter on my behalf to the insurance company's solicitors; he notified them that I intended to resist the order and asked for their affidavit. They replied asking for a postponement, as they were not prepared. We agreed. We then heard nothing for some weeks following which my solicitor suggested that we close the case. I agreed. I was very relieved that it was all over.

During this time, I can remember a growing awareness of the extent of my patient's desire to see my notes and of his increasing irritation at my not making them available to him. His excitement at the possibility of someone in authority (me) falling off my pedestal was clear. I think he found relief from his fear, feelings of powerlessness and rage by pushing them into me before joining the dominant group of tormentors, in which the lawyers were his only-too-willing allies. Although this was a familiar defensive maneuver for my patient, I think that had I been firmly supported in my stand to protect the treatment, in the way that a mother might be helped by a father with the destructive and intrusive behavior of a disturbed child, the patient might have been contained in the therapeutic relationship. I had the impression that he was disturbed by the turn of events and that seeing me face-to-face made him uncomfortable and threatened his manic defense.

Some weeks later, out of the blue, the insurance company's sworn affidavit arrived. It demanded disclosure of my notes and was accompanied by an order that I appear in court in ten days' time. The affidavit was long. It contained copies of notes on the patient and a number of reports; the patient's history was described in full detail. The central argument advanced by the insurance company was that the treatment with me concerned the patient's long-standing difficulties and had nothing to do with the accident; the solicitors declared that the absence of mention of the accident in my notes would prove their point.

It was days before I could reach my solicitor; a great deal of time was then wasted in my having to go over once again all the reasons why I thought I should fight the case. He, having read the insurance company's affidavit, now thought that I had no case. It was very close to another holiday, I applied to change the date of the hearing to a day when I could cancel as few patients as possible. The solicitor helped to prepare my affidavit and to apply for an adjournment. This turned out to be on a day when he was unable to attend. He offered to send his assistant solicitor, but I felt anxious about being accompanied by someone unqualified who was likely to be unfamiliar with my position and might even disagree with it.

My affidavit contained, elaborated, and expanded on my earlier explanations of confidentiality. I said:

> The psychoanalyst tries to understand the way the patient feels and thinks, so as to shed light on the reasons for the patient's behavior. Because the analyst is trying to understand what is going on in the patient's mind and how things appear from the patient's point of view, patients are encouraged to speak about anything that comes into their minds. This means that patients often reveal matters of an intimate nature and breach of confidentiality by the psychoanalyst would be acutely damaging to the essential relationship that must develop between the patient and the psychoanalyst.

I explained why I felt it crucial to remain neutral:

> In a world where a patient is being pushed and pulled by others, particularly in the litigation process, a psychoanalyst provides a solid, unmoving, and secure reference point from which a patient can begin to examine himself and the way he thinks and behaves. From this, a patient develops his own capacity to think and exercise judgment and take responsibility for his own actions.

I added: "It might be that one of you or a member of your family could find yourselves in a situation in which you need help. Would you not feel it important that there were available to you a profession with a very strict code of practice with regard to neutrality and confidentiality?" I also described that my notes were to myself, that they were an extremely incomplete record, and that they were in no way the same as clinical notes in a hospital, which are made accurately to record specific details of the patient's condition and as a communication to other colleagues. I sought costs from the insurance company.

Because much of English law is based on precedent, I thought that winning the case would uphold the Society's stand on confidentiality, but I did not think that going to prison and paying a fine would be of any benefit were I to lose. Having seen the psychiatrists' reports, it was clear to me that there was nothing in my notes that was not already known to all those involved in the case. I thought it unlikely that either side would find anything in my notes to use in court. The setting, my patient's privacy, and my privacy were already violated. On the other hand, I still wanted to protect the principle of the setting and had the image of an "ideal analyst" who would to go to prison rather than compromise on confidentiality. Furthermore, I felt very strongly that my notes were my private property and, as such, I wanted to protect them.

It seemed that whatever I did would be wrong; I felt trapped between the forces of two uncompromising figures who refused to listen to reason. It was a paranoid-schizoid situation, dominated by moralism. On the one hand, there was the "ideal psychoanalyst" who would lay down his life for confidentiality and who would not have gotten into this position in the first place; on the other, there was the divine right of the legal establishment to have access to whatever they wanted, regardless of the consequences. The plight of the analyst has been likened by Caper (1999) to Bion's description of the way in which a tank commander in the First World War had to guide the driver by walking in front of the tank. If hit by enemy fire, he was at risk of being run over by his own tank—in my case the ideal psychoanalyst.

I was, however, not completely trapped. I could think about my situation and so could my Society. Some funds had been provided, and I felt supported to put up a fight but not to let myself come to harm. A reality sense prevailed. I decided that I would put up a fight but that if I was ordered to hand over my notes I would argue for a restriction and then give them up. I could have argued for a postponement because of the lack of time to respond and because of my solicitor's inability to appear on that date. But I had a date that I could manage clinically, and I now wanted to get the thing over.

This was not a straightforward case about the degree of psychological damage caused by an accident but more an opportunity for the enactment of a confused and confusing perverse sadomasochistic relationship. I had thought that I must resist being pulled into the court case. But I was mistaken in thinking that in doing so I could keep myself, or the patient, safe. The series of events that took place in my dealings with lawyers were very intrusive; they took up time, crowded my mind, and caused me to feel anxious, angry, and helpless. I was a player in my patient's exciting drama.

My barrister friend kindly spent the weekend with me preparing a skeleton argument, a second document in which he set out in greater detail, quoting statute and case law, the reasons why my notes should not be disclosed and the reasons why I should be awarded costs. This document was sent to the applicant's solicitors and the judge the day before the hearing. Some confidence was expressed in my having a case and in my capacity to manage on my own. A miscalculation.

The case was heard by a judge in Chambers. I went to court with my skeleton argument, some photocopies of the relevant points of law, some notes, and some anxiety. On my arrival at the court, I was handed the insurance company's skeleton argument. This was a shock, as was the fact that they were represented by a solicitor and a barrister. I had been advised that there would be no skeleton argument and that they would be represented only by a mild-mannered solicitor. The insurance company was taking the case seriously. I could have stopped in my tracks at that point, asked for a postponement to read their skeleton argument, and engaged a barrister. I decided to continue.

It took barely seconds for me to realize the near impossibility of my task. I attempted, while listening to the arguments advanced against me, to read the skeleton argument, work out my replies, and locate the relevant points of law on my photocopies. It was a horrible experience. I felt the solicitor and barrister to be very hostile, and they attempted to denigrate me. They were angry at the delay and extra work that I had caused and were determined to win. They were doing their job. The situation was mitigated by the judge, who treated me with respect. Toward the end, the judge said that he found himself uncertain about what to do, and I felt hopeful that I might win. He concluded, however, that it was impossible to know the relevance of my notes until they were seen, and even though the two psychiatrists had told me that they were not needed he felt that he must order that I disclose. The two previous court orders for disclosure in this case influenced his decision. The insurance company was to pay its own costs. My request that access should be limited to the solicitors and their experts was granted, despite the barrister's insistence that the patient should also be allowed access. The restriction order did not allow for this. I failed to get a judgment that they pay my costs.

I sent my notes to the solicitors, but the wrangling continued for a further three months. They found it hard to believe that what I had given them really were my notes. My patient's solicitors then wanted the notes, but refused to put in writing an undertaking to restrict the access to themselves and their experts. They became increasingly belligerent and threatened me with further court proceedings. I refused, they finally agreed to the restriction, and I sent them my notes.

The situation was difficult on many levels. I started with little knowledge of my legal position, and no knowledge of my insurance situation; I had to learn about both as events unfolded. I repeatedly found myself put under pressure to respond quickly, which made it difficult to think. Had I been better prepared in advance with a more realistic view of my legal and insurance position and with a more considered view about confidentiality, I might have found myself more able to step back from the situation and think.

It is well known that part of a patient's motivation for treatment is to find someone into whom they can project aspects of themselves and into whom they can export their problems. The patient has conflicting wishes; wishes for the analyst to succeed, survive the experience, and find a way of coping against wishes for the analyst to fail and be destroyed. There are shifts and reverses in the balance between these wishes, which are partly dependent on the degree to which the patient retains awareness of having a problem and needing help. Interference from outside agencies can unbalance the whole enterprise.

My patient switched between a rather fragmented state that he found unbearable, in which he felt afraid and upset, to a slightly more bearable one in which he seemed to feel more held together. In the latter, he was cut off from knowledge of his own difficulties, either coldly indifferent to the difficulties of those around him or visibly excited and entertained. I am sure that the experience of being trapped and defenseless in the cruel presence of someone who took pleasure in his failure, was one with which my patient was familiar and one that drove him into perverse activity. I think that he had experienced the accident as a violent forced reintrojection of all that he had managed to project out. I then became the object into whom he could evacuate as much of his difficulty as possible. My suitability as such an object was increased by the precariousness of my position: no insurance, no lawyer, no defense in law, and initially little support from my Society. All this reduced my capacity to offer the needed containment and protection.

It is questionable whether it was ever possible or even right for me to have continued trying to contain the situation once it had spilled to such an extent outside the sessions. I felt on my own in a conflict with my own moral and professional standards. Where did my loyalties lie—to the patient, to my other patients, to my professional community, or to my family and myself? I was, however, not alone and not completely without funds; I could think and communicate, and my Society was able to hear. Nor was the judge indifferent to my arguments; he listened thoughtfully and agreed to my request for a restriction. I was not caught between enemy fire and my own tank, but was involved with others on whom I could make an impression, even if only slowly.

To return to the point that I made at the beginning: if we as psychoanalysts are to take the IPA statement on confidentiality seriously, then it has practical consequences. We need to give much more thought to the issues involved. We need greater clarity about when, with what backup, and in what way we are to take a stand. To what lengths are we as individual psychoanalysts, as Societies, or as an international body prepared to go?

Postscript

These questions are being debated currently within the British Psychoanalytical Society, the British Confederation of Psychotherapists, and within the European Psychoanalytic Federation. The provision of support for psychoanalysts and psychotherapists who become involved in legal proceedings is being addressed, as is the crucial matter of providing the legal profession and those drafting legislation with clear and understandable explanations of the nature of our work and our reasons for placing so high a value on confidentiality and neutrality.

References

Bollas, C. (2000), The Disclosure Industry. Opening Plenary Address, Conference on "Confidentiality and Society: Psychotherapy, Ethics, and the Law," Montreal, Quebec, Canada, October 13.

Caper, R. (1999), *A Mind of One's Own*. London: Routledge.

Hayman, A. (1965), Psychoanalyst subpoenaed. *Lancet,* October 16:785–786.

Introduction to CHAPTER 14

❧

Outing the Victim: Breaches of Confidentiality in an Ethics Procedure

A complainant at an ethics hearing faces a potentially daunting challenge to his or her reputation, and the situation is potentially graver if the complainant is a member of the analytic community. In this account of the unravelling of confidentiality within a North American psychoanalytic institute, David Sundelson narrates an astonishing cascade of betrayals resulting from professional smugness, pseudoprocedures, and the condescending "helpfulness" of colleagues who are unable to contain themselves and to maintain strict confidentiality. Coauthor with Christopher Bollas of the groundbreaking *The New Informants*, Sundelson brings to this account the acuity of a lawyer with a keen interest in confidentiality issues and a deep familiarity with psychoanalysis.

Many of the indiscretions Sundelson describes occurred in a casual manner, and many of the decisions were taken ad hoc, in a placid and unquestioning way. Strung together in real time, however, these seemingly insignificant events add up to a massive invasion of individual privacy and a serious collective failure of professional responsibility. Sundelson's contribution raises difficult issues about the all-too-human risks of interanalytic communication, underlining the need for much more careful thought, systematic investigation, and "vigilance" in the area of confidentiality, not least in analytic societies and institutes.

CHAPTER 14

༺✲༻

Outing the Victim: Breaches of Confidentiality in an Ethics Procedure

David Sundelson

Knowing Your Siblings

*A*t the international conference, "Confidentiality and Society," which inspired some of the chapters in this book, including this one, a psychoanalyst, whom I shall name X, spoke about case conferences at his institute where the patient under discussion was also a candidate. Those participating in the case conferences were, of course, analysts and other candidates, and often, as a result, "everyone in the room knew who the patient was." Gossip about who was in analysis with whom was common and, even without it, details of the discussion often made the patient easy to recognize.

Training analyses at that institute were thus regularly contaminated by breaches of confidentiality, the analyst said, but no one ever talked about the problem. His comments produced murmurs of recognition and assent from the audience but no suggestions for change.

My own experience, as an analysand and also as a friend and colleague of candidates and analysts, suggests that the erosion of confidentiality within psychoanalytic institutes (and the social and professional circles connected with them) is not unique to X's institute. Many years ago, I told an analyst friend who my own analyst was. "Don't you want to know who your siblings are?" he asked. The question caught me off guard. Before I could stop him, he proceeded to name several of my analyst's other patients. Some of them, it turned out—not surprisingly in a small community—were people I knew socially.

Since then, I have heard more of such gossip and the half-conscious sadism it expresses. I don't think "sadism" is too strong a word here. To demonstrate secret knowledge and a willingness to disclose it seems sadistic both toward those whose confidence is betrayed and toward the recipient of unwanted information. That recipient becomes a kind of dumping ground and must also wonder if his or her own confidence will soon be violated in the same way with some other "sibling."

The casual, even routine quality of what are at least akin to ethical violations is striking, especially in a profession that purports to place a high value on confidentiality and privacy. It may be that with his question in Montreal, analyst X shined a light on one cause of this behavior. How can any analyst who trains in a fishbowl, where everyone in a case conference often knows just whose symptoms, history, and conflicts are being discussed, learn to value the critical role of confidentiality in psychoanalysis or the value of privacy in general?

Dr. Brook and Dr. Schwartz

The atmosphere described by analyst X may also help to explain the multiple betrayals of confidentiality that I want to consider in this chapter. I will refer to the patient, who is herself an analyst, as Dr. Brook. The disclosures took place in connection with an ethics complaint Brook brought against her analyst, whom I will call Dr. Schwartz. Disciplinary proceedings resulted from the complaint. Some disclosures were made by psychoanalysts and lawyers in the course of those proceedings; others were connected to the proceedings less directly.

It is ironic that for many years, Brook's treatment with Schwartz, a successful and highly respected senior analyst, featured Schwartz's wholesale violations of confidentiality. Dr. Schwartz regularly discussed his other patients and his colleagues with Brook, identifying them by name and describing, often in vivid, anecdotal detail, their professional, marital, and sexual difficulties. Eventually, Schwartz found an easier way to convey this information. He left his answering machine on during Brook's sessions so that she could hear any mes-

sages that came in: messages from Schwartz's colleagues and patients and also from his wife and children. Particular messages often
provided a starting point for further gossip.

The treatment with Schwartz eventually included other unethical
conduct, including sexual boundary violations. After a long time,
Brook stopped seeing Schwartz. Some time later, she filed an ethics
complaint with the American Psychoanalytic Association and also
brought ethics charges with the state licensing board.

It was hard for Brook to take these steps. She was no longer
Schwartz's patient but was still confused by what remained of her
transference. She blamed herself for what had happened in her treatment, and she was also desperately worried that her husband would
leave her if he found out about it. Even after she confided in him and
was reassured by his response, she was still worried about her professional and social reputation.

As a result of these concerns, when she finally managed to seek
help, first from an analyst in a distant city and then from some of
Schwartz's local colleagues, Brook insisted on assurances that everything she said would be confidential. The two analysts she consulted
in her own city, the president of the local institute and the chair of its
ethics committee, told her that they could not guarantee her confidentiality. The president put the problem bluntly: "analysts talk."
However, they promised to do everything in their power to protect
Brook. Only after receiving these assurances did she tell them
Schwartz's name.

Due Process

Both the local and the out-of-town analysts Brook consulted advised
her to send her letter of complaint directly to the Ethics Committee of
the American Psychoanalytic Association, not to the local institute.
They told her that this strategy would help to protect her privacy. It
would also prevent Schwartz from using his local influence and pres-
tige to fend off disciplinary action. Brook followed their advice. Several
months later, the chairman of the national ethics committee informed
her that five members would consider her complaint at a formal
"investigative hearing." The committee would then determine what,
if any, disciplinary action to recommend regarding Schwartz.

The chairman also invited Brook to write to him if she had any
questions. In response, she and her husband sent various letters to

the chairman and also to the association's lawyer. In the letters, they asked questions that revealed their particular fears about the hearing. They also expressed their frustration with the slow pace of the ethics process and included personal information about the strain on themselves and their children. A short time before the hearing, the lawyer informed Brook that copies of all letters had been sent to Schwartz and his lawyer. Neither Brook nor her husband had ever given permission for any such disclosure.

When the investigative hearing took place, Schwartz was present from beginning to end. He heard all of Brook's testimony about her treatment, including her account of the facts and her psychological analysis. He heard the testimony by her husband and friend, and he heard the committee's questions to Brook as well as her responses. When Schwartz testified, the chairman asked Brook and her witnesses to leave the room. The chairman explained that Schwartz's presence was intended to protect his right to due process. The exclusion of Brook during Schwartz's testimony was to protect his confidentiality.

Six weeks after the hearing, the committee informed Brook that it had voted unanimously to recommend the most severe sanction at its disposal: permanent expulsion of Schwartz from the association. Brook immediately contacted the two local analysts she had consulted. She wanted to know what action the local institute would take in light of the decision by the national ethics committee.

She met with the local ethics chair, who told her that the institute would comply with the decision made by the national association. In light of the vote following the hearing, she said, the local institute "didn't want" Schwartz as a member any more. However, she didn't know exactly what steps the institute would take or when it would take them.

"The One Person He Trusted"

In the months before and after the hearing, Brook's husband John confided in an old friend ("Dr. French"), an analyst in a distant city. The two spoke many times over the phone, and John found French helpful and sympathetic. In one of these conversations, John was especially agitated as he talked about the stress on his wife and him as they waited for some action by the local institute. A day or two later, they spoke again. French told John that because he was concerned about him, he had called a psychoanalyst he knew and liked—"the one person he trusted" where John and Brook lived—and asked if he was available if John wanted to see him. French added that he had told his colleague Brook's story. He had identified Brook and John as well as Schwartz.

John felt stunned and betrayed. However, he was reluctant at first to confront the friend who was his one confidant, and he said only that he wished French had asked his permission before using any names. French seemed surprised by the reproach. He had expected John to be grateful, he said, but perhaps he had made a mistake by not consulting him first. He could understand why John was upset.

John subsequently received an apologetic e-mail from French, but when he called back to express his anger more directly, his friend's tone had changed. He and the local analyst he had consulted were clinical colleagues, he said. Such disclosures were routine among colleagues, and information that was confined to the clinical community was still confidential. He insisted that he had not violated Brook's confidentiality or John's. Moreover, it had been essential to reveal their names to determine if his colleague had any conflict of interest that would make him unavailable to John. He hadn't wanted to arouse John's hopes only to disappoint him.

"Substantial People"

Several months later, Brook still had not heard what action the local institute planned to take regarding Schwartz. Frustrated by the prolonged uncertainty, she arranged to meet again with the president of the institute ("Dr. Kahn"), whom she had previously consulted. John went with her.

Kahn told Brook and John that no action had been taken yet—there had been various delays caused by Schwartz's lawyer—but that the institute's board of directors was to meet with Schwartz the following evening in an attempt to reach some sort of agreement. The president would not tell Brook what position Schwartz or his lawyer were taking or anything about the board's decision-making procedure, insisting that such information was confidential.

As Brook and John were preparing to leave and almost in passing, Kahn mentioned that at the board meeting she intended to distribute copies of Brook's formal letter of complaint as well as the written statements that she and John had presented at the investigative hearing. Brook had given copies of the statements to the president after the committee reached its decision.

"Will you use our names?" Brook asked. Kahn said that she would. Both Brook and John objected strongly. Brook reminded the president that in previous consultations, she had spoken again and again of her fears about loss of confidentiality, and that Kahn had promised to do everything in her power to protect it.

Like French, the president seemed surprised by the objection. She thought Brook and John would be pleased, she said. Their statements were very eloquent, and their names were necessary to preserve the full effect. She wanted the board members to read them, and she refused to remove the names even after Brook repeated her objections in a faxed letter and a follow-up telephone call. It was her decision, the president said, and she took full responsibility for it.

The board meeting took place as scheduled the following evening, and after it was finished the president called Brook. She had distributed the statements from the hearing (but not the letter of complaint—it was "too long"). At her request, each board member had signed a promise to protect Brook's confidentiality. In considerable distress, Brook left a telephone message with each board member, objecting to the disclosure of her name and begging each not to disclose it further. No one returned her call.

She then made two more calls, to the local ethics committee chair and to the institute's lawyer. The lawyer insisted that the waiver Brook signed when she sent her letter of complaint justified the president's disclosure. The ethics chair said that the president had simply been trying to show the board that Schwartz's victims were "substantial people." When Brook asked what that meant, and how, in any case, the identity of his patient was relevant to any judgment about Schwartz's ethical lapses, the chair tried a different tack. The president had used their names because she was trying to add "that extra something" to her presentation.

"Taking an Action"

For a long time, Brook didn't talk to any local friends about her treatment with Dr. Schwartz. (The old friend who testified at the investigative hearing lived in another city.) Many were analysts or therapists themselves; many knew Schwartz socially or professionally.

Brook was still ashamed of what had happened to her and worried about her reputation in the professional community. She wanted desperately to protect her own and her family's privacy.

When she did confide in a friend who was also a clinician—I will call her Wilson—she did so with much hesitation, and only after Wilson assured her that she had listened to many secrets over the years and was utterly scrupulous about protecting confidential information. When Brook told the story of her treatment, Wilson reacted with shock and sympathy. She also mentioned that she knew some of Schwartz's other patients.

A week or two after she confided in Wilson, Brook received a message from her. Her friend wanted. Brook to "take an action." That is, she wanted her to tell her story to another friend of Wilson's who was in analysis with Schwartz. In light of what Brook had told her, she wanted her friend to know that her psychoanalyst was dangerously unethical so she could extricate herself from her treatment.

The request made Brook angry, but she told Wilson only that she didn't want to discuss Schwartz with anyone else. She also reminded Wilson that she was worried about her confidentiality. Wilson didn't press the issue.

Some weeks later, Wilson reported to Brook that her friend had asked her about rumors that Schwartz had "legal trouble." She reported that she had told her friend that she needed to take these rumors seriously and had then evaded further questions. However, it was clear that Wilson had said enough so that her friend would be able to identify Brook as the source of Schwartz's "legal trouble." In fact, Wilson subsequently told Brook that her friend had learned Brook's identity in some unspecified way.

Privacy and Confidentiality

This case presents issues of both confidentiality and privacy. Confidentiality is a principle of professional ethics that protects certain relationships: priest-penitent, lawyer-client, analyst-analysand. In psychoanalysis, the right to confidentiality arises from the analyst's ethical duty and the analysand's expectations, the latter based on the analyst's assurances and on a mutual understanding of the work to be done. Confidentiality protects trust. Without that trust, as Christopher Bollas and I have argued elsewhere (1995), free association cannot take place. Confidentiality is thus essential for psychoanalysis.

Confidentiality is a rule intended to protect privacy in particular circumstances, but the right to privacy is broader and is recognized in law. Its cultural sources are respect for individual dignity and awareness of what nourishes or harms it. Like sexual misconduct, breaches of privacy violate the victim's sense of psychic integrity and safety. Both kinds of violation are abuses of power.

Outside the strictly clinical relationship of analyst and analysand (or other professional relationships), one would ordinarily find violations of privacy, not confidentiality. However, some nonclinical situations include what one could call quasi-clinical conditions: a sharply increased sense of vulnerability, elements of transference, and specific assurances from one person to another. I would argue that in such situations, the ordinary legal obligation to respect privacy moves toward an ethical duty of confidentiality. For example, even though Brook was not a patient of the local analysts with whom she discussed her grievances, or of French, or of Wilson, I would say that their disclosures of her identity violated not only her privacy but an ethical duty of confidentiality.

Schwartz's boundary violations, including his extensive violations of privacy and confidentiality, generated poisonous feelings of shame, guilt, and self-loathing in Brook. For that reason, the preservation of her privacy—and her confidentiality—was especially urgent for her, and she brought it up again and again with the two local analysts she consulted. The assurances they gave her make their subsequent disclosures especially hard to fathom.

Due Process (2)

Confidentiality received some careful attention in the rules under which the investigative hearing was conducted, but that confidentiality is the analyst's, not the patient's (who in this context of course is not just a patient but a "complainant"). Due process does provide a rationale for allowing the analyst to be present during the complainant's testimony, notwithstanding any discomfort caused to the complainant. Due process protects the right to be heard and the right to confront adverse witnesses. Because the investigative hearing may result in significant professional (and ultimately, economic) sanctions imposed against the charged analyst, it is akin to a criminal proceeding, and due process is a guarantee of fairness.

However, even in a criminal proceeding where the possible

sanctions include fines and imprisonment, due process does not give the accused the right to an ex parte hearing—a private consultation— with the judge or jury. There was no reason to believe that Schwartz received any benefit from his private session with the Ethics Committee; certainly the unanimous vote to expel him from the association indicates that he did not. I suggest, however, that giving such a right to the charged analyst but not to the complainant creates at least the appearance of potential bias and the opportunity for cronyism—an appearance the profession might prefer to avoid.

In addition, a show of tenderness for the analyst's confidentiality seems unwarranted without at least some regard for the complainant's. The complainant is a former patient, after all, toward whom the parent association may well have a duty of care second only to that of the analyst himself.

The decision by the association's lawyer to provide copies of Brook's and John's prehearing correspondence to Schwartz is a simpler matter. The letter informing Brook that the correspondence had been sent is, of course, no substitute for adequate notice at the start, before she and John accepted the invitation to confide in the chairman of the hearing committee. To send that correspondence to Schwartz without permission was a clear violation of Brook's and John's privacy. That it was committed by counsel for the association reflects poorly on both.

Substantial People (2)

The decision by Kahn, the president of the local institute, to disclose Brook's and John's names at the board meeting is even harder to excuse. Kahn knew how worried Brook was about her confidentiality and her privacy, and Kahn assured Brook more than once that she would do her best to protect them.

The lawyer's attempt to use the release Brook signed to justify the president's disclosures is not persuasive. First of all, John signed no release. He did not waive his privacy rights, and no one could waive them for him. Second, the release Brook signed covered only her letter of complaint (which Kahn did not distribute to the board). The release did not apply to the substantially more personal and detailed statements she and John made at the investigative hearing. Finally, the release was not a blanket permission to use Brook's name at the president's or the institute's discretion. It permitted only "necessary" disclosures.

In this instance, no such necessity existed. Attempts to articulate a need by the local ethics chair (the president wanted to show the Board that Brook and her husband are "substantial people" or, alternatively, to add "that extra something" to her presentation of the case) can fairly be described as desperate. The first rationale is simple snobbery. Obviously, whether his patients are or are not "substantial" is irrelevant to any judgment of Schwartz's ethics. With respect to the second, one would be hard pressed to imagine what "extra something" could justify such a blatant violation of privacy and confidentiality.

It would have been a minor secretarial chore to remove names and personal references from the short statements that were distributed to the board members. Law firms routinely perform this chore in the course of discovery proceedings. Since the names added nothing of legitimate value and would have been so easy to remove, it is hard not to wonder why Kahn insisted on carrying out her plan to disclose them. Perhaps her decision was punitive. Kahn complained several times to Brook and John about the difficulty of her position and the burdens placed on her by the ethics proceeding. She made it clear that she resented any criticism of her administrative lapses (she often failed to return phone calls), and several times was openly and intensely angry at Brook. When Brook objected to the plan to disclose her name at the board meeting, the president accused her of trying to "orchestrate" the meeting, and insisted that such an attempt was unacceptable.

Clearly, the ethics proceeding and the underlying charges generated strong feelings in everyone concerned. It is hard not to suspect that Kahn wanted to punish Brook for her presumption and troublemaking and at the same time to prove her own authority once and for all. Brook would not choose whether or not to reveal her name at the board meeting; the president would. Brook would not orchestrate the meeting; the president would. Brook would not decide how to protect her privacy; the president would.

Unfortunately, her method of doing so—to have each board member sign a promise to maintain confidentiality—was a poor substitute for not disclosing the names in the first place. After all, as Kahn herself observed, "analysts talk."

The Titillation Factor

It may be that the ethics chairman's second rationale was correct: Kahn was trying to add "that extra something" to her presentation at the meeting. What could the extra something have been?

When she first consulted the ethics chair, Dr. Brook mentioned that she had once wanted to become a candidate at the institute: years before, she completed an application but didn't submit it. In response, the ethics chair wondered if bringing a complaint against Schwartz would prevent any future application by Brook from being accepted. Brook asked what she meant. The ethics chair answered that she was "thinking of the titillation factor."

Perhaps the titillation factor was in effect when Dr. Kahn made her presentation to the Board. Titillation feeds on the specific, after all. Perhaps the president could not resist an opportunity to identify the patient with whom Schwartz had transgressed. In any event, her disclosures not only violated the privacy she had promised so earnestly to protect. They also added needless sensationalism to the proceeding and created richer opportunities for *schadenfreude* and gossip.

The result was the "outing" of Brook. Lesser outings, driven in some part by the titillation factor, took place at the hands of John's friend French and Brook's friend Wilson. Each of these outings exposed Brook's private self at its most vulnerable, causing an overwhelming sense of helplessness and shame.

French's Disclosures

French offered two justifications for his disclosure of Brook's and John's names. First, the disclosure was necessary to protect John from potential disappointment. Second, it wasn't really a breach of confidentiality at all because French revealed their names only to another psychoanalyst—to a colleague.

The first rationale is one version of the patronizing—even infantilizing—stance that Brook encountered more than once. (She was told, for example, that "it would not be her decision" to send her complaint to the local institute or the parent association and, another time, that she had no right to know what administrative steps would follow the decision of the ethics committee.) In this instance, the infantilizing had more than one layer. French assumed that John wanted a referral even though he never asked for one. He also assumed that John would be unable to tolerate the disappointment of obtaining a referral only to find that the particular analyst was unavailable. Finally, he assumed that it was more important to save John from even so hypothetical a disappointment than to protect John's—and Brook's—confidentiality and privacy.

The basis of French's second defense of his disclosures is not an ethical precept but a professional need. Psychoanalysts need to consult each other about their work, to teach, and to write, and examples from their clinical work are useful and perhaps even essential to all these activities. However, none of them requires the sacrifice of confidentiality. Analysts can—and, if they are to follow the ethical principles of their profession, must—become adept at concealing the identity of their patients, not just by changing name or gender but with an assortment of more sophisticated methods.

To teach or write about one's patients without these safeguards is to eviscerate the principle of confidentiality. Consultation is no different, especially when the patient in question is also a clinician. To reveal a patient's identity in consultation is to pretend that psychoanalysts do not, like everyone else, talk to their spouses, friends, and colleagues. It is to pretend that they belong not to small, incestuous, and gossip-ridden professional and social communities but to a priesthood so disciplined that secrets conveyed to a fellow member never travel any further.

French's argument was based on a grandiose fairy tale about the profession, and comments by analyst X, which I mentioned at the start of this chapter, suggest that belief in the fairy tale is not confined to French. Such belief may provide the justification, more or less conscious, for arrangements like the case conferences in which everyone recognizes the patient under discussion. In any event, the fairy tale provided little comfort to Brook or John for a flagrant and disturbing betrayal of trust.

Theft of Narrative

To borrow a phrase from Jonathan Lear (this volume), psychoanalysis depends on a belief in the transformative power of words. This power comes in part from the construction of alternate narratives. It is too simple to say that an analysand, working with her analyst, constructs a new personal narrative of the self, its history, and its interactions with the world, including and especially the analyst. A single new narrative may seem true for a time, but psychoanalysis often contains multiple narratives, more or less provisional, subject to continuous or intermittent revision.

Psychoanalytic narratives are a serious form of play. Ideally, they create a restorative experience of mastery and dignity, which brings relief from the hopelessness of feeling trapped in a single story. Several elements contribute to the experience, including the collaboration of analyst and analysand and the trust and sense of freedom produced by confidentiality.

The loss of confidentiality extinguishes that freedom. First, there is a loss of control. Another narrator takes possession of one's story, turning it to some purpose that is not one's own. In addition, the provisional quality is lost. The possibility of many narratives, each with some truth, gives way to a single story, unchangeable and inevitably reductive.

When a treatment is contaminated by unethical conduct, as was Brook's, all provisional narratives disappear into a single tale, not restorative but shameful, that threatens to swallow the analysand. If she is to recover from the trauma, she will have to interpret the shameful narrative as false and discard it in favor of new narratives so that she can once again feel like the author of her own identity.

This new construction will be unusually difficult, because trauma has seriously undermined the analysand's belief in her narrative powers. Much revision will be needed, and the meanings that emerge may be especially fragile. Control of the new narratives is crucial, for in the hands of someone else they cease to be provisional and threaten to become, once more, a dominating "true" story that permanently defines the self as shameful, guilty, or damaged. For all these reasons, analytic work following a trauma of the kind Dr. Schwartz caused requires the private space created by confidentiality, and the loss of that space is especially harmful.

The president of the local institute was surprised when Brook objected to the plan to distribute the statements she and her husband had written. After all, hadn't they already read those statements at the investigative hearing?

They had, of course, but Kahn missed the difference between speaking one's own words in one's own voice, face to face with an audience for whom they are intended, and having those same words presented by someone else to an audience one did not choose. The first position is one of authorship and connection, the second of theft. The first is active, the second passive. The first allows the speaker to do everything a storyteller does: to modify her voice and tone and also to hear, evaluate, and answer responses. It therefore restores a sense of at least partial control. The second position is of exclusion, helplessness, and psychic emptiness.

In a small way, my friend's question—"Don't you want to know who your siblings are?"—induced the same sense of helplessness. Instead of stealing my narrative, my friend injected one of his own. For an unpleasant moment, I became a figure in his cartoon of psychoanalysis. The distinctive, amorphous meanings of my transference vanished, replaced by the single hackneyed meaning he stamped on it. ("The analyst is your father. His other patients are your siblings. Get used to it.")

Of course, my friend's question was only a minor intrusion into the private space of psychoanalysis. The disturbing effects of even so small an intrusion give one some sense of the damage inflicted by more substantial narrative thefts.

Actions and Principles

When Wilson asked Brook to "take an action" by telling her story to another one of Schwartz's patients, she failed to consider that Brook had already taken action of a very different kind. Brook did not act out her more dramatic fantasies of revenge. She did not confront Schwartz in a restaurant, forcing him to flee in embarrassment. She did not picket his office. She did not sit in his waiting room and tell each of his patients what he had done. Instead, she put her faith in disciplinary procedures established by the profession and by the state.

For Brook, the act of bringing charges was an attempt to reestablish connections with other colleagues and with a profession that was hers as well as Schwartz's, connections that had atrophied as she became more and more involved with him. In a larger sense, she sought to reestablish her sense of a morally ordered world. In such a world, everyone is protected by principles. When those principles are violated, an individual victim has no need to strap on a sixgun, because society takes action. Justice replaces revenge.

Wilson pushed Brook toward the very methods she was trying to avoid: those of the vigilante. In effect, she asked Brook to police the profession, to take over the job of protecting Schwartz's other patients in spite of the legal and professional machinery that Brook had already set in motion.

Her request thus had the flavor of lawlessness. It suggested, if not outright contempt for process, a preference for private remedies. The same reliance on private judgment and "action" instead of principle and procedure appears many times in this story. It appears in Wilson's disclosure of just enough information to let her friend identify

Brook. It appears in Kahn's decision to disclose Brook's and John's names to the board of the institute. It appears in French's decision to disclose their names to his colleague.

Of course, none of these psychoanalysts intended to harm Brook, and each claimed to have her best interests at heart. As I have noted, Kahn seemed genuinely surprised by Brook's and John's objections to her plan to reveal their names at the board meeting; she thought they would be pleased. French admitted that he expected John to be grateful to him for taking the trouble to consult a colleague. Wilson claimed that she was trying to protect both Brook and her other friend who was also Schwartz's patient. Each, when confronted, resolutely denied having done anything wrong.

In spite of unshakable belief in their own good intentions, each of these psychoanalysts committed a serious violation of Brook's (and her husband's) confidentiality and privacy. Each violation compounded and in some ways repeated the trauma caused by Schwartz's unethical treatment. The cause of these violations remains a mystery. Did Kahn, French, and Wilson act as they did because Brook's vulnerability elicited their unconscious sadism? Psychoanalysts are not, exempt from sadism, any more than from professional vanity or the impulse to gossip, and the unconscious, even for them, is stubbornly unconscious. Should we instead blame the persistent ideological divisions within the profession? Perhaps such divisions generate skepticism not just about principles of theory and practice but about ethical principles as well. If such skepticism exists, it may leave a vacuum too easily filled by the inflated self-confidence of those who rarely face criticism.

Whatever the cause, the profession would be well advised to redouble its vigilance with regard to confidentiality and privacy. The best and perhaps the only protection against unconscious sadism, abuses of authority, the impulse to gossip, and other common human failings is strict adherence to principle. In cases like Brook's, obviously, the greatest scrupulousness is required to avoid adding trauma to trauma. The same scrupulousness is needed in the overheated, incestuous atmosphere of psychoanalytic communities. If the profession is to retain its integrity and the respect of those it claims to serve, psychoanalysts must place principle first, whatever the temptations of "action."

References

Bollas, C. & Sundelson, D. (1995), *The New Informants*. Northvale, NJ: Aronson.

SECTION 4

⤛⤜

Professional Ethics and the Law

Introduction to CHAPTER 15

❧

Confidentiality and Professionalism

In "The Question of Lay Analysis," Freud (1925) went to great lengths to demonstrate that competency to practice psychoanalysis can only be acquired through a specifically psychoanalytic kind of training which has no intrinsic links to any other profession, even medicine and psychology. This argument would seem to give great weight to a view of psychoanalysis as a profession in its own right, but for historical and other reasons, psychoanalysis has tended to regard itself as a specialized extension of other professions, in either elite or subordinated relation to psychiatry and psychology. In the following trenchant analysis, originally delivered to the IPA Congress in Nice, France, in 2001, Christopher Bollas argues that contemporary uncertainty about the status of confidentiality is directly related to this problematic of the ambiguous and tentative professional status of psychoanalysis. Deepening the arguments of his seminal book on confidentiality, *The New Informants*, written with lawyer David Sundelson, Bollas exposes fundamental conflicts within the psychoanalytic movement which have produced the symptoms of the confidentiality crisis, and traces them to deeper psychic levels of the profession's social history.

CHAPTER 15

❧

Confidentiality and Professionalism

Christopher Bollas

*I*t might be argued that because people qualify as psychoanalysts, house themselves in training organizations and societies, congregate once every two years in an international arena, and publish a journal that they are formed as a profession. Certainly much of value can be said to occur through these forms of organization, but the constitution of a profession is not necessarily one of them. Indeed, the comparative lassitude around the question of confidentiality and privilege within psychoanalytical organizations could be taken as evidence of the reluctance of psychoanalysis to profess itself.

It is difficult to establish standards of practice for a profession if it has yet to exist. A group is a profession when it is self-regulating in educational, ethical, organizational, and economic matters; self-defining for state licensing; self-promoting in its expertise and contribution to society; and self-protective in appropriately vigorous ways when its ethos and organization are under challenge.

What are the obstacles preventing those who practice psychoanalysis from organizing it into a profession? What are the foundations of this reticence to exist? I think what we discover—at very first glance—is an obvious attachment to *other* professions that has stunted the growth of psychoanalytical professionalism.

What one finds in many countries is the explicit or tacit argument that psychoanalysis is *a branch* of psychiatry or psychology. Matters pertaining to standards of practice are often referred back to the *discipline of origin* that is seen as having set the criteria by which psychoanalysts must practice.

But even a cursory examination of the ethical guidelines of national associations of psychology and psychiatry will in certain countries reveal already-existent schisms between ethic codes of the original discipline and those of psychoanalysis. For example, it is now a guideline of practice in the United States for all psychologists who have a patient whom they deem to be a candidate for civil action to take notes suitable for use in a court of law. Not to do so constitutes a failure to maintain one's professional standards. A psychologist who is a member of the American Psychoanalytic Association (APsaA) would be in direct conflict with the psychology profession's standard of practice if he or she agreed with a recent recommendation of the APsaA that psychoanalysts not keep clinical notes (APsaA, 1994).

In North America and in Europe, legislative and regulatory bodies are establishing criteria for the qualification, practice, and account-ability of psychoanalysis. Many psychoanalysts have argued that psy-choanalysis was more a frame of mind and could never become a profession, but did they envision a time when the state would set the terms of reference for psychoanalytic qualification and practice? In-deed, in the United States, two state legislatures—Vermont and New Jersey—have already legislated the qualifications and standards nec-essary for the practice of psychoanalysis, stimulated to do so not by the APsaA or the International Psychoanalytical Association (IPA) in-stitutes but by rival organizations that sought to take possession of the future of psychoanalysis in the United States.

It may very well be that other states in the United States will codify psychoanalysis, just as it is highly likely that the European Union will eventually do the same. At the heart of the issue, it seems to me, is the question of who will determine the nature of psycho-analysis as a profession. However much one sympathizes with the argument that psychoanalysis is a state of mind and should not be standardized, this point of view will only collude with state interven-tion in the formation of the profession. The more serious obstacle to the formation of a profession of psychoanalysis (which among other things, would set its own standards for confidentiality), however, is the view that psychoanalysis is not a separate profession but simply a branch of the other, primary, disciplines of origin.

This view is promoted by psychologists and psychiatrists who between them constitute by far the largest number of practitioners of psychoanalysis within the IPA. And although psychoanalysis continues to benefit from its historic links to psychiatry and psychology, it is time to act on the recognition of these last 40 years that the original disciplines are too ambivalent toward psychoanalysis for it to survive as their derivative. And although the interest by psychoanalysts in neuroscience and cognitive studies will no doubt benefit psychoanalytical creativity, it may also unwittingly serve lost libido that would romance the parent disciplines with their true love objects. How many departments of neuroscience or cognitive psychology have honored psychoanalytical interest in these areas by appointing psychoanalysts to their departments?

Psychoanalysis should broaden its intellectual, cultural, economic, and political base by opening its doors to members from other disciplines who wish to become psychoanalysts. One obstacle to this growth, however, is the dependent relation of psychoanalysis on psychiatry and psychology.

We certainly cannot invite others to join in psychoanalytical training if an entire country banishes anyone other than a psychiatrist or a psychologist from training to be a psychoanalyst, as is true in many IPA member countries. The failure of psychoanalysis to thrive in too many countries in the world, its marginalization in certain cultures, and its mockery by large areas of the media may have less to do with forces hostile to psychoanalysis than to the failure of the psychoanalytical movement to forge links with other disciplines in society.

Until psychoanalysis becomes an independent profession, it cannot adequately lobby national legislatures because it will be lumped into the practice standards of the original disciplines. Furthermore, psychoanalysts who are also psychiatrists or psychologists may find themselves in a conflict of interest when called upon to represent psychoanalysis, as the interests of psychiatry or psychology are not equivalent to those of psychoanalysis.

When Anne Hayman, the English psychoanalyst and member of the British Psycho-Analytical Society, was subpoenaed in the middle 1960s she refused to testify about a patient. Looking back, Hayman (1965) is sure that the reason the judge did not find her in contempt of court was because he knew she was prepared to go to jail, and he did not want to do that.

Anne Hayman knew that she could not testify. For her it was not a matter of choice, but a visceral conviction: she could not do otherwise.

Counsel assisting someone like Anne Hayman would have to construct a legal defense around the psychoanalyst's professional code of conduct. Such a defense would not ordinarily be a problem, except that as psychoanalysis is not yet a profession, psychoanalysts—individually or in groups—ask the legal profession for guidance, not simply on what to do, *but what to believe!* Think about the transferential implications of this act.

It looks as if psychoanalysts are simply trying to educate themselves in legal procedure. But by asking another profession to define their fate in the courts, psychoanalysts continue to refer themselves for definition to yet another discipline. The continued dependence on an originary other to define their identity is transferred now to the legal profession, which is asked to tell psychoanalysts what they can or cannot believe in and practice.

Because of the extraordinary influence of psychoanalysis on Western culture, the man on the street has wrongly assumed that psychoanalysts were formed into a profession that would vigorously advocate its position in the social order. But when mandatory reporting laws were passed in different countries, with not only no opposition from psychoanalytical societies but also often active collaboration in the formation of these laws, it was striking to members of the legal and medical profession that psychoanalysis did not argue *its* case against these laws. It had been wrongly assumed that psychoanalysis was as well organized as the law or medicine. One of the outcomes of this lack of professionalism was a slowly developing contempt within at least the legal profession for the failure of psychoanalysts to argue their case.

What *was* one to make of a collection of people of such outstanding qualifications who yet remained innocents in the social order? Dependent upon original objects that held psychoanalysis in contempt, it sought its future from yet another profession—the law— that had developed its own bemused view of psychoanalysis. Perhaps psychoanalysts are projectively identifying doubts about themselves as professionals into other professions, doubts further exacerbated by leaving it up to others to determine the position of psychoanalysis in society.

It is often argued that as psychoanalytical organizations are much smaller than realized, one cannot expect of them a high level of organization—equivalent, say, to legal or medical associations. For example, the public might assume that the American Psychoanalytic Association is a large organization—comparable to the American Bar Association—but in fact its full-time staff is quite small. The same could be said of the IPA.

Indeed, these bodies would collapse were it not for the mostly unpaid voluntary work of scores of psychoanalysts who fill important administrative posts. Although this is admirable, it is also, in the best sense, but regrettably, amateurish. Psychoanalysis is not forming a profession through these organizations but instead, collections of

amateurs miming the functions of professional life. Indeed, the continual rotation of presidents of local societies, national organizations,
and the IPA (often accompanied by the concomitant rotation of chairs
of important committees as part of presidential patronage) comes
closer to the honorary activity of a club than a professional function.
The kind of work needed to form the profession of psychoanalysis,
especially in the arenas of national and international legislative and
regulatory bodies, requires organizational continuity, but is hampered
by the culture of a "gold-watch" rotation.

Is the size of these organizations a cause of the limitations of
IPA psychoanalysis up to this point? The size of the APsaA is indeed
disappointingly small in comparison to what we might think of as the
average expectable number of members, because for decades the
APsaA only trained psychiatrists. Because psychoanalysis in the United
States and in most other countries has tended toward a senselessly
self-serving elitism, individuals who wished to become psychoanalysts or simply those who were deeply influenced by analytical thinking
were compelled to become psychoanalytical psychotherapists or non-
IPA analysts. If, however, we *include* all those who practise within
the realms of psychoanalytical thinking in the community, then it is
very clear that the number of "psychoanalysts" is indeed very considerable relative to the paltry organizations that represent them.

If we look at the curricula of psychoanalytic psychotherapy training courses, we will not find seminars or workshops on psychotherapy. Where do they discuss, for example, the characteristics of
once-weekly psychotherapy, distinguished from twice or three times
a week? What we see are courses on psychoanalysis by candidates
usually in analysis with a qualified psychoanalyst. The majority of
these courses are, in effect, unrecognized psychoanalytical trainings.

Lacanian psychoanalysis has blossomed since the middle 1970s
in many countries around the world, not only because of the interest
found in Lacan's thinking but also because Lacanian institutions were
prepared to train non medical psychoanalysts. One result has been a
birth boom from Lacanian trainings, which have a vigor, intellectual
energy, and public presence rare among IPA institutions.

It is not accidental that Lacanian societies are competing around
the world with IPA and other psychoanalytical organizations for the
right to represent psychoanalysis in national and international forums. The struggle, in part, is about who shall constitute and operate
this profession.

I understand the arguments for high standards, but IPA

exclusionism is a disaster for the preservation of psychoanalysis. IPA psychoanalysis must awaken from its anaclitic relation to primary objects (i.e., psychology, psychiatry) to define, advocate, and develop psychoanalysis. To do so requires a minimum recognition of the consequences of dependence on original objects, which continue to disable psychoanalysts from taking the lead in determining their standards—nowhere more important than over the issue of confidentiality.

The IPA should also foster a new spirit of inclusion, one that follows the life instincts, rather than the history of its exclusionism under the sway of a death instinct. Psychoanalysis should invite other organizations to join the IPA (either as members or in a confederation) to define, promote, and struggle for psychoanalysis as an independent profession.

Psychoanalysts can, *if they wish*, find legal counsel who will construct a defense of strict confidentiality. If, like Anne Hayman, psychoanalysts are prepared to go to jail rather than to compromise their practice—as happens with journalists who refuse on similar grounds—they will eventually earn de jure privilege. Psychoanalysts have de facto privilege in many parts of the world, because one can see during the sentencing phase of contempt of court for noncompliance with a court order, in the overwhelming number of cases, the judiciary's recognition of the psychoanalyst's privilege. Legal proceedings may be applied against such civil disobedience, but judges and others recognize the integrity of the psychoanalyst who by virtue of conscience—and I hope profession—cannot violate any of his patients' confidence or the pledge of confidentiality. Without an uncompromising position on confidentiality, psychoanalysis cannot exist in any meaningful form.

The new IPA ethics code not only separates psychoanalysis from formal definition by some other from which it originated, but it also puts psychoanalysis in a position to define itself. The new code is simple and to the point: psychoanalysis is a confidential relation.

The psychoanalysis that saw itself as a branch of psychiatry, psychology, or social work has long since died. To thrive, psychoanalytic training must in principle be open to *anyone* who wishes to train: from linguists, mathematicians, and fine artists to filmmakers, anthropologists, historians, philosophers, and many others. Other disciplines bring vital additional perspectives to the project of comprehending the human mind and its expressions in the analytical space.

We may linger a bit over the curiosity of a group—of psychoanalysts—remaining attached to its original disciplines long after the remains of any primary affection is gone—indeed, attached not only to objects that are disinterested in psychoanalysis but also, in the case of departments of psychiatry and psychology, that have no meaningful comprehension of psychoanalysis.

What are we to make of the lack of both anxiety and the appropriate impetus to separate from such objects, which so characterizes the last four decades of the twentieth century? Perhaps psychoanalysis as a profession inhabits the realms of the negative hallucination, residing in the original discipline's negation of psychoanalysis. This death trap may be curiously comforting, as it were "life" with no future—indeed, life as death. The passion of psychoanalysis thus far, then, may be in the wish to be a dying profession or a profession that died before it ever really came to life.

From this point of view, psychoanalysts would have to find some form of analytical consensus about their plight. They would have to privilege a type of interpretation that analysts could be invited to consider, a comment that would of course find its resistances as all troubling comments do but one that, if correct, could prove mutative as it entered the here and now of psychoanalysis.

The interpretation that I believe awaits us is that psychoanalysis is not a profession because it has found itself enamored of the original discipline's forms of hate, that it resides in the *other's death trap*, and that it is allied with the death instinct as passion. To proceed with this enactment is to come to the orgasm-death of psychoanalysis as a practice, thus fulfilling the desire of the other that this progeny be cast off. The story of Oedipus it would be, but with the son accepting the death throw of the father, never to be rescued, never to return, and never to engage in the killing of the death-bearing father.

If the group of people who call themselves psychoanalysts, but who derive from psychology and psychiatry, could find insight into this enactment, then, as with the analysand, there is potential freedom from pathological structures. But the death-love at the heart of analysis is not so easy to influence. Analysts know that there is a compelling idea, a passionate idea, to which too many analysts adhere. It is something like: "Well, analysis may die out, but if so, then at least this is its truth. Those of us in this generation are the last analysts, anyway, who practice true analysis: those of the younger generations do not practice true analysis." With the death of a generation, psychoanalysis too is meant to die. What remains is simply something else, a kind of false analysis. Like a funerary amulet, psychoanalysis then has been repeatedly going to the grave of the generations of dying analysts.

This desire is the desire of the *other*, in this case the death wishes of psychiatry and psychology, which now barely conceal their hatred of psychoanalysis. Analysts bear the hatred in their own unconscious structures, to be revealed through a strange type of passivity, an indifference to their fate, all of which is an enactment aimed at fulfilling the *other's* death work.

To break free, the group who call themselves psychoanalysts need to mull over comments such as these—and the comments will crop up in differing form in differing parts of the world of analysis—and they must enter the public mind of analysts so that a working-through process can begin to transform the analytical *malaise*.

In addition, psychoanalysis must form itself into an independent free-standing profession, seek legal counsel that comprehends it and is prepared to form a strong legal argument for its ethics, represent it in courts of law, lobby in legislatures for its position, and advocate it before national and international regulatory bodies that are meeting now to consider its fate.

A challenge for the prospective leaders of the IPA is to realize not only that the continuation of the gold-watch culture—a society serving more to honor its leaders, colleagues, and friends—does not serve the formation of a profession but also is a kind of unconscious funerary ritual, the ceremonies simply enactments of the death throes of the group who call themselves psychoanalysts. Psychoanalysts would have to satisfy the wish for such celebration by relocating this ritual from its organizational structures to new forms of ceremony, perhaps linking its international ceremonial structures with aging and preparation for death. In turn, it would have to foster an organizational leadership with long-term stability and with coherent legal and technical support able to implement a sustained strategy for the entrance of psychoanalysis in the legal, legislative, and regulatory complexities of the modern world.

Psychoanalysis can develop important strategies for the preservation of confidentiality, but only after it has worked its way to "a sense of profession."[1]

---

[1] From "How the concept of profession evolved in the work of historians of medicine" by John C. Burnham (p. 10). Downloaded from the Internet: http://muse.jhu.edu/demo/bhm/70.1burnham.html.

References

American Psychoanalytic Association (1994), *Practice Bulletin #2: Charting Psychoanalysis.*

Bollas, C. & Sundelson, D. (1995), *The New Informants.* Northvale, NJ: Aronson.

Freud, S. (1926), The question of lay analysis. *Standard Edition,* 20:183–258. London: Hogarth Press, 1959.

Anon. (Hayman, Anne). (1965) Psychoanalyst Subpoenaed. *The Lancet,* October 16:785–786

Introduction to CHAPTER 16

❧

Psychoanalytic Ethics:
Has the Pendulum Swung Too Far?

Ray Freebury has played a key role in the development of an appropriate ethics for psychoanalysis and psychiatry in Canada. His essay provides an exceptional overview of the evolving legislative situation in the province of Ontario. Strongly influenced by the legal theories of Catherine McKinnon, Ontario is in many ways a microcosm of the value conflicts occurring all over the Western world around the issues of confidentiality, professional ethics, and the scope of professional responsibility. Freebury documents the advantages and disadvantages of professional self-regulation and oversubservience to the political pressures increasingly placed by the law and government bodies on the psychoanalytic profession. His reflections are a model analysis for similar situations developing in other jurisdictions and are a guide to future policy formation for the International Psychoanalytical Association.

CHAPTER 16

⚮

Psychoanalytic Ethics: Has the Pendulum Swung Too Far?

D. Ray Freebury

*T*his chapter attempts to demonstrate the need for a specifically psychoanalytic code of ethics and to explore some of the difficulties that face the profession in devising and implementing this. I argue that the challenge of a psychoanalytic code of ethics arises primarily from the unique role played by confidentiality not only as an ethical principle of psychoanalysis but also even more fundamentally as a practical precondition of psychoanalytic psychotherapy.

Because confidentiality is so basic to the conduct of psychoanalysis, it permeates every phase of psychoanalytic life in a way that finds few meaningful parallels in other fields of professional activity. Psychoanalytic training and teaching, supervision and peer review, research and scientific reporting, and politics and administration— and even its social life—are all deeply affected in their substance by the problem of confidentiality. Whereas other professional groups understand confidentiality as an ethical obligation toward clients that must be weighed with other ethical obligations, psychoanalysis presupposes confidentiality even before it begins to consider what is and is not ethical. This supposition does not mean that psychoanalysis considers confidentiality to be an absolute in some idealistic sense beyond the practical needs of society, but it does mean that the ethical framework of psychoanalysis will have unique characteristics determined by the special role that confidentiality plays in psychoanalytic practice and professional life. Since these are by no means obvious to the general public, it is important for the profession to develop very clear ideas about them and, wherever possible, to develop credible methods of ensuring that its own professional and ethical standards are being met by its practitioners. If we fail in this effort, the public and its representatives will insist that the conduct of psychoanalysis be regulated according to the principles and precepts most prevalent in other domains, which may be at odds with psychoanalytic practice.

In my opinion, the pendulum of the ethical codes of some of our sister professions has gone too far in righting previous professional abuses in our field and in the process puts the complex emotional interaction between analyst and therapist at risk of being misunderstood as well as distorted. The lack of a specifically psychoanalytic ethic as an indigenous guide to good practice has created difficulties for us in the past when we have engaged in complex relationships with governments, allied professions, insurance companies, and the law.

The Rationale for Ethical Codes

There is still a debate among psychoanalysts on the merits of ethics codes and ethics committees. Some suggest (Haas, 2000) that a moral supervisory agency, such as an ethics committee, inevitably results in damage to psychoanalytic societies. It is suggested that the requirement to report suspected misconduct or impairment in a colleague would create an environment of mistrust that is particularly destructive of control analyses and supervision. Such a requirement would be considered potentially destructive of any psychoanalytic relationship because it would involve a betrayal of confidentiality. There are undoubtedly problems with the reporting of an impaired or unethical colleague because it frequently involves information that is secondhand or thirdhand. Without an ethics committee, however, there are no procedures in place for handling reports by analysands of sexual misconduct, and the accused psychoanalyst will have no recourse within the psychoanalytic community. In this context, it is noteworthy that false complaints are not rare (Gutheil, 1992) and that in these circumstances the accused psychoanalyst would greatly benefit from having to face a jury of his own peers.

It must be acknowledged that some of the most respected members of our profession have been guilty of egregious and cynical violations of the traditional psychoanalytic respect of interpersonal boundaries. When a respected senior training analyst, who has influenced the thinking and practice of many members of a society, is revealed to have committed such indiscretions, disbelief and denial are the initial reactions (Gabbard, 2001), perhaps explaining why it took so many years for us psychoanalysts to acknowledge that such conduct could occur within our ranks. Underlying this disbelief is the assumption that the training analysis makes such misconduct unlikely among analysts.

It is naïve—one might alternatively say grandiose—to think that the process of psychoanalytic training, even with all its safeguards, excludes or inhibits those who would use their influence to gain personal advantage. As an association of professionals, we cannot absolve ourselves of responsibility for correcting such abuses. One can, however, argue that correcting abuse with laws, trials, and penalties is inferior to education and prevention (Margolis, 1997).

Modern psychoanalysis acknowledges that if we are to be effective as psychoanalysts, we often tread a demandingly narrow path as we endeavor to acknowledge the powerful emotions, such as sexual and nonsexual love, hatred, and rage, as they emerge in the analytic situation. The "impossible profession" is also a dangerous profession in the present climate. The majority of us are under ethical guidelines that prohibit for life psychoanalysts from entering into a sexual relationship with a patient. Although most of us find this prohibition acceptable, there are serious-minded colleagues who see it as an infringement of basic civil rights and a message to analysands that they will not ever be able to make healthy choices about future relationships. These colleagues see the latter assumption as an indictment of the effectiveness of psychoanalysis (Hamilton et al., 1992).

On the subject of confidentiality, the Canadian Psychoanalytic Socity (CPS) ethical code contained, until 2001, an escape clause that committed us to maintain confidentiality except where the law dictated otherwise. Bollas (Bollas and Sundelson, 1995) and others consider that psychoanalytic codes of ethics should not be unquestioningly subservient to legal requirements. If they were, we would permit other disciplines to dictate conditions for the frame of psychoanalysis and we would fail to support colleagues with the courage to oppose legal demands that confidentiality be betrayed. In fact, strictly speaking, until the code was revised in 2001, we would have been in breach of our own ethics code if we had resisted legal pressures to provide our records. Bollas (2000) takes a firm position, believing that anything short of absolute confidentiality with respect to third parties makes psychoanalysis impossible.

In contrast to Haas (2000), I conclude that in today's social climate an ethical code and a means of implementing it are necessary evils. The public, and indeed government, views us as having a fiduciary responsibility to our patients. The public tends to view this responsibility along strictly medical lines. We might see our primary responsibility as belonging to the analysis, which cannot guarantee symptom relief or happy-ever-after endings. However, if we relinquish the responsibility attributed to us by the public, how are we to defend those aspects of the frame that are vital to the practice of psychoanalysis? Shall we say to the judge that we psychoanalysts do not consider that we have a fiduciary responsibility? If we disclaim this responsibility, how do we then respond to his request that we hand over all of our records?

We do need a code of ethics with a foundation independent of prevailing laws. Local circumstances, which in Canada may vary from province to province, and changes in social climate and sensibility can have destabilizing and counterproductive effects on the establishment of an ethical framework for psychoanalysis. My role in the development of a code of ethics and procedures for implementation for both the Toronto Psychoanalytic Society (TPS) and the CPS, has provided me with experience of the dilemmas that arise for a national organization when both provincial regulations and cultural attitudes vary considerably. As history has illustrated, laws are not always just: we may need to disobey the law if we feel that it contaminates the integrity of the treatment we offer. Furthermore, we must assert the responsibility of psychoanalysis to distinguish an individual's legal rights as a citizen from the moral right to an ethically bounded treatment.

When I began to work in this area, I must admit it was with a somewhat self-righteous and zealous enthusiasm. Experience has tempered my zeal without inducing the need to jettison the whole works. Since Freud (1930) drew our attention to it in "Civilization and Its Discontents," we have been well aware of the tendency to defend our own virtue by attributing our less benevolent impulses and desires to others. This tendency can result in excessive zeal and deference to the laws of the land. Haas (2000) suggests, quoting Freud, that "so-called natural ethics has nothing to offer except the narcissistic satisfaction of regarding oneself as better than others." One can only agree that it is not only others who are abusing patients and that there are forms of abuse other than sexual. (If we exclude ourselves as potential abusers, we would not need ethical codes.) Surely, however, as psychoanalysts, we do have a strong sense of what is objectionable in the conduct of a person who enjoys the title "psychoanalyst." That is not to say that gray areas do not exist. In the arena of technical neutrality, for example, there is considerable disagreement about what constitutes a breach of neutrality (Adler and Bachant, 1996; Renik, 1995). The same can be said of abstinence. A responsible ethical code and reasonable, clear, and fair procedures should protect us from the potential for abuse from within.

The francophone analytic community in Canada has been an ongoing source of constructive debate about our ethical code. French Canadian analysts have been opposed to an unduly legalistic code, and they also consistently resist defining psychoanalysis as a medical discipline. They are as protective of the art of psychoanalysis as the anglophones are of its therapeutic aims. My impression is that they are inclined to be more forgiving of human frailty without being any less ethical.

The Consequences of Regulation by Others

Psychoanalytic training in Canada has always been open to non-medical disciplines. As a result, we have become familiar with the reality that, as individuals, we are subject to regulation by our primary disciplines. This continues to be the case for the majority of Canadian psychoanalysts. In the past, we tended to rely on the regulatory functions of those disciplines to draw our attention to unethical conduct by our members. Differences among members have also been created by the advent of universal health care in Canada, which resulted in physician psychoanalysts also becoming answerable to the government as a third-party payer. All these circumstances have serious implications for the maintenance of confidentiality in the treatment relationship.

The Impact of Professional Regulatory Bodies

The research on the frequency of patient-therapist sex was published in the early 1980s (Bohoutsos et al., 1983; Gartrell et al., 1986; Herman et al., 1987). This research followed heightened public awareness of the high incidence of incest along with its devastating effects (Spencer, 1978; Rosenfeld, 1979; Herman, 1981). Despite the early warnings from Freud in his papers on technique (Freud, 1915), psychoanalysts have contributed to the denial of professional responsibility by alluding to "wish-fulfilling fantasies"on the part of their patients as a way of sidetracking suspicions about their transgressions. The sexual violation of a patient is indefensible, and the trauma for the patient can be devastating, but societal pressures for rapid punitive response may serve vengeance more than it serves justice for both parties.

Many factors have contributed to the development of demands for draconian regulations and extreme and unforgiving punishment for the various transgressions that may occur in professional relationships, especially in psychotherapeutic and psychoanalytic relationships. Included among these factors are society's reaction to the extreme permissiveness of the sixties, the need to externalize guilt and to find culprits to punish for one's own forbidden desires, and the high-profile and egregious offenses of some psychoanalysts. Along with our historical attempts at denial, these highly publicized events make psychoanalysts convenient containers for society's propensity to project its unwanted impulses. These factors have contributed to the focused attention we have received from lawmakers. I will elaborate on the consequences we face.

In response to the growing evidence that psychoanalysis was not immune to professional misconduct, the TPS began to develop an ethical code in 1985. When the finished product was approved at the 1989 annual meeting, it was the first psychoanalytic code of ethics in Canada. During this period, the government of Ontario was categorizing the health professions with a view to replacing the existing Health Disciplines Act with the Regulated Health Professions Act (RHPA). In 1991, the College of Physicians and Surgeons of Ontario (CPSO) published the report of an independent ad hoc task force on sexual abuse of patients. Headed by a feminist lawyer, this task force (McPhedran et al., 1991) adopted a "zero-tolerance" position, proposing a series of prohibitive commandments. The task force undertook no consultation with organized psychoanalysis. After the passage of the bill establishing the RHPA, the government presented Bill 100, which was an amendment based on the recommendations of the McPhedran task force.

Under the act, sexual abuse of a patient by a member of a regulated health profession was categorized on three levels, namely, sexual violation, sexual transgression, and sexual impropriety. These categories were defined respectively as sexual intercourse or other forms of physical sexual relations, touching of a sexual nature, and behavior or remarks of a sexual nature. These very different levels of sexual offenses were all to become subject to mandatory reporting. The government also directed the colleges of the regulated professions to establish programs to fund therapy and counseling for persons who, while patients, were sexually abused by members. There is no statute of limitations and, in the case of psychoanalysts and psychotherapists, the prohibitions are for life. Psychotherapists and psychoanalysts, despite many briefs to the relevant committees arguing for exceptions, are now also obliged to report on these three levels of transgression if they are described during treatment. The reporting must take place over the patient's objections with the additional proviso that failure to report could lead to suspension of the therapist's licence to practice.

Several years ago, when the McPhedran task force on sexual abuse was adding "suggestive language" to its hierarchy of sexual abuses, I was supervising a candidate on a very difficult male patient. The candidate was a sincere, warm, and empathic therapist. An aggressive, schizophrenic brother, who had abused the patient as a child, frequently screamed at him, "Suck my cock." In response to a very alarming and threatening tirade from the patient, the candidate defused the rage with the simple interpretation "I think that you are saying to me 'suck my cock.'" If this patient had chosen to report this interpretation to his family physician, the latter would, in principle, have been obliged to report the incident to the college. It would have meant, at the very least, a visit from a college investigator.

Unfortunately, members of regulatory bodies are not well versed in psychodynamic principles, are biased against psychoanalysis, or have no knowledge about it. They usually know nothing about the projection of unwanted personal evils and have a "guilty until proven otherwise" position with respect to an individual who is the subject of a complaint. Despite government efforts to relegate psychoanalysis to the status of a cosmetic procedure, the same bureaucrats leaped on the McPhedran bandwagon in attributing an increased potential for harm in psychoanalytic relationships, thereby, in effect, acknowledging the great psychological influence of the process.

Of course, there are other mandatory reporting laws that have applied to health professionals over the years, such as the duty to report sexual or physical abuse of children and the duty to report on patients who have disorders (e.g., epilepsy or alcoholism) rendering them unsafe to operate machinery and motor vehicles. An expert medical panel in Ontario determined that the need to protect the public from serious risk of harm is a paramount concern that should supersede the duty of confidentiality (Ferris et al., 1998). Regardless of the rationale, it must be pointed out that every condition that undermines complete confidentiality also undermines the fundamental rule of free association.

The main difficulty with all mandatory reporting laws is that they have been implemented with little thought for the consequences for therapeutic relationships. The one concession that was made regarding the reporting of sexual misconduct in Ontario was probably the result of parliamentary presentations by the TPS and others prior to the passage of Bill 100. The reporting patient can decline to place a charge, and he or she need not be named. In this case, a file is created on the alleged abuser in the event that other complaints come forward, at which time the therapist would be directed to request the patient making the allegations to formally complain. Even with this modification, the very fact that the psychoanalyst is obligated to act against the patient's wishes creates a major obstruction to free association and to the psychoanalytic process.

Extreme forms of intolerance have permeated society's attitudes to the slightest impropriety. Witness the community's potential for hysterical response in the suspension of a six-year-old boy from school for kissing a girl classmate on the cheek. More recently, in Ontario, two nurses have been charged with criminal negligence causing death, when a ten-year-old died unexpectedly. These charges were laid by police before the professional association of nursing had been given the opportunity to evaluate either the circumstances or the professional competence of the accused nurses.

In the face of the exaggerated intolerance of the McPhedran report, and feeling inexperienced in the regulatory field, the CPS decided to hire the services of a lawyer to help in developing the national code of ethics. As a consequence, the ethical code developed, and the procedures for dealing with violations of the code were, in retrospect, too obedient to the law. There is no doubt that individuals who are developing ethical codes are greatly influenced by current societal attitudes, especially when these are adopted by governments and the courts. I believe that this is a reason for us to maintain an analytic stance when we are developing codes and procedures. It is not, however, a reason for us to abdicate responsibility for deciding what constitutes unethical practice in psychoanalysis.

The Impact of Universal Health Care

As governments have increasingly taken on the task of developing privacy laws, their explicit goal is touted as being the preservation and security of health-care records. Implicitly, however, these new statutes serve the purpose of increased government scrutiny of health care. Very recent experience in Ontario, where the government proposed to introduce Bill 159, a Personal Health Information Privacy Act, is a reminder that we can no longer be apolitical. This provincial act, presented under the guise of protecting confidentiality, would have provided government officials and police with unprecedented access to personal health information. Thanks to lobbying by the Section on Psychiatry of the Ontario Medical Association and a strong response from the Medical Association itself, the act was withdrawn for further study. The Section on Psychiatry has had strong representation from the TPS for almost 20 years, sensitizing that group to the importance of confidentiality in all therapeutic relationships.

The intrusion of third-party payers into the analytic frame creates an additional threat to confidentiality. When the founding fathers of the Toronto Institute of Psychoanalysis (TIP) persuaded the Ontario government to include psychoanalysis as an insured service, they indentured physician analysts to the provincial government. On one hand, they guaranteed the growth of our society, as many candidates, both physicians and nonphysicians, enjoyed an insured training analysis to offset the costs of didactic training. On the other hand, the creation of two categories of psychoanalysts, the medical analysts whose services are insured and the nonmedical analysts whose identical services are not, had unforeseen consequences with respect to confidentiality.

The preservation of confidentiality is much more difficult for physician psychoanalysts. Under the agreement with the Ontario Health Insurance Plan (OHIP), they have a primary responsibility for the relief of symptoms and may be called on by OHIP or the College of Physicians and Surgeons of Ontario (CPSO) to demonstrate symptomatic improvement on file! They are also subject to random peer review of their standard of practice, a process now conducted, after much protest by the TPS, by psychoanalysts who, in support of the protest, volunteered as scrutineers. OHIP has the legal right to perform medical audits, reviewing files to ensure that services claimed have actually been provided. To a lesser degree, psychoanalysts who are members of other health professions are also under occasional scrutiny from their colleges. In general, however, it appears that nonphysician psychoanalysts enjoy a more undivided primary responsibility to the analysand and the analysis. They are not burdened in establishing a clear framework for the analysis and can set a fee commensurate with their experience unencumbered by written contracts. Finally, there are those analysts who are not members of a regulated health profession and who do not therefore place their careers at risk when they choose not to comply with mandatory reporting requirements in order to protect confidentiality.

Disciplinary Hearings: The Advantages of Holding Our Own

In today's social climate, the analyst may run afoul of regulatory bodies as a result of actions we would consider among ourselves to be good analytic practice. Given that the Ontario government has adopted the proposal of the McPhedran task force stipulating that there be no statutory limit to complaints of sexual misconduct, conduct which may have been acceptable 20 or 30 years ago could today result in charges of ethical misconduct. Moreover, the definition of sexual misconduct now includes suggestive language, which is not clearly defined. In the case of Ontario, financial arrangements between physician psychoanalyst and analysand are also intruded on by government through the health-insurance plan; this highlights the need for a psychoanalytic prescription for what constitutes ethical practice.

Undoubtedly, psychoanalysis needs protection in these arenas, and I use the word "arena" advisedly. If a complaint against a physician reaches the stage of a disciplinary hearing, several years may have passed since the date the complaint was first received. The discipline hearing is a formal legal procedure and the complainant will have had much support from college investigators and skilful lawyers who may endeavor to portray any evidence of transference-countertransference interaction as misconduct. Every deviation from the traditional frame of psychoanalysis may be regarded as evidence of the "slippery slope." I have observed lawyers for the complainant suggest that even the acceptance of a small gift constitutes unethical practice. In this, they will often get a sympathetic hearing from members on the disciplinary panel that includes appointed members of the public but never a psychoanalyst. The analyst's lawyers will often need a great deal of instruction about the practice of psychoanalysis in order to defend the member.

One such hearing concerned a complainant who had been enrolled in a support group. It was after her experience in this group

that the list of sexual acts supposedly committed by her former analyst grew exponentially. Years after the fact, these could neither be
substantiated nor disproved. However, the psychoanalyst was a credible and consistent witness, and his clinical practice was clearly in
accordance with our ethical code. Fortunately, he was exonerated,
but not until after several years of anxiety. It is perhaps also tragically
relevant that when asked about successful long-term relationships,
the patient could only list her relationship with the analyst!

My experience in providing expert testimony before the courts
and before medical licensing bodies further fuels my concern about
how prevailing social attitudes can influence the disciplinary process. In fact, the courts provide more safeguards for defendant's rights
than some medical regulatory bodies do. The cases with which the
author has had personal experience have ranged from predatory sexual
abuse by a therapist and naive, inappropriate practice by a psychiatric
resident, to a patently false allegation by a patient against a psychoanalyst. The case of predatory sexual abuse led to a civil suit. The
therapist's conduct was indefensible, and the patient, an anxious
dependent woman whose marriage had almost been wrecked as a
result of her victimization, was severely traumatized. There was no
injustice in bringing this case to a civil hearing.

My appearance as expert witness for the defense has been in
regulatory hearings of the discipline committee of the CPSO. In the
two other cases I referred to, I was appalled at the conduct of the so-
called independent college investigators. In the case of the psychoanalyst, the investigator revealed on the witness stand that she had
clearly made up her mind that the member was guilty when she first
visited his office. The purpose of this visit was to inform him of the
complaint and to collect his files. The psychiatric resident was less
fortunate. Here, a supposedly unbiased investigator, in the guise of
making it easy for the victim, is observed on videotape, coaching and
exhorting the complainant to pursue her claim whenever she showed
any sign of acknowledging indebtedness to the doctor. The inter-
view culminated in the complainant revealing the vengeful aspect of
her complaint. She said, "Yeah and even if I don't win, I bet it will
fuck the hell out of him." To this, the investigator replied, "Yes, and
we will know he is someone for us to be on the lookout for."

In our own national association, we have had occasion to expel
several members. One of them was a member who had indulged in
a sexual relationship with a patient who, he claimed, pursued him
sexually. He paid the price for his indiscretion with his career both as

a physician and a psychoanalyst. Nevertheless, the punishment was evidently not enough because attempts were made to have the former member thrown out of the university where he had begun studies towards developing a new career. Wherefore the quality of mercy? There is no doubt that these examples are testimony to individual and group motivations for needing culprits and for needing to extract severe punishment from them.

In 1986, the Ontario government passed Bill 94, making it illegal for a physician to charge patients a fee that exceeded the amount paid by OHIP for the service provided. This meant that physician analysts could no longer set a mutually agreeable fee with the analysand if it exceeded what the government determined the service was worth. However, the physician analyst could and can chose to have OHIP reimburse the patient directly for his services, in which case the patient has the responsibility for the direct payment to the analyst.

There is also a third financial arrangement that has been chosen by a number of physician analysts. In addition to the tariff allotted by OHIP, these analysts have elected to charge a fee for services that are not covered by OHIP in the event that they are required (examples are providing medical reports for insurance purposes, provision of prescriptions for drugs, and consultation with other psychoanalysts). In my view, the contortions necessary to make this procedure conform to the law create a greater distortion of the frame than that created by the patient recovering the full fee from the government. Some psychoanalysts feel so strongly about this practice of billing for uninsured services that they deem it unethical. To my knowledge, however, the majority of psychoanalysts in Ontario who are billing patients for uninsured services are doing so in good faith, in the belief that they are maintaining the integrity of the frame by establishing their own fee with the patient. Yet requiring patients to sign a contract agreeing to pay for services they may never require, and to agree despite having the right to decline, risks putting them in the position of pleasing or submitting to the analyst. Anxious to begin analysis on good terms and perhaps trying to preserve an idealized transference, they may have to deny to themselves the thought that they are conspiring with their analyst in creatively circumventing the fee structure provided by the health plan. My difference with these colleagues is on both technical and theoretical grounds. While I do not consider the practice unethical, I do think of it as a standard-of-practice issue because it creates a potentially unanalyzable collusion. Thus, it is incumbent on those who bill for uninsured services in this way to shoulder the responsibility of protecting the purity of the psychoanalytic frame from potentially conflicting monetary self-interests.

Let me nuance my thoughts further. Making the practice of billing for uninsured services an ethical misconduct would represent a repetition of the act that created the problem in the first place. It would be typical of the overzealous, intolerant reactions of society in its need to attribute blame. Further, who will decide what technical devices constitute unethical practice? Shall we decide that individuals like McLaughlin (1995) who do not preclude nonsexual touching on appropriate occasions or Renik (1996), who are not averse to the use of self-revelation, are breaching acceptable standards of neutrality or abstinence? For good reasons, have we shied away from establishing formal standards of psychoanalytic practice except where the conduct clearly breaches the moral standards expected by society or clearly does harm. If we have formal standards along with disciplinary procedures to ensure that the standards are maintained, we could risk stifling creativity, and with it the innovations that permit today's psychoanalyst a realistically human interaction, in contrast to the austere approach of earlier generations.

Experience has taught those of us who have served on the CPS ethics committee that poor communication frequently leads to unnecessary difficulties. It may be that an independent arbitrator could settle misunderstandings and disputes in a shorter time and with a great reduction in angst for both parties than would be the case in a formal discipline process. This alternative would require the consent of both complainant and accused member. The ombudsman role that Margolis (1997) has espoused, which we formerly opposed out of concerns about confidentiality, has now been adopted by the CPS, albeit on an ad hoc basis. We have yet to have the opportunity to use it, however.

In our own disciplinary hearing panels, we are not obliged to hear legal arguments, although we may permit both complainant and defendant to be advised by counsel. In this setting, more clinical than legal, a panel of psychoanalysts can better determine the merits of the psychoanalyst's actions and the veracity of the patient's complaint. This setting is also more likely to avoid further abuse, which can occur during the aggressive cross-examination of a disciplinary hearing, of those who have been victimized and ensures that the defendant is fairly treated by individuals who understand the nature of our practice.

Conclusion

In the history of science, courageous men and women have shown a level of ethics that demanded uncommon courage. Darwin, Galileo, and Freud are examples of individuals who have shown great resolve in persevering with the pursuit of knowledge and the enlightenment of society in the face of scorn and humiliation from their contemporaries. One must also agree that the likes of Gandhi and Mandela have shown equally high ethics in opposing both inequities and iniquities in the law. Most psychoanalysts, while trying to do good work and earn a living, however, are subject to the usual human frailties. We hope in most cases where we or our colleagues fail that it is not the result of self-serving action that disregards the consequences for our patients.

Psychoanalysts are not the infallible guardians of "higher ethics" and we can only strive toward something approaching it. I believe that we do this best by having an ethical code, fallible though it too may be. Haas is certainly correct when he argues that the crisis within and without psychoanalysis will not be solved by some "primal parricide" (Haas, 2000). It will also not be solved, however, by denying that fathers are capable of acts deserving of excommunication. We witnessed the serious consequences of denial in the TPS after the ethical misconduct of one of the founders, a psychoanalyst of international repute who was exonerated in the early 1970s only to be expelled 20 years later after several subsequent offenses. He was a man who had been personal analyst or supervisor to a generation of psychoanalysts. After his extreme misconduct was exposed, they faced guilt, grief, rage, resentment, shame, self-doubts, and uncertainties about their identities as psychoanalysts.

If we have no ethical code or ethics committees, we leave the disciplinary colleges as the only option open to patients who feel that they have been victimized by their psychoanalyst. We must have our own code and procedures. They will be imperfect, but they will be refined over time as we gain the experience of using them. As I have indicated, a psychoanalyst appearing before a medical regulatory body faces the disadvantage of not being judged by his peers. These discipline panels are conducted in a formal legal manner complete with discovery, examination, cross-examination, and the like. Descriptions of countertransference may end up being viewed as misconduct by ill-informed panel members. Scatological language, sometimes the currency of psychoanalysis and interpretation, will be viewed with suspicion. The acceptance of small gifts or the exchange of small symbolic gifts, which occasionally might sustain an alliance during an absence, will require strenuous expert defense if they are also not to be considered examples of misconduct. Psychoanalysts must be prepared to assist in the defense of colleagues in such situations particularly because false allegations are not rare in our present social climate (Gutheil, 1992).

The experience of developing and modifying ethical codes and procedures is a humbling experience. It has the potential to modify zeal as well as a tendency to reflexive subservience to legal demands. One must learn from one's colleagues and become aware of the risk of attributing one's own forbidden desires to them. In developing these codes, there is always a risk of them becoming as oppressive as the various laws and statutes that intrude into the analytic relationship in harmful ways. In setting down our codes and procedures, we must be mindful of the fact that regulations are only as good as those administering them.

References

Adler, E. & Bachant, J. (1996), Free association and analytic neutrality: The basic structure of the analytic situation. *J. Amer. Psychoanal. Assn.*, 44:1021–1046.

Bohoutsos, J., Holroyd, J., Lerman, H., Forer, B. & Greenberg, M. (1983), Sexual intimacy between psychotherapists and patients. *Professional Psychol.: Research & Practice*, 14:185–196.

Bollas, C., (2000), The disclosure industry. Presented at the conference "Confidentiality and Society." October, Montreal.

———— & Sundelson, D. (1995), *The New Informants*. London: Aronson.

Ferris, L. E., Barkun, H., Carlisle, Hoffman, B., Katz, C. & Silverman, M. (1998), Defining the physician's duty to warn: Consensus statement of Ontario's Medical Expert Panel on Duty to Warn. *Canad. Med. Assn. J.*,158:1473–1479.

Freud, S. (1915), Further recommendations in the technique of psychoanalysis: Observations on transference love. *Standard Edition*, 12:159–171. London: Hogarth Press, 1958.

———— (1930), Civilization and its discontents. *Standard Edition*, 21:64–145. London: Hogarth Press, 1961.

Gabbard, G. O. (2001), Boundary violations by training Analysts. *J. Amer. Psychoanal. Assn.*, 49:659–673.

Gartrell, N., Herman, J., Olarte, S., Feldstein, M. & Localio, R. (1986), Psychiatrist-patient sexual contact: Results of a national survey. *Amer. J. Psychiat.*, 143:112–131.

Gutheil, T. (1992), Approaches to forensic assessment of false claims of sexual misconduct by therapists. *Bull. Amer. Acad. Psychiat. Law*, 20:289–296.

Haas, E. (2000), Does the IPA need an ethics code or an ethics committee? Ten arguments against. *Internat. Psychoanal.,* 9:25–27.

Hamilton, J., Freebury, D. R., Johnston A., Reisman A. L. & Finlayson, R. (1992), OMA section on psychiatry position statement. *Ontario Med. Rev.,* 59:17–24.

Herman, J. (1981), *Father-Daughter Incest.* Cambridge, MA: Harvard University Press.

———— Gartrell, N., Olarte, S., Feldstein, M. & Localio, R. (1987), Psychiatrist-patient sexual contact: Results of a national survey. II: Psychiatrists' attitudes. *Amer. J. Psychiat.,* 144:164–169.

Margolis, M. (1997), Analyst-patient sexual involvement: Clinical experience and institutional responses. *Psychoanal. Inq.,* 17:349–370.

McLaughlin, F. (1995), Touching limits in the analytic dyad. *Psychoanal. Quart.,* 64:433–465.

McPhedran, M,. Armstrong, H,. Edney, R., Marshall, P., Roach, R., Long, B. & Homeniuk, B. (1991), *The Final Report.* Toronto: College of Physicians of Ontario.

Renik, O. (1995), The ideal of the anonymous analyst and the problem of self disclosure. *Psychoanal. Quart.,* 64:466–495.

———— (1996), The perils of neutrality. *Psychoanal. Quart.,* 67:566–593.

Rosenfeld, A. (1979), Incidence of a history of incest among 18 female psychiatric patients. *Amer. J. Psychiat.,* 136:791–795.

Spencer, J. (1978), Father-daughter incest. *Child Welfare,* 57:581–590.

Introduction to CHAPTER 17

We Have Met the Enemy and He (Is) Was Us

This chapter by Paul Mosher draws on extensive research and experience related to the interaction between psychoanalytic and legal concepts of confidentiality. Mosher provides an informative and detailed historical account of the post-World War II background and contemporary aftermath of the crucial 1996 *Jaffee v. Redmond* decision of the United States Supreme Court on confidentiality. Two of the key elements in Mosher's historical analysis concern the initial failure of psychoanalysis to differentiate psychoanalytic from other forms of confidentiality and its failure to react in a principled as opposed to defensive manner to the growing threat under "managed care" to confidentiality and patient privacy. The historical turning point in *Jaffee v. Redmond* was strongly influenced by the amicus curiae brief of the American Psychoanalytic Association, whose production was steered by Mosher. The 1996 decision established a strong precedent for a psychotherapy privilege, potentially beyond "judicial balancing," which is unique in the common-law tradition.

Chapter 17

❧

We Have Met the Enemy
and He (Is) Was Us

Paul W. Mosher

*T*he erosion of confidentiality protection for psychoanalysis in the United States is common knowledge. Analysts themselves to some degree have been responsible for this deterioration (Bollas and Sundelson, 1995). The purpose of this chapter is to discuss, within the context of recent history, some negative and positive occurrences contributing to the current state of confidentiality protection in the United States. Among the negative factors have been analysts' somewhat anachronistic reliance on the ethical guidance of other professional groups, a failure to distinguish between privacy needs of psychoanalytic and medical data, and timidity in taking an assertive stand within the legal system and third-party reimbursement systems. On the positive side are the emergence of revisions of ethics codes, a federal privilege for psychotherapeutic data, and a new federal privacy law that extends special stringent protection to psychotherapy information.

Psychoanalysis and the derivative psychotherapies gained preeminence in the middle 50 years of the 20th century, largely embedded within the health-care professions. Until recently, U.S. psychoanalysis appeared to be a subspecialty of psychiatry and thus more a branch of medicine than a separate profession. Most psychoanalysts were first trained as physicians and psychiatrists and hence were socialized in the American medical profession. Understandably, the development of the ethics, legal framework, and organization of the health-care system in the United States has had an enormous influence on the development of psychoanalysis (Hale, 1995).

Psychoanalysts, as members of their "core" professional organizations, such as the American Medical Association (AMA) and the American Psychiatric Association (APA), relied on the concomitant ethical precepts of these groups to provide a concept of confidentiality. The one-to-one nature of the practice of psychoanalysis generally mirrored the organization of the entire health-care system, because medicine was mostly practiced by individual general practitioners who had long and trusting relationships with patients. As late as the 1960s, a congenial definition of confidentiality meant the ethical understanding that the physician would not disclose information obtained from the patient to any other person.

Subsequent transformations in the health-care system have altered the common usage and meaning of the term "confidentiality." These transformations include the specialization of medical care with shared information among multiple physicians per patient, the increased use of third-party payment, a decrease in the paternalistic role and authority of physicians, an increasingly mobile population, the evolution of health-care systems using treatment teams, the development of managed care systems in which confidential information is shared with nonprofessional case managers, and networked computerized record-keeping systems (Siegler, 1982).

The health-care professions adapted their confidentiality practices to these changes, but "confidentiality" could be maintained only by altering the meaning of the term to encompass the sharing of information among a widening circle of individuals involved with the patient's care. In general, there is little evidence that this changing concept of confidentiality has resulted in an erosion in the overall quality of health-care. However, psychoanalytic treatment continues strictly to be based on a trusting one-to-one relationship and, consequently, it is no longer sensible for analysts to rely solely on ethical codes of other health care professions to articulate standards of confidentiality for psychoanalysis. Psychoanalysts have been slow to respond to the changes by defining their own ethical principles and guidelines.

External pressures have brought increased demands for access to confidential psychotherapeutic information. Information disclosed to psychotherapists forms a rich repository of highly sensitive personal data that, if available, could be used for many purposes unrelated to psychotherapy. For example, psychotherapists have been legally obliged to report past, present, and possible future child abuse to state authorities, to testify in divorce proceedings and child-custody hearings, to participate in disability determinations, to assume legal liability if they fail to take measures to protect intended victims of potentially violent patients, and to disclose sensitive information to representatives of third-party payers. As earlier requirements that physicians and others report certain information such as communicable diseases and gunshot wounds to the state have gradually been expanded, psychotherapists have been carried along in a creeping process of expanded disclosures. Bollas and Sundelson (1995) have pointed out that the psychotherapy professions have been participants to an alarming degree in this redefinition of their roles.

Additionally, beginning in 1974 with the first Tarasoff decision in a California state court, some state courts have held that psychotherapists have a "duty" to protect intended victims of imminently dangerous patients, a "duty" that overrides the obligation to maintain the confidentiality of the treatment relationship. Such rulings are widely misunderstood to "require" psychotherapists to intervene in such instances. In fact, Tarasoff rulings establish the principle that in certain situations the psychotherapist can be held liable (i.e., sued) by a third-party victim to whom he owed, but did not fulfill, a "duty to protect" (Slovenko, 1998; Buckner and Firestone, 2000).

Distinguishing Psychotherapy Information from Medical Information

The way in which confidentiality was conceptualized by the mental-health professions began to diverge from the views of other health-care professionals in the early stages of the cold war. The divergence first surfaced in 1950 in response to a request from the director of the Federal Bureau of Investigation published in the *Journal of the American Medical Association* (JAMA) that physicians should report subversive inclinations on the part of their patients to the FBI (Hoover, 1950). Psychiatrists and psychoanalysts protested Mr. Hoover's request (Slovenko, 1998). Prior to 1957, American physicians were bound to avoid nonconsensual disclosures of confidential information except to protect the *health* of another individual or group, or if *required* by law. In 1957, the ethics code of the American Medical Association was changed to allow disclosures "necessary to protect the *welfare* of the individual or the community."[1] This was inter-

---

[1] To the extent that the 1957 modification of the AMA's ethics code made physicians "agents of the state," the views of the American medical profession were opposite to those expressed by European physicians. These physicians were all too familiar

preted as allowing the disclosure by physicians of confidential information for political and "national-security" purposes. That code remained in effect until 1984 when the wording was changed to require physicians to "safeguard patient confidences within the constraints of the law" (Graber, Beasley, and Eaddy, 1985).

Ten years after Mr. Hoover's *JAMA* editorial, a second high-profile cold war event played a significant role in fostering the divergence of thinking on the subject of professional allegiance. In 1960, Bernon F. Mitchell, a young cryptographer at the top-secret National Security Agency in Washington, defected to the Soviet Union along with a male friend. Both turned up at a high-profile Moscow press conference a few months later. This incident has been described as the "worst scandal in the history of the NSA." When it was discovered that shortly before his defection Mitchell had consulted Dr. Clarence Schilt, this Silver Springs, Maryland psychiatrist was interviewed by investigators from the controversial House Un-American Activities Committee (HUAC). Schilt had gathered no material related to the matter of a planned defection during his three sessions with Mitchell. However, Schilt voluntarily agreed to testify in closed session before the Committee, where he disclosed details of his interviews with Mitchell. The next day, many details of the interviews appeared on the front page of the *Washington Post*. Thirty-seven psychiatrist members of the Maryland Medical and Chirurgical Faculty signed a petition raising an ethics complaint about Dr. Schilt. The Faculty's Professional Conduct Committee exonerated Dr. Schilt, however, concluding that the interests of the nation "transcended those of the individual" (Sidel, 1960, 1961).

Disclosure to Third-Party Payers

After World War II, the growth of health insurance with generous, virtually no-questions-asked coverage of analytic treatment provided a powerful inducement for psychoanalysts to associate themselves with the health-care system. There was little incentive in such a system

---

with the collusion between medical professionals and the state in Nazi Germany and the Soviet Union. In 1949, the World Medical Association stated in its ethics code, "A doctor owes to his patient *absolute secrecy* on all which has been confided to him." In 1954, the following statement was adopted: "Professional secrecy by its very nature must be *absolute*. It must be observed in all cases. A secret which is shared is no longer secret" (Seidel, 1961).

to establish a separate professional identity for psychoanalysis with its own ethical and record-keeping standards. Such separate standards would have implied a recognition of the differences between the confidentiality requirements of psychoanalysis and that of medical and psychiatric care.

Disclosure to third-party payers has become a serious factor in the breakdown of the protection of confidentiality in the United States. For psychoanalysts, this disclosure problem can be traced to their attempts to maintain a position within the health-care reimbursement scheme. Indeed, published evidence (Goodman, 1973) supports a view that analytic organizations, toward whom others look for a model of confidentiality protection, actually fostered the development of intensive case management (sensitive information is disclosed by telephone to "case managers" on a regular basis). Other psychotherapists face today what, ironically, is now avoided by most United States analysts.

In the early 1970s during the Nixon Administration, with the first hint of a publicly supported health-care system, the American Psychoanalytic Association (APsaA) made an explicit decision to play down differences between psychoanalysis and other health-care modalities to gain third-party coverage for analysis (Goodman, 1973). As a result, APsaA developed *a very detailed reporting form* for third-party utilization management based on an existing protocol intended for a different purpose. The protocol originated as a guide to candidates who were writing case reports for progression or certification (Gray, personal communication via e-mail, 2001). The original hope was to provide a standard mechanism by which a psychiatrist employed by the insurer could carry out confidential case reviews. Even this plan was controversial, because prior to that time any disclosures by analysts of identifiable case material would have been unthinkable. However, the forces within the profession favoring cooperation with the imagined new third-party payment system prevailed.

This APsaA form was reproduced in a widely circulated peer review manual (American Psychiatric Association, 1976), thereby conveying the message that filing detailed case reports by therapists as part of the third-party payment system had the profession's approval. Before long, what had been intended to be a confidential "peer" review mechanism mutated into a system in which therapists' reports were reviewed within insurance companies by subdoctoral reviewers from professions such as nursing and social work. The reporting forms were retained in files, and eventually information taken from the forms was entered into computer databases. As insurers requested more and more confidential treatment information, a backlash developed.

Around the time that these events were occurring, an attempt was made to prohibit such disclosures and to create a mechanism for claims review more respectful of confidentiality. In 1978, a law became effective in Washington, DC (District of Columbia, 1978) that prohibited third-party payers from requesting confidential mental-health information and instead spelled out a mechanism for confidential reviews of disputed claims by independent professional peers. A similar statute (New Jersey, 1985), applicable only to patients of psychologists, was passed in New Jersey in 1984. Although these statutes continue to be in effect, they are not widely known and have not been duplicated in other jurisdictions.

In the early 1990s, the APsaA issued a new practice guideline because experience with the prior protocol supported the need to limit the amount of information that could be disclosed (American Psychoanalytic Association, 1992), but it failed to rescind the old reporting form. Finally, as the 1990s reached a close, APsaA rescinded the former protocols and reporting form; a utilization review protocol truly protective of patient privacy was adopted (American Psychoanalytic Association, 1999).

Reporting Child Abuse

For several decades, health professionals have been required by state statutes to report to authorities patients who reveal evidence of child abuse and have generally been willing to make such reports. Bollas and Sundelson (1995) point out that this requirement, which now exists in some form in all 50 states, is one of the most difficult dilemmas to confront psychotherapists. They trace the evolution of these statutes, in which the physician first was *permitted* to report, to a contemporary form in which physicians are now *required* to report such evidence.[2] The fundamental rule of psychoanalysis, which asks the patient to say everything that comes to mind and withhold nothing, places the patient in an untenable position. A patient cannot say

---

[2] "The obligation to comply with statutory requirements is clearly stated in the Principles of Medical Ethics. In addition, physicians have an ethical obligation to report abuse even when the law does not require it" (American Medical Associataion, 1997, p. 5).

"everything" if certain things that are said require the filing of a report with state authorities. Such reporting requirements imposed on the psychoanalytic relationship cannot be anything but detrimental.

The APsaA finally has responded by including in its ethics code provisions that *permit* but do *not require* psychoanalysts to make such reports, deferring to the discretion of the analyst, often after confidential collegial consultation (American Psychoanalytic Association, 2001, Sec. VIII.10).[3] The reasoning behind this provision is similar to that underlying a similar provision in the code of ethics of the North Carolina Bar Association. That code addresses the question of whether an ethical attorney must report child-abuse information obtained in those situations where the North Carolina reporting law overrides the attorney-client privilege (North Carolina Bar Association, 1995):

> [The ethics code] prohibits a lawyer from revealing the confidential information of his or her client except as permitted under [a part of the rules that says that a lawyer] "may reveal" the confidential information of his or her client . . . "when . . . required by law or court order." The rule clearly places the decision regarding the disclosure of a client's confidential information within the lawyer's discretion. While that discretion should not be exercised lightly, particularly in the face of a statute compelling disclosure, a lawyer may in good faith conclude that he or she should not reveal confidential information where to do so would substantially undermine the purpose of the representation or substantially damage the interests of his or her client. . . .
>
> It is recognized that the ethical rules may not protect a lawyer from criminal prosecution for failure to comply with the reporting statute.

The disagreement between ethics codes and statutes is by no means resolved. Professionals who disobey the law risk, among other things, losing their licenses to practice. A courageous analyst and a dedicated professional organization will be required to confront this disagreement in the courts.

---

[3] A nearly final draft of the new code of ethics of the American Psychoanalytic Association, however, reads: "When a psychoanalyst becomes convinced that abuse is occurring, the psychoanalyst *should report* adult or child abuse of a patient or by a patient to the appropriate governmental agency in keeping with local laws. In this circumstance, confidentiality may be breached to the extent necessary." This provision, fortunately, was changed to *permit*, but *not require* such reporting, before the final code was approved (American Psychoanalytic Association, 2000).

Privileged Information and Privilege Rules

Although professional ethical codes offer the strongest protection for confidentiality, a protective legal framework also exists. In addition to statutes that spell out the obligations of professionals to protect patient confidences, there are privilege rules within the justice system that are meant to shield certain confidential information from disclosure without the patient's consent, particularly in court proceedings.

The court is seen within the legal system to be crucially reliant on the availability of all information necessary to decide the outcome of a case, and therefore every citizen has a legal obligation to make available information the court requires. The few exceptions to this rule, called privileges, are expressions of a societal consensus that the value of protecting the privacy of certain relationships outweighs the imperative need for truth-seeking in the courts.

Mental-health professionals often misunderstand the significance of privilege rules and are often warned, for example, that privilege rules do not govern disclosures to third-party payers where the relationship is governed by private contractual arrangements. In issuing cautions emphasizing the limits of privilege rules, legal advisors have often erroneously created the impression that privileges have no effect outside the courtroom. This is not the case. Privilege rules tend to be controversial for the very reason that these rules have ramifications that affect interactions outside the courtroom situation. For instance, participants in conversations that are privileged tend routinely to take precautions to avoid losing the privileged status. This might take the form of scrupulously avoiding behavior that could be interpreted as indicating that the conversation did not take place "with an expectation of privacy," or of strengthening professional ethics codes to encourage behavior consistent with the privilege (Imwinkelreid, 1994).

Privilege rules can, however, be eroded by an accumulation of loopholes and exceptions. In the United States, about forty-two states currently have a physician-patient privilege statute, but these statutes have so many exceptions that legal scholars tend to view them as relatively unimportant (Slovenko, 1998).[4] The Federal courts do not recognize a physician-patient privilege at all.

---

[4] In the State of New York, which has the country's oldest physician-patient privilege statute dating from 1828, the following exceptions to the privilege are created by statutory reporting rules: dental information to identify a patient; information indicating that a patient under age 16 has been the victim of a crime; information about the mental or physical condition of a deceased patient that will not disgrace

In 1952, two years after Mr. Hoover's editorial appeared in *JAMA*, a local court in Chicago ruled that the information conveyed by a patient to a psychiatrist was *privileged;* that is, unlike almost all other information including ordinary medical information, psychotherapy information is not subject to compelled disclosure. The court's sophisticated articulation of the special privacy requirements of psychotherapy based on psychoanalytic principles in this landmark case (Binder v. Ruvell, 1952) began a trend within the American legal system toward increased protection of psychotherapy information, during the same era in which confidentiality within general health care was eroding.

In the 25 years following *Binder,* proposals were made to create a statutory (by legislation) psychiatrist-patient (or psychotherapist-patient) privilege applicable in state courts, which resulted eventually in the passage of privilege statutes in all 50 states. These statutes vary from state to state, some being modeled on the highly respected and centuries-old common-law attorney-client privilege and others on the less certain physician-patient privilege. For example, in the State of New York, patients of psychologists are protected by a privilege directly based on the attorney-client model, but patients of psychiatrists are protected only under the general physician-patient privilege.

In the early 1960s, the Supreme Court of the United States started a process of rewriting the rules of evidence (including privilege rules) for the federal courts, which are governed by a separate set of rules from those in the various state courts. After years of study, the advisory committee proposed a set of federal evidence rules including, among others, a specific privilege for patients of psychotherapists. A privilege for patients of physicians was explicitly *not* included in the proposal. The proposed rules were sent to Congress in the early 1970s with the expectation of legislative approval.

Instead, the proposed privilege rules became the subject of enor-

---

the memory of the deceased; clinical information about the subject of a guardianship proceeding in which the court has ordered disclosure; information about the mistreatment of children in child-abuse or neglect proceedings; information about gunshot wounds; information about communicable diseases; the names and addresses of drug users, sent to the commissioner of public health; psychiatric records, sent to enumerated persons or agencies for specified purposes; and information pursuant to a court order finding that the interests of justice significantly outweigh the need for confidentiality. In addition to these, courts have noted precedents for several implied waivers, including grand-jury investigations, governmental investigations, and in criminal cases in respect to a defendant's constitutional due-process rights (*Amin v. Rose,* 2000).

mous controversy. Hearings were held, and many interest groups submitted testimony. The proposed privilege rules became so invested with symbolic meaning, pitting professional and other groups against each other, that the controversy threatened to interfere with the passage of all the new evidence rules. On one hand, some argued that, because privilege rules have ramifications that reach far beyond the courtroom, such rules were rightly established through a legislative and political process rather than in the courts. On the other hand, because privilege rules were so controversial, a national political resolution of all the disputes about privileges seemed out of reach.

Consequently, Congress deleted all the specific proposed privilege rules from the new federal evidence code and instead created a single general privilege rule that in effect empowered the federal courts to evolve privilege rules through a common-law process. Importantly, in adopting this approach, Congress declared that the deletion of the specific privileges should not be perceived as disfavoring a psychotherapist-patient privilege or any of the other specific proposed privileges. The revised rules were signed into law by President Ford in 1973 and became effective in 1975 (Svetanics, 1997).

The passage into law of the new rules of evidence set in motion a decades-long process in which the lower federal courts considered the question of a privilege for psychotherapist-patient communications. A few appellate courts, accepting the reasoning in *Binder v. Ruvell*, the relatively uniform approval of *Binder* by legal scholars, and the existence of the privilege in the states, held that such a federal privilege was justified. A greater number of appellate courts evidently thought that the Congressional mandate was to recognize only long-standing common-law privileges such as spousal and attorney-client privilege. The Supreme Court demonstrated a conservative attitude toward the creation of new privileges, and disapproved virtually all proposed privileges.

The specific issue of the psychotherapist-patient privilege reached the U.S. Supreme Court for the first time in 1995 in the case of *Jaffee v. Redmond*. Four years earlier a female police officer named Mary Lu Redmond shot and killed an African-American man, Ricky Allen Sr., while on duty. After the shooting, officer Redmond began psychotherapy with Karen Beyer, a social worker, whom she saw two or three times a week for at least six months. Ms. Beyer was employed as a psychotherapist by the same village as the police officer (*Jaffee v. Redmond*, 1995).

In a subsequent federal civil-rights suit against the officer and the village, surviving relatives of the deceased man (represented by a relative named Carrie Jaffee) sought access to Ms. Beyer's testimony and psychotherapy notes. Ms. Beyer, lacking officer Redmond's consent to disclose information, demurred on the grounds that the information was protected by a privilege. That privilege claim was rejected by the trial court. However, on appeal, the federal appellate court for the 7th circuit joined a minority of other federal appellate courts in holding that a privilege did exist for psychotherapy information in the federal courts. The privilege rule fashioned by the seventh circuit court was modest in that it allowed a trial judge to make a case-by-case determination of the relative value of protection of the patient's privacy on one hand versus the need for the information on the other (a "balancing test"), a so-called qualified privilege (*Jaffee v. Redmond*, 1995).

The Supreme Court, recognizing that the lower federal courts were clearly in disagreement on the issue of a privilege for psychotherapy patients, accepted *Jaffee v. Redmond* in 1995 and issued its decision in the case in June, 1996 (*Jaffee v. Redmond*, 1996). In that decision, the Court, by a majority of seven to two, ruled that a psychotherapist-patient privilege exists in the federal courts.

Had the Court done nothing more than endorse the holding of the appellate court, *Jaffee* would have been considered a landmark case. The Supreme Court, however, went beyond the appellate court by establishing the foundation of a much stronger privilege. In language that was utterly explicit, the Court rejected the imposition of a "balancing test" as proposed by the lower courts and instead insisted that the privilege must be "absolute" (i.e., not subject to case-by-case balancing) and placed the new privilege in the same group as the highly respected absolute common-law privileges (*Jaffe v. Redmond*, 1996):

> We part company with the Court of Appeals on a separate point. We reject the balancing component of the privilege implemented by that court and a small number of states. Making the promise of confidentiality contingent upon a trial judge's later evaluation of the relative importance of the patient's interest in privacy and the evidentiary need for disclosure would eviscerate the effectiveness of the privilege. As we explained in *Upjohn*, if the purpose of the privilege is to be served, the participants in the confidential conversation "must be able to predict with some degree of certainty whether particular discussions will be protected. An uncer-

tain privilege, or one which purports to be certain but results in widely varying applications by the courts, is little better than no privilege at all" [p. 1932].

In reaching its decision, the Supreme Court carried forward the view originally set forth in *Binder,* which differentiates the psycho-therapist-patient relationship from the physician-patient relationship.

The Court, recognizing that details of the privilege would have to be worked out by the common-law process through which the privilege was created, declined to specify the "contours" of the Jaffee privilege. The Court, however, made it clear that the privilege could be "waived" by the patient. Like other existing privilege rules, the Court "[had no] doubt that there are situations in which the privilege must give way, for example, if a serious threat of harm to the patient or to others can be averted only by means of a disclosure by the therapist" (*Jaffee v. Redmond,* 1996).

In the first five years following *Jaffee,* the psychotherapy professions in the United States were slow to understand its importance. *Jaffee* was decided at a time when psychiatry as a medical specialty was undergoing rapid change from a professional population dominated in the 1960s by psychotherapy practitioners to a "medicalized" specialty more concerned in the 1990s with hypothetical brain pathology and psychopharmacology. Most of the psychotherapy in the United States is now practiced by social workers. Because *Jaffee* differentiates the treatment of "physical ailments" from psychotherapy, it has thus intersected sensitive "turf issues."

Some legal commentators, examining *Jaffee* with a literal eye, asserted that the existence of the privilege in all 50 states prior to *Jaffee* meant that *Jaffee* would make little difference in most courts. Others believed that the privilege was of little consequence because it would likely be eroded by accumulating exceptions, as the physician-patient privilege had been in the states (Slovenko, 1974; Slovenko, 1997; Shuman and Foote, 1999). Whether the privilege will evolve along the lines of the porous state physician-patient privilege rules or the more protective attorney-client privilege is an open question. However, the wording of the *Jaffee* opinion appears to signal the Supreme Court's intent that the new privilege develop in a way that would render it both robust and reliable.

Since *Jaffee,* the lower federal courts have begun to render opinions not only demonstrating how the privilege might evolve but also showing that the courts' view of the privilege is anything but uniform. Generally, lower courts have been rather expansive in applying the privilege. No court has dealt with the issue of whether the privilege extends to all forms of psychotherapy or only to those forms that rely in some way on psychoanalytically informed approach. The courts appear inclined to view the privilege as applying to all verbal treatments of mental disorders.

The originally proposed federal privilege applied only to psychotherapeutic relationships between licensed physicians (treating a mental disorder) or psychologists and their patients. *Jaffee* extended the privilege to the patients of licensed social workers as well. Lower courts since *Jaffee* appear inclined to extend the privilege even further to include, for example, Employee Assistance Program (EAP) counselors. Considerable difference of opinion exists as to which psychotherapists are included in the federal privilege. In *Jaffee*, the Court combined the "license-based" approach with a "functional" approach: " . . . confidential communications between a licensed psychotherapist and her patients in the course of diagnosis or treatment . . . " Whether the privilege will be found eventually to extend to psychoanalysts who are not licensed in a mental-health discipline is unclear (Dubbleday, 1985; Aronowitz, 1998; Nelken, 2000).

The lower courts have differed on two important issues affecting the privilege. The first is whether there is a "dangerous patient" exception to the privilege—that is, whether a therapist having set aside the confidentiality of the relationship to warn or protect an intended victim thereby also makes the contents of the therapy available as evidence in a subsequent court proceeding (*United States v. Glass*, 1998; Harris, 1999; *United States v. Hayes*, 2000). The second issue is whether the patient having entered her mental state into a claim or defense thereby automatically waives the privilege protecting all psychotherapeutic conversations in her past (the "patient-litigant exception").

In general, privilege considerations cease to apply when a patient voluntarily waives the privilege. For example, if a patient *requests* that a therapist make a disclosure, the therapist may not assert the privilege on his or her own behalf. However, even where the patient requests a disclosure, other considerations, such as ethical constraints, might come into play where the therapist believes that the disclosure could be harmful (Mosher and Swire, 2002).

Federal Policy Regarding Confidentiality of Psychotherapy

Despite the initial lack of awareness within the psychotherapeutic professions, the *Jaffee* ruling has had a major influence in shaping the U.S. government's policy toward the confidentiality of psychotherapy information. Until 2001, the United States had no overall federal legal protection for the privacy of most medical information. Congress attempted to enact legislation providing some degree of protection on a federal level, but a decade's worth of such attempts was stalemated by conflicting interest groups that disagreed sharply as to the extent of privacy protection that is warranted and practical. The gathering momentum for computerized health-record systems, however, added a note of urgency to the debate about health-care privacy.

On one hand, some privacy advocates urged the creation of a set of legal standards based on a seemingly idealistic wish to return to a simpler time when true medical-record confidentiality could be reasonably expected by patients. More than one professional organization enacted a position statement urging that no patient should be required to have his medical data entered into a computerized record system. On the other hand, management-oriented groups viewed such standards as naive and impractical. These groups advocated instead the use of "fair information practices" as a standard for the protection of health data. Such standards are used for the protection of commercial information and are viewed by many privacy advocates as little better than no protection. It seemed that the only way to break the logjam of legislative paralysis created by the polarized positions was to impose a compromise.

The forcing of a compromise came about when Congress passed The Health Insurance Portability and Accountability Act of 1996 (HIPAA), one part of which is entitled "Administrative Simplification." The intent of that section is to mandate the standardization, and hence promote the computerization, of the vast amount of largely administrative data exchanged throughout the health-care system, in the hope of increasing efficiency and lowering costs. The "Administrative Simplification" section acknowledged the requirement for federal privacy protection for the developing new systems and therefore empowered the Executive Branch to issue binding federal health privacy rules with the force of law if Congress failed to agree on legislation for the same purpose by 1999. The 1999 deadline passed without Congressional agreement, and so the U.S. Department of

Health and Human Services (HHS) began a Herculean two-year effort to create new rules for the federal protection of private health information. Once in place, these rules would have the force of federal law and would apply to all medical information in the United States (Gostin, 2001).

In attempting to create such rules, HHS was placed in the position of achieving the compromise that had eluded the Congressional political process for many years. A particularly difficult issue was the status of especially sensitive information (such as AIDS-HIV status, genetic information, and mental health data), each category of which had patient and professional advocacy groups urging that it be treated as an exception from the general rules by being given a higher order of protection. Those responsible for implementing and operating the data systems, however, believed that it would be impractical to designate subsets of information within medical records for special treatment.

Ultimately, HHS decided to treat all information (with a single exception) uniformly. The general rule, which became law in April 2001 and must be complied with by April 2003, provides that most information in a medical record may be disclosed, with no special notification to the patient or specific authorization, for purposes related to what are called "treatment, payment, and health-care operations." Other kinds of disclosures would be subject to a complicated set of rules, but in general unauthorized use of a patient's information for nonmedical commercial purposes would be prohibited.

The precise amount of protection that the new federal rule should impose on disclosures of medical information (other than psychotherapy information) within "treatment/payment/health-care operations" has been subject to a protracted and emotional political struggle. That struggle illustrates how difficult it is to impose a workable compromise of privacy protections on the health-care system and how difficult it is for many people to understand the difference between the terms "prohibit," "allow," and "require." The issue boils down to the question of whether the federal government should prohibit, allow, or require a generalized written consent in every patient file before any health information can be used for more or less routine purposes within the health-care system.

The 1999 first draft of the HHS privacy rule prohibited such "consent forms," except in jurisdictions where such forms were required by a state or local law. Several reasons were given for the prohibition. HHS pointed out that such forms, which are routinely used in many institutions, are usually read and signed in a perfunctory manner and are therefore meaningless. In addition, it was argued that insisting on such forms would create a false sense of protection among patients who would not realize that in the complex modern health care system their confidential data would be routinely shared among a wide group of health-care workers and others (United States Department of Health and Human Services, 1999a). The law did allow for the creation of special legally binding arrangements with patients to protect specific parts of their record, but this was a voluntary arrangement between patients and practitioners that practitioners were not obliged to accept. Privacy advocates, however, took the position that the requirement of a consent form is a "core protection" that at the very least offered an opportunity for the patient to discuss the handling of information with the physician and at most offered the opportunity to exercise a supposed legal "right" to give or withhold the consent.

The original proposal was subject to a torrent of protest during the public-comment period. In response to this criticism, the Clinton administration did a complete reversal of position in its final version of the privacy rule issued in the closing days of that administration in December 2000. In that "final" version, the presence of a general consent form in the patient's file, rather than being prohibited, was now required for every routine use and disclosure of health information.

Almost as soon as the Bush administration assumed office, the "final" rule, which was not actually due to take effect for more than a year, was reopened for additional comment and eventual revision. The mandatory consent requirement, in particular, came in for severe criticism from almost all the medical organizations in the country (other than psychiatrists), in addition to hospitals, researchers, pharmacists, and insurers, who saw the requirement as an administrative nightmare. In its revised final April 2002 version of the rule, which now must take effect with no further change in April 2003, the Bush administration adopted a middle-ground position, eliminating the mandatory consent forms but permitting practitioners who desired to use such forms to do so (United States Department of Health and Human Services, 2002). This led to an outcry from the most zealous of the country's privacy advocates who have been resorting to arguing that the federal government had then "taken away the traditional right to give consent" even though no such right had ever existed. No practitioner's habit of obtaining consent, or any local law requiring consent forms, is in any way affected by the rule's lack of a federal mandate for a consent form. Nevertheless, the Democratic Party tried to make the lack of a consent requirement a major political issue in the fall 2002 campaign.

Clearly, the compromise for general health information falls short of the protections hoped for by many privacy advocates who now view the new federal protection as severely weakened. The single exception in the privacy rule was the creation of a new category of information called "psychotherapy notes" which remained unchanged throughout the above revisions.[5] Psychotherapy notes must be "separate from the rest of the individual's medical record." Once so segregated, information in these notes is accorded stringent protection unlike that provided for other data. With some narrow exceptions, no disclosure of "psychotherapy notes" for treatment, payment or "health-care operations" can take place without the patient's specific written authorization. In addition, third-party payers (insurance companies) are prohibited from requiring a patient to disclose such information either when selling an insurance policy or processing an insurance claim. Finally, an important provision of the rule that requires physicians to grant patients access to their entire medical record does not apply to "psychotherapy notes." In the documents accompanying the publication of the privacy rule, HHS gave the following reason for the special protection of psychotherapy information (United States Department of Health and Human Services, 2000):

> Generally, we have not treated sensitive information differently from other protected health information; however, we have provided additional protections for psychotherapy notes because of *Jaffee v. Redmond* and the unique role of this type of information. There are few reasons why other health-care entities should need access to psychotherapy notes, and in those cases, the individual

---

[5] The definition of "psychotherapy notes" in the HHS Rule is as follows:

> Psychotherapy notes means notes recorded (in any medium) by a health-care provider who is a mental-health professional documenting or analyzing the contents of conversation during a private counselling session or a group, joint, or family counseling session and that are separated from the rest of the individual's medical record. Psychotherapy notes excludes medication prescription and monitoring, counseling session start and stop times, the modalities and frequencies of treatment furnished, results of clinical tests, and any summary of the following items: diagnosis, functional status, the treatment plan, symptoms, prognosis, and progress to date [United States Department of Health and Human Services, 2000, p. 82805].

is in the best position to determine if the notes should be disclosed [p. 82652].

In December 1999, the Surgeon General of the United States issued a major report on the subject of mental health (United States Department of Health and Human Services, 1999a). Chapter 7 of that report is devoted entirely to confidentiality and opens with a passage from the Supreme Court majority opinion in *Jaffee*. The section that deals with disclosure to third-party payers points out that the state laws that permit disclosure of mental-health information to insurers were, for the most part, written in an era before managed care and did not anticipate the current demands for disclosure of detailed information. The report goes on to suggest that such permissive statutes need to be revised and offers the New Jersey statute (as previously discussed) and the similar District of Columbia statutes as a possible model.

Although there are many ambiguities and uncertainties in these new federal initiatives, it appears that after a delay of several decades during which the confidentiality of psychotherapy has been severely eroded, the tide may be turning. Policy makers, the judicial system, and ordinary citizens are becoming aware of the enormous stakes in the protection of confidentiality in the psychoanalytic and psychotherapeutic process.

References

American Medical Association (1997), *Code of Medical Ethics: Current Opinions and Annotations.* Chicago: American Medical Association.

American Psychiatric Association (1976), *Manual of Psychiatric Peer Review.* Washington: American Psychiatric Association.

American Psychoanalytic Association (1992), Reporting information for claims review of psychoanalysis. In: *Manual of Psychiatric Quality Assurance*, ed. M. Matteson. Washington: American Psychiatric Press, pp. 237–238.

——— (1999), Practice bulletin 3: External review of psychoanalysis. *Amer. Psychoanal.*, 34(2).

——— (2001), *Principles and Standards of Ethics for Psychoanalysts.* New York: American Psychoanalytic Association.

Amin v. Rose (2000), *New York Law J.*, December 7, 2000: 31, col. 1.

Aronowitz, S. (1998), Following the psychotherapist-patient privilege down the bumpy road paved by *Jaffee v. Redmond. Annual Survey Amer. Law*, 1998:307–348.

Binder v. Ruvell, Civil Docket 52 C 25 35, Circuit C. of Cook County, IL (1952). Reported in full: *J. Amer. Med. Assn.*, 150:1241–1242.

Bollas, C. & Sundelson, D. (1995), *The New Informants:*. Northvale, NJ: Aronson.

Buckner, F. & Firestone, M. (2000), "Where the public peril begins" 25 Years after Tarasoff. *J. Legal Medicine,* 21:187–222.

District of Columbia (1978), *District of Columbia Mental Health Information Act of 1978.* DC Code, sec. 6–2001 et seq.

Dubbleday, C. (1985), The psychotherapist-client testimonial privilege: Defining the professional involved. *Emory Law J.,* 34:777–826.

Goodman, S. (1973), Report of the secretary of the executive council. *Bull. Amer. Psychoanal. Assn.,* 29:435–453.

Gostin, L. O. (2001), National health information privacy: Regulations under the Health Insurance Accountability and Portability Act. *J. Amer. Med. Assn.,* 285:3015–3021.

Graber, G. C., Beasley, A. D. & Eaddy, J. A. (1985), *Ethical Analysis of Clinical Medicine.* Baltimore: Urban

Hale, N. G. (1995), *The Rise and Crisis of Psychoanalysis in the United States, Vol. 2.* Oxford: Oxford University Press.

Harris, G. (1999), The dangerous patient exception to the psychotherapist-patient privilege: The Tarasoff duty and the Jaffee footnote. *Washington Law Rev.,* 74:33–68.

Hoover, J. E. (1950), Let's keep America healthy. *J. Amer. Med. Assn.,* 144:1094–1095.

Imwinkelried, E. J. (1994), An Hegelian approach to privileges under federal rule of evidence 501: The restrictive thesis, the expansive antithesis, and the contextual synthesis. *Nebraska Law Rev.,* 73:511–523.

Jaffee v. Redmond, 51 F. 3d 1346 (1995).

Jaffee v. Redmond, 116 S. Ct. 1923 (1996).

Jaffee v. Redmond, 518 U.S. 1 (1996).

Mosher, P. W. & Swire, P. P. (2002), The ethical and legal implications of *Jaffee v. Redmond* and the HIPAA medical privacy rule for psychotherapy and general psychiatry. *Psychiat. Clin. N. Amer.,* 25:575–584.

Nelken, M. (2000), The limits of privilege: The developing scope of federal psychotherapist-patient privilege law. *Rev. Litigation,* 20:1–43.

New Jersey (1985), *Practicing Psychology Licensing Act.* New Jersey Stat. 45:14B-2–45:14B-46 .

North Carolina Bar Association (1995), *Rules of Professional Conduct,* Opinion #175.

Shuman, D. W. & Foote, W. (1999), *Jaffee v. Redmond's* impact: Life after the Supreme Court's recognition of a psychotherapist-patient privilege. *Professional Psychol. Research & Practice,* 30:479–487.

Sidel, V. W. (1960), Medical ethics and the cold war. *The Nation,* 191:325–327.

———— (1961), Confidential information and the physician. *New Eng. J. Med.,* 264:1133–1137.

Siegler, M. (1982), Confidentiality in medicine: A decrepit concept. *New Eng. J. Med.,* 307:1518–1521.

Slovenko, R. (1974) Psychotherapist-patient privilege: A picture of misguided hope. *Catholic University Law Rev.,* 23:649-673.

———— (1997), The psychotherapist-patient testimonial privilege. *Amer. J. Psychoanal.,* 57:63–68.

———— (1998), *Psychotherapy and Confidentiality.* Springfield, IL: Thomas.

Svetanics, M. L. (1997), Beyond "reason and experience": The Supreme Court adopts a broad psychotherapist-patient privilege in *Jaffee v. Redmond. Saint Louis University Law J.*, 41:719–759.

United States Department of Health and Human Services (1999a), *Mental Health: A Report of the Surgeon General.* Rockville, MD: U.S. Department of Health and Human Services, Substance Abuse and Mental Health Services Administration, Center for Mental Health Services, National Institutes of Health, National Institute of Mental Health.

———— (2000), Standards for privacy of individually identifiable health information: Final rule. *Federal Register,* 65:82461-82829.

———— (2002), Standards for privacy of individually identifiable health information: Final rule. *Federal Register,* 67:53181–53273.

United States v. Glass, 133 F. 3d 1356 (1998).

United States v. Hayes, WL 1289028, 6th Cir. (2000).

Introduction to CHAPTER 18

❦

The American Psychoanalytic Association's Fight for Privacy

Robert Pyles's chapter summarizes the legal and philosophical basis for the extraordinarily effective American Psychoanalytic Association intervention on the question of patients' privacy and psychoanalytic confidentiality. Although Pyles emphasizes the importance of privacy rights, his discussion of *Jaffee v. Redmond* and the Bierenbaum and Hayes cases makes it quite clear that success in the courts has been based on the pragmatic or utilitarian argument for a special psychotherapy privilege. The argument is grounded less on the right of privacy than on society's overriding interest in preserving the benefit of psychotherapy for its individual citizens. According to the argument in *Jaffee vs. Redmond*, this benefit depends on the professional promise of confidentiality.

Pyles's comparison of the very different Canadian Supreme Court approach of balancing privacy rights against trial rights in confidentiality cases raises some interesting questions about the appropriate philosophy and strategy to be used in establishing this ethical principle. If confidentiality is defined mainly as a privacy right, it would seem inevitable that it be subject to judicial "balancing." A certain protection from court disclosure of psychotherapy files has been provided in Canadian criminal law, but this applies almost exclusively to complainants in sexual-assault cases. U.S. jurisprudence seems to provide greater protection for all its citizens.

CHAPTER 18

❦

The American Psychoanalytic Association's Fight for Privacy

Robert L. Pyles

*I*n all our efforts in the American Psychoanalytic Association (APsaA), whether political, legal, or clinical, we have taken the very firm position that the quality of psychotherapeutic care depends completely on the privacy of psychoanalytic and psychodynamic communications and records. We maintain that privacy is the cornerstone of care and that no good care can take place without the assurance of privacy for the information passed between patient and therapist. For 2000 years, it has been understood that privacy and medical treatment go hand in hand. The Hippocratic Oath, which most of us took, states:

> whatever in connection with my profession . . . I see or hear, in the life of men, which ought not to be spoken of abroad, I will not divulge, as reckoning that all such should be kept secret. While I continue to keep this Oath unviolated, may it be granted to me to enjoy life and the practice of the art, respected by all men, and all times. But should I trespass and violate this Oath, may the reverse be my lot.

This is a solemn oath, meant to be taken very seriously. It also contains a punishment, a curse really, should the practitioner fail to keep it.

Moving to relatively contemporary times, the Constitution of the United States contains language that most feel defines a basic right to privacy. First, it should be understood that the overriding concern of the Founding Fathers was to ensure that the civil rights of citizens would be protected, especially from incursions *by the government.*

In particular, the right to privacy is protected by two amendments, and its preservation is one of the basic purposes of the Constitution. The Fourth Amendment protects "the right of the people to be secure in their persons . . . against unreasonable searches and seizures." The Fifth Amendment protects any person from being deprived of "liberty . . . without due process of law."

The Preamble to the Constitution sets forth that it was intended to "establish Justice" and "secure the Blessing of Liberty to ourselves and our posterity," among other things. The "Pledge of Allegiance," which many of us used to recite daily in school, promises "one nation, indivisible, with liberty and justice for all." The problem, however, is that "liberty" and "justice" exist with a certain basic dynamic tension to each other, particularly in the area of privacy. Whereas "liberty," or the freedom of the individual, involves the guarantee of privacy, "justice," or the right to a fair trial, can require the mandated disclosure of private information. Thus, the tension between the protection of individual rights and the public good is inherent in the basic precepts of the Constitution.

The Supreme Court, in the *Whalen v. Roe* (1977) case, found that privacy was an essential element of liberty. The American Psychoanalytic Association has commissioned two white papers outlining the argument for the constitutional right to privacy, the special need for privacy of mental health information particularly in therapist-patient communications ("The Right to Medical Privacy: An Indispensable Element of Quality Health Care," 1997; "Comments of the American Psychoanalytic Association on Standards of Individually Identifiable Health Information", 2000).

Crucial for us, and one of the most fascinating issues, is the nexus between constitutionally protected freedom and the privacy of communications between patient and therapist. The analysis following Chief Justice Louis Brandeis, as stated in his 1890 law-review article, could be outlined as follows: the right to freedom encompasses the right to privacy, and the right to privacy is essentially the right to be let alone (Brandeis, 1890). A fundamental principle of our system of government is that the government has no right to detain or interrogate law-abiding citizens in the absence of probable cause to believe that they have committed a crime. Whereas the right to privacy may vary with the setting, nowhere is the right stronger than in the context of one's thoughts about oneself. A recent Supreme Court decision is instructive.

In *Kyllo v. United States* (June 11, 2001), the Court (in an opinion by Justice Scalia, who wrote the dissent in Jaffee) found that it was a violation of the Fourth Amendment's prohibition on unreasonable searches and seizures for agents of the Federal Department of the Interior to use a thermal imaging device to determine (without a warrant) whether an individual was growing marijuana in his home (he was). In determining whether a privacy right under the Fourth Amendment protected the interior of the individual's home, the Court observed, "At the very core of the Fourth Amendment 'stands the right of a man to retreat into his own home and there be free from unreasonable governmental intrusion' . . . With few exceptions, the question of whether a warrantless search of a home is reasonable and hence constitutional must be answered no."

The Court noted that the protection afforded by the Fourth Amendment exists where "the individual manifested a subjective expectation of privacy in the object of the challenged search" and where "society [is] willing to recognize that expectation as reasonable." Clearly, the right of someone to have privacy within their own mind should be as strong as the right to privacy in his home. Patients clearly manifest the subjective expectation in therapy sessions that the information will be kept private without their consent for disclosure, and the Court in *Jaffee v. Redmond* (1996) noted that society has recognized that expectation as reasonable.

It is the position of the American Psychoanalytic Association, and one that we have espoused in clinical, political, and legal arenas, that control of mental-health information must remain in the patient's control and should only be released with the patient's fully informed consent. This right cannot be overridden except in the most extreme of circumstances. The right to access all possibly relevant information in the name of a full and complete defense is not *necessarily* one of them.

The crux of the question is the concept of "balancing" the individual's right to privacy with society's right to demand disclosure of the individual's private information. It appears that until recently the courts in the United States and those of Canada have been going down entirely different paths in regard to this question. In case after case, it would appear that the Canadian courts have decided that the right of a person to a full defense overrides the right of the individual to maintain the privacy of psychiatric records. This has been true in the two criminal cases of *O'Connor* (1995), *Carosella* (1997), and partially true in the civil suit of *M. (A.) v. Ryan* (1997) where a more limited disclosure was ordered. In all these cases, vigorous dissents, arguing squarely for the right to privacy, have been written by Madame Justice L'Heureux-Dubé.

In these questions, the Canadian courts customarily rely on something known as the Wigmore (1961) criterion, which has four elements:

1. The communication was made with an expectation of confidentiality.
2. Confidentiality is an essential aspect of the therapeutic relationship.
3. It is in the public interest to protect the confidential nature of the therapeutic relationship.
4. The permanent damage incurred to the relationship by disclosure must be considerably greater than the advantage to be gained by a "fair and just decision."

The General Evidentiary Rule is the usual standard for what evidence is required for a full and fair judicial process. That rule states that "[the] court and the public is entitled to every man's evidence." This rule, however, cannot apply if psychotherapy is to be possible. The Wigmore criterion attempts to resolve this apparent conflict through the use of the "balancing test." Indeed, the fourth element of the Wigmore criterion is the embodiment of the "balancing" concept.

In stark contrast to resolution by "balancing" is the position taken by the U.S. courts in a series of decisions, most notably in the *Jaffee v. Redmond* Supreme Court decision of 1996. It should be noted that the American Psychoanalytic Association filed an amicus curiae brief[1] in this case. The Court reviewed the entire history of the privacy issue and made its decision based on that survey. In reaching its decision, the Court quoted the holding of the Seventh Circuit:

> reason and experience, the touchstones for acceptance of a privilege under the 501 Federal Rules of Evidence . . . compelled recognition of a psychotherapist-patient privilege (51F.3d 1346, 1355, 1995). Reason tells us that psychotherapists and patients share a unique relationship, in which the ability to communicate freely

---

[1] An amicus curiae brief, a "friend of the court" brief, is filed about a particular court case by interested parties or organizations not otherwise directly involved with the case but that are interested in providing information and legal arguments to the justices to try to influence the ultimate decision made by them.

without the fear of public disclosure is the key to successful treatment [p. 4].

The Court noted further:

> Effective psychotherapy . . . depends upon an atmosphere of con-
> fidence and trust in which the patient is willing to make a frank
> and complete disclosure of facts, emotions, memories, and fears.
> Because of the sensitive nature of the problems for which indi-
> viduals consult psychotherapists, disclosure of confidential com-
> munications made during counseling sessions may cause
> embarrassment or disgrace. For this reason, the mere possibility
> of disclosure may impede development of the confidential rela-
> tionship necessary for successful treatment [p. 8].

Thus, the Court found that any disclosure, actual or implied,
would result in the destruction of treatment. The Court specifically
rejected the "balancing" argument:

> The psychotherapist privilege serves the public interest by facili-
> tating the provision of appropriate treatment for individuals suf-
> fering the effects of a mental or emotional problem. The mental
> health of our citizenry . . . is a public good of transcendent im-
> portance [p. 9].

The Court then stated:

> We reject the balancing component of the privilege implemented
> by that court and a small number of States. Making the promise of
> confidentiality contingent upon a trial judge's later evaluation of
> the relative importance of the patient's interest in privacy and the
> evidentiary need for disclosure would eviscerate the effective-
> ness of the privilege. . . . An uncertain privilege, or one which
> purports to be certain but results in widely varying applications
> by the courts, is little better than no privilege at all [p. 16].

Thus, the Court found no conflict between the public and the private
interests and found that both were best served by protecting the
privacy of the patient's psychotherapy.

Wigmore 4 appears to be the major locus of the problem. To my
reading, it is a remarkably weak and narrow standard. In addition to
the fact that it is the embodiment of the balancing test, another major
problem with Wigmore 4 is that, even if we grant the unlikely premise

that a judge would have the professional expertise to make such an impossible determination, the massive amount of psychotherapy data that he would need to peruse in order to do so would already have destroyed the psychotherapy process.

The Court also held that the public gain from disclosure would be limited:

> In contrast to the significant public and private interests support-ing recognition of the privilege, the likely evidentiary benefit that would result from the denial of the privilege is modest. If the privilege were rejected, confidential conversations between psy-chotherapists and their patients would surely be chilled, particu-larly when it is obvious that the circumstances that give rise to the need for treatment will probably result in litigation [p. 9].

Although this decision occurred in a civil case, the reasoning is being widely applied to a variety of cases, and it appears that the privilege is being expanded, according to the several surveys the American Psychoanalytic Association has conducted of cases in which *Jaffee v. Redmond* has been cited.

For example, in the *Swidler and Berlin v. United States* judgment of 1998, the Justice Department attempted to obtain private notes from the lawyer of Vince Foster (special counsel to President Clinton) for purposes of determining whether someone in the White House had engaged in obstruction of justice in the investigation of the ap-parent suicide of Foster. In that case, two possibly conflicting aspects of the preamble to the Constitution were discussed, one being to "secure the Blessing of Liberty" for the individual and the other being to "establish Justice." The focus was on several questions, one being whether the privilege continued even after the death of the indi-vidual. The court concluded that it did. The second was the question of what the client would have preferred had he been in a position to make this decision. The court decided that Foster would have pre-ferred to maintain the privilege. Much of the reasoning that the court employed in this case was based on *Jaffee v. Redmond.* It rejected the "balancing" component and cited the importance to the indi-vidual of maintaining his right to the privilege, and therefore his privacy. As in *Jaffee v. Redmond,* the court recognized the impor-tance to both the citizen *and* the public of preserving the privacy of communications between individuals and their counselors.

The Katz-Bierenbaum (*The People of the State of New York v.*

Robert Bierenbaum, 2000) case is a high-profile one in New York concerning a plastic surgeon with a history of violent outbursts, accused of murdering his first wife who disappeared about 15 years ago.[2] Prior to her disappearance, he was evaluated by a psychiatrist, Dr. Michael Stone. As a precondition of the evaluation and in accordance with the Tarasoff (1976) "duty to warn," Stone obtained consent from the patient to contact his wife or parents in case of imminent danger. After examining Bierenbaum, Stone felt that he *was* a threat to the wife and warned her and the parents of that fact. There was a complex negotiation as to the conditions for further treatment, which ended with the patient refusing treatment. Two years later, the wife disappeared, never to be seen again, presumably dead.

When Bierenbaum was charged with the murder, Stone stated publicly that he would like to testify in the murder trial and strongly implied in media interviews that he had reason, based on his examination of the patient, to think that Bierenbaum was in fact guilty, or at least capable of murdering his wife.

Bierenbaum's lawyers contended that Stone's testimony was inadmissible because it was privileged and the patient had not given consent. The prosecution claimed that the privilege had been waived when Bierenbaum consented to let Stone warn his wife and parents. Of course, under Tarasoff, Stone would have been obligated in any event to have warned the wife and parents, or to have found another way of fulfilling the duty to protect, if he considered them to be in potential danger. The point at issue was whether the issuing of a Tarasoff warning caused the privilege to be waived.

Although this was a state court and *Jaffee v. Redmond* holds only in federal courts, the Confidentiality Committee of the American Psychoanalytic Association felt that the confidentiality of the patient-therapist communication was under attack. It was decided to file an amicus brief to advance the *Jaffee v. Redmond* argument as a guiding principle in this case. This brief was filed and appears to have influenced the outcome. The presiding judge ruled that the reasoning in *Jaffee v. Redmond* was compelling and applied it to the patient's communication with Stone. The judge concluded that the privilege remained intact and was not waived by the Tarasoff warning. She

---

[2] Thanks to Howard Levine (chair of the Joint Committee on Confidentiality of the American Psychoanalytic Association) and Paul Mosher for bringing the case to the attention of the committee. I am also indebted to Dr. Levine for this description of the Bierenbaum case.

refused to allow Stone to give testimony based on his evaluation of the patient, because he did not have the patient's consent to do so.

This case and the following one present the most extreme test of the psychotherapist-patient "privilege" and the issue of "balancing." There are two competing public interests: the essential need for privacy for successful psychotherapy, as outlined in *Jaffee v. Redmond*, and the duty to protect a potential victim, as outlined in the Tarasoff case. In the Bierenbaum case and the following one, the court took very clearly into account on one hand the nature of the public good at issue and the broad need for individual privacy, and on the other hand the extreme and narrow duty to warn in urgent situations. In each case, the court rejected the idea that the issuing of a Tarasoff warning waived the privilege and specifically refused the idea of a "balancing" test.

In a federal case in the Sixth Circuit, *United States v. Hayes*, which was argued on April 26, 2001, the court cited the *Jaffee v. Redmond* rejection of the "balancing component":

> In this appeal, we are required to decide whether there is a "dangerous-patient" exception to the federal psychotherapist/patient testimonial privilege under the federal rules of evidence 501 (*Jaffee v. Redmond*). We hold there is not.

The court argued the following:

> Recognition of a "dangerous-patient" exception surely would have a deleterious effect upon the "atmosphere of confidence and trust" in the psychotherapist-patient relationship . . . Thus, if our nation's mental health is indeed as valuable as the Supreme Court has indicated, and we think it is, the chilling effect that would result from the recognition of a "dangerous patient" exception, and its logical consequence, is the first reason to reject it. Second, we think that allowing a psychotherapist to testify against his or her patient in a criminal prosecution about statements made to the therapist by the patient for the purposes of treatment, arguably "serves a public end," but it is an end that does not justify the means. Thus we conclude that the proposed "dangerous patient" exception is unnecessary to allow a psychotherapist to comply with his or her professional responsibility and would seriously disserve the "public end" of improving the mental health of our nation's citizens. . . . To conclude, "reason and experience," teach us that a "dangerous-patient" exception which would allow a

psychotherapist to testify against a patient in criminal proceedings should not become part of the federal common law.

We hold, therefore, that the federal psychotherapist-patient privilege does not impede a psychotherapist's compliance with his professional and ethical duty to protect innocent third parties, a duty which may require, among other things, disclosure to third parties or testimony at involuntary hospital proceedings. Conversely, compliance with the professional duty to protect does not imply a duty to testify against a patient in criminal proceedings or in civil proceedings, other than directly related to the patient's involuntary hospitalization, and such testimony is privileged and inadmissible if the patient properly asserts the psychotherapist-patient privilege [IV, para. 9].

In other words, the court held that both public interests of protecting a particular individual and of maintaining the privacy of another were not mutually exclusive, *could not be balanced, and did not constitute an exception to the privilege.*

The court continued:

It is one thing to inform a patient of the "duty to protect"; it is quite another to advise a patient that his "trusted" confidante may one day assist in procuring his conviction and incarceration. None of Hayes' psychotherapists ever informed him of the possibility that they might testify against him, and therefore, Hayes cannot be said to have "knowingly" or "voluntarily" waived his right to assert the psychotherapist-patient privilege here. We conclude therefore that the government's constructive waiver argument is meritless [p. 10].

The "constructive waiver" position of the government argued that the Tarasoff warning, in effect, waives the psychotherapist-patient privilege.

In conclusion, the "balancing" argument is a dangerous and slippery slope. The patient's rights and the privacy of his psychotherapy and psychoanalytic records must be as complete as possible. Once started on the road of the "public good" becoming a justification for state-sanctioned breaching of privacy, there is no end. For example, in both Canada and the United States, there is a crisis of health-care delivery caused by the rising costs of health care. There is no question that the "public good" might be served and health-care costs reduced by making certain medical tests mandatory. For example, colonoscopy could be mandated for patients above a certain age. For the state to have the right to impose medical procedures, for the pubic good, without patient consent, is little different in principle than to argue that for the public good the state should have a right to obtain private psychotherapy information without patient consent. Surely, the forceful invasion of a person's most private thoughts is a more serious violation of privacy than even an invasion of the body without consent.

In the United States, "managed care" has created private for-profit corporate medicine. Profit depends on controlling and reducing the amount of care given. Managed care companies demand more and more information for the purpose of determining "medical necessity," the euphemism for health care rationing. There is no medical or psychiatric information that is so private that it is not desired and sought after by various corporate and marketing interests in the United States.

Another example—who could argue with the idea that the "public good" is served by medical research? Therefore, should not all medical and psychiatric information be made available in fully identifiable form for such research? This is no hypothetical argument. We have had many legislative bills introduced for the mandatory wholesale collecting of all medical data on every encounter between a healthcare professional and a patient in the United States. This would include a specific code number to be assigned to each citizen, a number that we have come to refer to as "the national tattoo."

We are just at the beginning of these debates. Think, for example, of what we face with the question of genetic information. The citizenry of Iceland has decided to turn genetic information on each of their citizens over to the government in order to aid in the carrying out of genetically based research. Consider, for the sake of argument, that this is in the public good. Is the court now going to have access to this information based on the "balancing" argument? Should the government have access to this information based on "public good"? Should the police be able to scan these data banks to identify DNA residues? Such is the magnitude of the dilemmas facing us in the next few years.

I would like to say a word about the responsibility of our professional organizations in these public policy matters. In the American Psychoanalytic Association, we have come to feel strongly that our professional organizations must take the lead in protecting our patients, our profession, and even ourselves as patients. We have developed a vigorous and effective effort in three arenas. The first has been to devise clear "standards of practice." The practice bulletin "Charting Psychoanalysis" (1994) issued by our Committee on Peer Review, holds that any accountability of psychoanalytic documentation, be it to a third party or to the patient, will "distort the process of evenly hovering attention that characterizes classical psychoanalytic technique." To be specific, we embrace the standard of no psychoanalytic notes, and therefore no record of psychoanalytic communications that could be accessed by third parties of any description. This guideline aims at promoting the idea of a "safe haven" for analytic clinical material.

The second arena has been that of political representation. The APsaA has become a serious presence on Capitol Hill and has played a major role in helping to halt dangerous legislation that would have required the disclosure of psychiatric records. We have worked hard to see that the principles of *Jaffee v. Redmond* are included in new legislation and have succeeded in having those principles incorporated into privacy regulations being promulgated by the Department of Health and Human Services, largely through the efforts of John Fanning (of the Health and Human Services Office of Assistant Secretary for Planning and Evaluation). Efforts by the APsaA have ensured special protections in the regulations for "Psychotherapy Notes" (United States Department of Health and Human Services, 2000). *Jaffee v. Redmond* is featured in the Surgeon General's report (United States Department of Health and Human Services, 1999) on mental health. We have also been instrumental in making privacy a major focus in the recent 2000 presidential campaign in the United States.

The third arena has been participation in key and selected legal cases. APsaA has filed amicus briefs in the *Jaffee v. Redmond* case and in the Bierenbaum case, and both have played an important role in a successful outcome. We have several other cases under consideration, including one that challenges the right of managed care companies to access patient records without consent in order to "manage" the therapist (*Daniel S. Shrager v. Magellan Behavioral Health*, 2001). We consider the political and legal arena our one-two punch, each part of which reinforces the other.

We conclude that our professional associations must develop standards of ethics for maintaining the privacy of records. In this era of third party and government intrusion, the individual cannot stand alone, though many courageous practitioners have, at great personal cost. Therapists who work for managed care companies are under constant pressure to divulge patient information without consent.

Corporate policy is often set up specifically to routinely violate patient privacy. This is done under the guise of "quality control" and "medical necessity." In fact, these are cost control measures designed to reduce patient access and utilization of mental health services. This is a particular problem in the so-called "carve-out," where mental health is isolated from the rest of health care and where discriminatory practices abound.

A therapist in such a system is forced into the position of becoming a "double agent." No longer can his sole concern be the welfare of his patient. He is pressured to become an agent of the company, a guardian of corporate profit and of his own job. If, as we believe, confidentiality is the cornerstone of quality mental health care, our psychoanalytic associations must ensure that our standards of the ethics of privacy are recognized by government and insurers alike.

Some have argued that such a code of ethics should include a requirement for members to obey all laws. To paraphrase Will Rogers, law and ethics are two different things. They might both reflect "reason and experience," but ethical standards are developed by members of a profession based on specialized knowledge of what is desirable or necessary in the practice of that profession. Laws might incorporate ethical standards, but they are enacted by elected representatives who generally do not have the specialized knowledge and experience of members of the profession. Not only would it be terrible policy to have a blanket requirement to obey all laws, but also it would abdicate the standard-setting responsibility of a profession to the most unenlightened legislative majority. If, however, certain laws also contain standards that the profession feels are important, they can adopt them as specific ethical standards.

The relationship between a patient and a therapist is in the nature of an unwritten pact. The patient agrees to make certain disclosures, which can be used in treatment, on the condition that those disclosures will not be revealed elsewhere without consent. In the absence of that pact, the disclosures would never be made.

Therapists should not be placed in the position where they have to inform their patients that their communications might be disclosed. Rather, they should be confirming the patients' wishes and expectations that communications will not be disclosed without their consent. If clinical information is to be disclosed against the patients' will, it would be little different than extracting damaging and embarrassing information with the enforced use of sodium pentothal.

In conclusion, I feel strongly that psychoanalytic organizations must take the leadership in this fight to protect the rights of our patients as well as to safeguard our ability to deliver high-quality private psychoanalytic and psychotherapeutic care. I believe that at its core psychoanalysis is about human freedom and the uniqueness of each individual. The mission of psychoanalysis should be to embrace and preserve the essential "humaneness" of individuals and society. Within the next few years, a course will be set that will determine how our society will grapple with these critical bioethical issues. Psychoanalysts and psychoanalytic organizations should not only participate in these debates but should play a leading role.

References

American Psychoanalytic Association (1994), *Charting Psychoanalysis.* Practice Bulletin #2.
———— (1997), *The Right to Medical Privacy: An Indispensable Element of Quality Health Care.*
———— (2000), *Comments of the American Psychoanalytic Association on Standards of Individually Identifiable Health Information.*
Daniel S. Shrager v. Magellan Behavioral Health, No.GD-015809, C.P. Alleghany County Court (2001).
Jaffee v. Redmond, 518 U.S. 1 (1996).
Jaffee v. Redmond, Amicus Curiae Brief, filed by the American Psychoanalytic Association, Division 39 of Psychoanalysis of the American Psychological Association, The National Membership Committee on Psychoanalysis in Clinical Social Work, The American Academy of Psychoanalysis (1996).
Kyllo v. United States, 533 U.S. (2001).
Miranda v. Arizona, 384 U.S. 436 (1966).
M. (A.) v. Ryan, 1 SCR (1997).
R. v. Carosella, SCR 80 (1997).
R. v. O'Connor, 4 SCR (1995).
Swidler & Berlin v. United States, 524 U.S. 399 (1998).
Tarasoff v. Regents of the University of California, 551 P.2d 334. California (1976).
The People of the State of New York v. Robert Bierenbaum, No. 8295/99, NY Superior Court, order preceding testimony (2000).
United States Department of Health and Human Services. (2000), *Standards for Privacy of Individually Identifiable Health Information: Final Rule*, Federal Register 65:82461.
United States Department of Health and Human Services, NIMH. (1999), *Report of the Surgeon General.*
United States v. Hayes, 227 F.3d 578, sixth circuit (2001).
Whalen v. Roe, 429 U.S. 589 (1977).
Wigmore, J. H. (1961), *Evidence in Trials at Common Law, Vol. 8*, revised by J. T. McNaughton. Boston: Little, Brown.

Introduction to CHAPTER 19

❦

Legal Boundaries on Conceptions of Privacy: Seeking Therapeutic Accord

Daniel Shuman raises the important issue of therapeutic agendas in the law. Tort law has an implicit therapeutic agenda, for example, as do, more explicitly, child-custody laws; but it is not always possible for the law to pursue therapeutic goals to the full, partly because these may conflict with deeply entrenched normative values basic to the law or because there is more than one legitimate therapeutic interest at play. With these considerations in mind, Shuman examines three different forms that psychotherapist-patient privilege might take in common law, analyzing their advantages and disadvantages: privilege with no exceptions; privilege with categorical exceptions, such as child abuse; and the balancing model, which leaves the onus on the courts to adjudicate between competing therapeutic and legal interests. Each approach differs significantly with respect to decisions about setting the boundaries between private and public information, who will make them, their predictability, and their likely consistency. Shuman concludes with some reflections on the kinds of arguments used in favor of psychotherapy privilege and the need for more empirical evidence to support these arguments.

CHAPTER 19

Legal Boundaries
on Conceptions of Privacy:
Seeking Therapeutic Accord

Daniel W. Shuman

At first blush, it may seem odd or unwise to consider the affinity between law and therapeutic practice. Charters and constitutions speak to considerations of fairness, justice, and due process. The goal of antitrust laws, for example, exemplified by the recent U.S. governmental effort to break up Microsoft, appears unrelated to what mental-health professionals regard as therapeutic considerations (*United States v. Microsoft Corp.*, 2000). The debate about breaking up Microsoft addresses the fairness of utilizing market power and its economic, not therapeutic, consequences for mental or physical health. In other instances, however, although not explicit, the law advances therapeutic goals. Consider, for example, tort law, a privately initiated system of law for seeking monetary damages from intentional and negligent wrongdoers. Although tort law does not explicitly invoke therapeutic considerations, its goals of deterrence and compensation, which seek to reduce the level of accidental injury and restore the injured through tort-law judgments, embrace a therapeutic agenda (Shuman, 1993a).

Tort judgments may have an effect on manufacturers' and service providers' willingness to make investments in safety (Shuman, 1993b) and victims' recovery from their injuries, in terms of both the ability of victims to purchase restorative goods and services as well as the impact on them of the process of assessing responsibility for harm (Shuman, 1994). Indeed, when therapeutic considerations are defined broadly, one might even reframe the Microsoft antitrust litigation as addressing the health of the market.

Other bodies of law have an explicit therapeutic agenda more recognizable to therapists. Child-custody and visitation law, for example, guided by the "best-interest-of-the-child" standard, explicitly embraces a therapeutic agenda (Goldstein, Freud, and Solnit, 1973, 1979). Invoking therapeutic rather than legalistic language that has precipitated a generation of controversy, the best-interest-of-the-child standard exalts the role of mental-health professionals in legal decision-making and transforms both the substantive law as well as the process of custody and visitation determinations (Champagne et al., 2001).

Ideally, one might assume, at least where the law has adopted a therapeutic agenda, it should maximize its therapeutic potential and minimize its antitherapeutic impact, advancing congruent legal and therapeutic agendas (Wexler, 1990; Wexler and Winick, 1991, 1996). However desirable, that will not always be possible for a multitude of reasons (Slobogin, 1995). Irreconcilable conflicts may exist between a therapeutic agenda and normative constitutional values. For example, although the best interest of a child might be served by removing the child from his or her biological parents and, absent a serious risk to the health or welfare of the child, placing the child with a couple who possesses superior parenting skills, the value our society places on the biological parent-child relationship rejects involuntary removal of a child merely because that child might be raised "better" by someone else.

Consider the following (*Wisconsin v. Yoder*, 1973):

> The history and culture of Western civilization reflect a strong tradition of parental concern for the nurture and upbringing of their children. This primary role of the parents in the upbringing of their children is now established beyond debate as an enduring American tradition [p. 232].

Normative constitutional values limit the application of the therapeutically driven best-interest-of-the-child standard in termination of parental rights to discrete circumstances such as abuse or neglect. These constitutional limitations on the power of the state to dictate parent-child relations are one reflection of a consensus in most western democracies that a therapeutic agenda, though in many contexts regarded as significant, should not be permitted to trump all other interests.

Even when therapeutic considerations appear to be controlling, however, a conflict may exist between competing therapeutic considerations. Consider, for example, a contested child-custody determination involving two young children in which one child is expected to fare better with the mother, the other with the father, and both children are expected to fare better if they remain together. Prioritizing therapeutic considerations does not necessarily determine the outcome of a legal proceeding that has adopted a therapeutic agenda. In some circumstances, advancing one set of therapeutic interests irreconcilably conflicts with another set of therapeutic interests, requiring a decision that will subordinate one set of therapeutic interests.

Recognition of a psychotherapist-patient privilege, which cloaks confidential communications between patient and therapist with protection from judicially compelled disclosure, is an instance in which the law has adopted a therapeutic agenda seeking to encourage (or to avoid discouraging) therapist-patient communications. Relational privileges do not advance the concerns of courts with accurate fact-finding by encouraging the receipt of all potential sources of relevant evidence; rather they advance a different set of interests. As the Supreme Court has summarized its jurisprudence:

> For more than three centuries it has now been recognized as a fundamental maxim that the public . . . has a right to every man's evidence. When we come to examine the various claims of exemption, we start with the primary assumption that there is a general duty to give what testimony one is capable of giving, and that any exemptions which may exist are distinctly exceptional, being so many derogations from a positive general rule [p. 332].

Although both utilitarian (consequentialist) and deontological (ethics of duty) arguments have been advanced in support of psychotherapist–patient privileges, common-law jurisdictions (e.g., England, United States, Ontario) have tended to rely on utilitarian considerations in choosing whether to recognize a privilege,[1] in contrast with civil law

---

[1] *Jaffee v. Redmond* (1996) states the following:

> Like the spousal and attorney-client privileges, the psychotherapist-patient privilege is "rooted in the imperative need for confidence and trust" (*Trammel*, 445 U.S. at 51). Treatment by a physician for physical ailments can often proceed successfully on the basis of a physical examination, objective information supplied by the patient, and the results of diagnostic tests. Effective psychotherapy, by contrast, depends upon an atmosphere of confidence and trust in which the patient is willing to make a frank and complete disclosure of facts, emotions, memories,

jurisdictions (e.g., France, Quebec) that have tended to rely on deontological considerations. Relying on the utilitarian justification for privilege, but without demanding rigorous scientific proof of its underlying assumptions, privileges have been recognized for psychotherapist-patient communications in many common-law jurisdictions, although the source of the common law, England, continues to refuse to do so. The rationale for the recognition of a psychotherapist-patient privilege in common-law courts is that the privilege is thought to decrease delay in seeking help, increase patient disclosure and the effectiveness of therapy, avoid premature termination of therapy, and prevent harm to patients by therapists' testimony (Shuman and Weiner, 1987). Yet, the decision to recognize a privilege is the beginning, not the end, of the attempt to accommodate legal and therapeutic considerations concerning therapist–patient communications.

The decision to privilege therapist-patient communications does not resolve when the privilege should apply. Competing legal and therapeutic claims to the information cloaked by the privilege remain. Privilege legitimizes the therapeutic claim; but it does not necessarily resolve the tension between legal and therapeutic claims in every case, let alone between competing therapeutic claims. Three models may be used to address this tension.

The first model, which has not been embraced by courts or legislatures (*M. [A.] v. Ryan*, 1997), is to accord an absolute protection to privileged communications that permits no exceptions. Always protecting communications cloaked by a psychotherapist-patient privilege requires no mechanism to balance competing claims for the information it cloaks. Thus, this model is easy to apply, and its results

---

and fears. Because of the sensitive nature of the problems for which individuals consult psychotherapists, disclosure of confidential communications made during counseling sessions may cause embarrassment or disgrace. For this reason, the mere possibility of disclosure may impede development of the confidential relationship necessary for successful treatment. As the Judicial Conference Advisory Committee observed in 1972 when it recommended that Congress recognize a psychotherapist privilege as part of the Proposed Federal Rules of Evidence, a psychiatrist's ability to help her patients "is completely dependent upon [the patients'] willingness and ability to talk freely. This makes it difficult if not impossible for [a psychiatrist] to function without being able to assure . . . patients of confidentiality and, indeed, privileged communication. Where there may be exceptions to this general rule . . . there is wide agreement that confidentiality is a sine qua non for successful psychiatric treatment" [pp. 15–17].

are easy to predict. Nonetheless, the prospect of an inviolate privilege claim that invariably trumps all competing public and private claims for access to that information has not produced a groundswell of support for an absolute psychotherapist-patient (or lawyer-client) privilege. Whether to advance national security, confront adverse witnesses, prevent child or elder abuse, defend a malpractice or professional disciplinary action, or collect an unpaid fee, all jurisdictions that recognize a psychotherapist-patient privilege also recognize some (although not always the same) circumstances under which the privilege should give way, just as the lawyer-client privilege is not absolute and gives way when the relationship is used to commit a crime or fraud, when a need arises to substantiate or defend a breach of duty arising out of the relationship, or in proceedings between joint clients.

It is not surprising that neither the courts nor legislatures have regarded the psychotherapist-patient privilege as absolute considering the legal, therapeutic, and moral premise for absolute privilege. The fourth-century B.C. Hippocratic oath is often touted as an unquestioned source of ancient wisdom about the importance of medical confidentiality to support recognition of a privilege. Consider the following quote (Edelstein, 1967): "What I may see or hear in the course of treatment or even outside of the treatment in regard to the life of men, which on no account one must spread abroad, I will keep to myself, holding such things shameful to be spoken about."

Close inspection reveals that the oath was never intended to be absolute. It only binds the physician to keep confidential that "which on no account one must spread abroad." By its terms, the oath recognizes that some information learned "in the course of treatment or even outside in regard to the life of men" may be "spread abroad," while some may not.

The context in which this text came about reinforces this conclusion. Medicine in the fourth century B.C. was practiced by physicians who treated their patients in the company of family, friends, and neighbors. The communal setting in which medicine was practiced at the time of the oath's origin belies the claim that physician-patient communications were intended to be accorded an absolute protection against revelation to others and supports the interpretation that the oath was in keeping with the Pythagorean tradition that sought to guard its trade secrets (Shuman and Weiner, 1987). The oath's author(s) made no claim for absolute confidentiality, as some current-day advocates of an absolute privilege maintain.

The absolutist approach to a psychotherapist-patient privilege is also devoid of a firm moral foundation. The moral foundation necessary for a claim of confidentiality to prevail over competing claims by the state for that same information requires good evidence that the claimant will make better, or at least as good use of the information as the state. In the case of disclosures about child abuse, those who claim that the state should not recognize a duty to disclose evidence of abuse learned in therapy have presented no sound research that psychotherapy is an effective treatment for child abuse. Instead, they ask us to assume that, whatever its efficacy, it must be preferable to the problems engendered by compelled disclosures (Bollas and Sundelson, 1995). Declining to take immediate action to protect a child at risk of imminent harm in favor of maintaining the confidentiality of that information is a cost that states have regarded as morally unacceptable, given the alternative held out by psychotherapists. Failing the legal, therapeutic, and moral case for an absolute privilege requires a mechanism to determine how competing claims for this information should be addressed.

The second model of resolving the tension between legal and therapeutic claims utilizes categorical exceptions determined in advance of the onset of therapy or litigation to address the competing claims. These exceptions reflect the judgment of the privilege's drafters regarding the accommodation of competing demands for information cloaked by the privilege. For example, the privilege may explicitly note that an exception will apply in cases of child abuse, based on the assumption that such communications are not worthy of protection or that the protection of children through effective prosecution, for which this information is regarded as necessary, outweighs the potential of the privilege to encourage effective therapy for abusers. Another common categorical exception is the patient-litigant exception, which regards it as unfair for a person who has instituted a claim to keep confidential relevant information about that claim in the ensuing litigation. Many other categorical exceptions exist in different jurisdictions. Not all jurisdictions recognize the same exceptions, and these differences reflect different judgments about the appropriate balance between legal and therapeutic demands. By determining the existence of these categorical exceptions in advance of the inception of therapy or litigation, this model purports to provide guidance to patients about the disclosures that they may hope to keep confidential (e.g., not those acknowledging abuse) and the conduct that may cause them to lose their claim to confidentiality (e.g., suing their therapist for malpractice). It also seeks to advance the principle of informed consent by permitting the patient to identify circumstances that will give rise to a risk of disclosure.

The third model of resolving the tension between legal and therapeutic claims requires courts to balance the importance of confidentiality and the importance of disclosing the information it cloaks on a case-by-case basis, as the issue arises (S.C. 1997, c. 30). Thus, in each case in which a privilege claim is made, the trial judge is called upon to assess the costs and benefits of sustaining the privilege. The balancing model purports to permit a more precise accommodation of the competing therapeutic and normative legal values presented in a specific case. Of course, if patients are sensitive to the risks of judicially compelled disclosure, the use of the balancing model does not permit them to make accurate predictions of the outcome of a prospective claim of privilege when choosing to enter therapy or when making disclosures in therapy.

The implications of the differences in these models for boundary-setting between public and private information, in seeking to harmonize judicial and psychoanalytic concepts of privacy, are significant in several regards. The models differ with regard to who will make the decision about boundaries between public and private information and the circumstances under which these decisions will be made. They also differ with regard to their precision in accommodating legal and therapeutic interests. And, they differ with regard to the consistency and predictability of decisions about boundaries between public and private information.

With regard to who will determine the boundaries between public and private and the circumstances in which that decision is made, the balancing model places the accommodation of competing interests in the hands of a trial judge whose discretion is unlikely to be disturbed on appeal and whose decision is not subject to democratic input. There is no popular vote on the boundaries between public and private information set by a judge in a particular case, and, typically, only the parties, not members of the public, are granted standing to raise or seek review of the issue. The categorical model places the decision about the categories that will be protected or excepted from the privilege's protection either in the hands of the legislature, democratically elected and officiated, or the high court, utilizing its rule making capacity, subject to public review and comment.

These models also differ as to their precision in accommodating competing interests. The categorical exception model assumes that it is possible to make an appropriate accommodation between competing interests in the abstract. For example, recognition of a categorical exception to the privilege for child abuse assumes that the privilege's application should always be excepted in this instance without regard to the likelihood that a particular therapy may reduce the risk of abuse for a particular patient or that alternative sources of equivalent evidence exist in a particular case that do not jeopardize the confidentiality of therapist-patient communications. The balancing decision permits the court to consider the necessity to compel disclosure of the specific information sought and its therapeutic costs against the evidentiary background of a particular case.

In addition, these models also differ as to their consistency and predictability. If privilege is important because patients do consider the state of the law before entering therapy or disclosing specific information (a matter about which some dispute exists), categorical exceptions will provide greater consistency and predictability about the risk of compelled disclosure than a balancing determination made on a case-by-case basis. The balancing approach requires a patient to predict not only the context in which an attempt to compel disclosure might arise but also what other evidence may be presented in the case, as well as which judge will be assigned the case and that judge's history of balancing decisions, to predict whether a particular confidential communication in therapy will be protected from compelled disclosure.

Choosing between these models, however, entails more than choosing among the advantages and disadvantages noted here. It also entails choosing between differing theoretical underpinning, for the privilege. The categorical approach, providing greater predictability and consistency, is more consistent with the utilitarian or consequentialist justifications for privilege, typically utilized in common-law jurisdictions, which assume that patients consider likely legal outcomes before making therapeutic choices. The balancing approach, providing less predictability and consistency but greater precision in accommodating competing interests, is more consistent with the deontological or ethics of duty justification for privilege typically utilized in civil-law jurisdictions. But is the public aware of the state of privilege law? Does it make choices about psychotherapy relying on the law of privilege? Have changes in the law of privilege resulted in changes in willingness to seek psychotherapy or in the conduct of therapy? There is good reason to question the role that privilege law plays in therapeutic decisions for most patients (Shuman and Weiner, 1987). In the absence of compelling empirical proof of these assumptions about the importance of privilege law in decisions about therapy, it is conceptually troubling to rely on a utilitarian rationale for a psychotherapist-patient privilege. This then requires that the argument for privilege rests on deontological claims that governmental intrusion into this private sphere is intrinsically wrong.

Shifting the rationale for the privilege from utilitarian to deontological grounds has important implications. Exalting the role of privacy in society, not because it has specific consequences but because of the value we place on the lines we draw between public and private, raises the prospect of a broader scope of protections not limited to communications between specific professionals and their clients or patients. Why should we regard governmental intrusion on parent-child relationships, absent claims of abuse or neglect, as any less pernicious than intrusion on psychotherapist-patient relationships? What of governmental intrusion on confidential communications between siblings or close friends? The concern that these more expansive demands for privilege may cause other privilege claims to collapse under their weight is not illusory. Consider the arguments advanced by Justice Scalia of the United States Supreme Court in his dissent in *Jaffee v. Redmond*, opposing the recognition of a psychotherapist-patient privilege:

> When is it, one must wonder, that *the psychotherapist* came to play such an indispensable role in the maintenance of the citizenry's mental health? For most of history, men and women have worked out their difficulties by talking to, inter alios, parents, siblings, best friends, and bartenders—none of whom was awarded a privilege against testifying in court. Ask the average citizen: would your mental health be more significantly impaired by preventing you from seeing a psychotherapist, or by preventing you from getting advice from your mom? I have little doubt what the answer would be. Yet there is no mother-child privilege [p. 22].

The more we expand the contexts in which our concerns with privacy translate into the recognition of a limitation on the ability of the courts to compel disclosure of relevant evidence, the less likely courts will be to accept limitations on access to this information to serve the court's business of correctly resolving disputed claims. Placed in perspective, the choice must be acknowledged to be normative, calling for a societal judgment—in the legislative, judicial, and executive branches of our governments—about the contours between public and private, guided, but not ultimately determined, by legal and therapeutic values.

References

Bollas, C. & Sundelson, D. (1995), *The New Informants.* Northvale, NJ: Aronson.

Champagne. A., Easterling, D., Shuman, D. W., Tomkins, A. & Whitaker, E. (2001), Are court-appointed experts the solution to the problems of expert testimony? A pilot study. *Judicature,* 84:178–183.

Edelstein, L. (1967), *Ancient Medicine.* Baltimore, MD: Johns Hopkins University Press.

Goldstein, J., Freud, A. & Solnit, A. (1973), *Beyond the Best Interests of the Child.* New York: Free Press.

———— ———— & ———— (1979), *Before the Best Interests of the Child.* New York: Free Press.

Jaffee v. Redmond, 518 U.S. 1 (1996).

S.C. 1997, c. 30.

M.(A.) v. Ryan, 143 DLR (4th) 1 SCC (1997).

Shuman, D. W. (1993a), Making the world a better place through tort law? Through the therapeutic looking glass. *NY Law Sch. J. Hum., Rts.,* X:739–758

———— (1993b), The psychology of deterrence in tort law. *Kansas Law Rev.,* 42:115–168.

———— (1994), The psychology of compensation in tort law. *Kansas Law Rev.,* 43:39–76.

———— & Weiner, M. F. (1987), *The Psychotherapist-Patient Privilege.* Springfield, IL: Thomas.

Slobogin, C. (1995), Therapeutic jurisprudence: Five dilemmas to ponder. *Psychol., Public Policy, & Law,* 1:193–219.

United States v. Bryan, 339 U.S. 323 (1950).

United States v. Microsoft Corp., 87 F. Supp. 2d 30 (DDC 2000), rev'd in part 2001 U.S. App. LEXIS 14324.

Wexler, D. (1990), *Therapeutic Justice.* Durham, NC: Carolina Academic Press.

———— & Winick, B. (1991), *Essays in Therapeutic Jurisprudence.* Durham, NC: Carolina Academic Press.

———— & ————, eds. (1996), *Law in a Therapeutic Key.* Durham, NC: Carolina Academic Press.

Wisconsin v. Yoder, 406 U.S. 205 (1972).

Introduction to CHAPTER 20

❀

The Right to Privacy:
A Comment on the Production of Complainants' Personal Records in Sexual-Assault Cases

The Honorable Madame Justice Claire L'Heureux-Dubé was appointed to the Supreme Court of Canada in 1987 after serving for 14 years as a trial and appellate-court judge. She was the second woman appointed to the Court and was, at her retirement in 2002, the Court's longest-serving justice. This chapter draws out the relationship between the notions of privacy, confidentiality, and equality; it examines this nexus in the particular context of issues surrounding the production, in sexual-assault cases, of complainants' personal records that are held by third parties. It follows three moments in the history of these issues in Canada and argues that this history provides vital lessons about the meaning and significance of equality rights. The first moment in this history is Justice L'Heureux-Dubé's dissent in *R. v. O'Connor*, the second is the legislative affirmation of those reasons in Bill C-46. The third is the majority confirmation of her position in *R. v. Mills*. Justice Berman of the United States Supreme Court spoke of dissents in which authors speak as "prophets of honor." The judicial and legislative history outlined in this chapter show that Justice L'Heureux-Dubé's dissent was indeed honorable and prophetic.

CHAPTER 20

⁂

The Right to Privacy: A Comment on the Production of Complainants' Personal Records in Sexual-Assault Cases

Claire L'Heureux-Dubé

*T*he legal, mental-health, and counseling professions share a concern for the privacy interest of patients in therapeutic relationships. However, law differs from the other professions in the way it conceptualizes the interest and in the scope and nature of other concerns that it considers. Legal professionals often frame the privacy interest in terms of the rights of the patient, and in the litigation context where the patient is a complainant or witness, in light of the rights of the accused. The legal analysis of the privacy interest also raises systemic issues, including those pertaining to the integrity of the trial process and the harms that result from society's inaccurate perceptions of vulnerable classes of patients. In this chapter, the discussion of patients' interest in privacy is limited to a particular set of legal issues, namely those surrounding the production, in sexual-assault cases, of complainants' personal records that are held by third parties.[1]

---

[1] The *Oxford Dictionary of Law* defines the production of documents as: "The act of a party in making available documents in his possession, custody, or power either for inspection by the other party or for use as evidence at trial in accordance with a notice to produce" (*Oxford Dictionary of Law*, 2002).

    Law of Evidence in Canada raises the particular issues of concern to this chapter: "When a party in a criminal proceeding serves a subpoena *duces tecum* to obtain documents in the custody of a third party, constitutional concerns also arise in relation to the production of confidential documents" (Sopinka, 1999).

I will set out how Canadian judicial and legislative actors have sought to protect a patient's dignity as well as to safeguard the defendant's right to a fair trial. Perhaps most important, I will show that pursuing the first of these objectives need not result in the devaluation of the second. In criminal trials, as elsewhere, dignity and fairness are not antithetical values.

Privacy, Confidentiality, and Equality

To understand the right to privacy in Canadian law as it relates to the production of patients' communications with their physicians, the general nature of the right as well as developments in Canadian equality jurisprudence require examination. Although these two discussions might seem unrelated, I will show that in the context of sexual assault they are inextricably linked.

The Two Faces of Privacy

Canadian jurisprudence has defined two aspects of the right to privacy, both of which are relevant to the present discussion.[2] The first speaks to the right to control information over which one has a reasonable expectation of privacy. In *R. v. Dyment* (1988), Justice La Forest underlined the importance of this aspect of the right to privacy in modern society (pp. 429–30). Justice Sopinka in *R. v. Plant* (1993) set out the contextual factors which should guide the analysis of the "biographical core of information which individuals in a free and democratic society would wish to maintain and control" (p. 293).[3]

---

[2] McNairn and Scott (2001) have commented on this judicial bifurcation of the right to privacy. For a general overview of different philosophical understandings of the right to privacy, see Schafer (1980).

[3] This element of the right to privacy finds its constitutional expression in Section 8, which states: "Everyone has a right to be secure against unreasonable search and seizure." The contextual factors set out by Justice Sopinka (*R. v. Plant*, 1993) include:

> The nature of the information itself, the nature of the relationship between the party releasing the information and the party claiming its confidentiality, the place where the information was obtained, the manner in which it was obtained and the seriousness of the crime being investigated to allow for a balancing of societal interests in protecting individual dignity, integrity, and autonomy with effective law enforcement [p. 293].

Under the second aspect, the right to privacy is subsumed within the rights to liberty and security of the person.[4] Justice Wilson expressed the privacy component of the right to liberty in *R. v. Morgentaler* (1988) when she held that Section 7 of the *Canadian Charter of Rights and Freedoms* "guarantees to every individual a degree of personal autonomy over important decisions affecting their lives." The Court in *Rodriguez v. British Columbia (Attorney General)* (1993) held that security of the person includes "protecting the dignity and privacy of individuals with respect to decisions concerning their own bodies." Finally, in *(M.)A. v. Ryan* (1997), I stated unequivocally that "the rights to liberty and security of the person as enshrined in Section 7 of the *Charter* include a right to privacy."

Confidentiality and Privacy: Trusting Relationships

In addition to the right to privacy, the present discussion raises related questions of confidentiality.[5] In the medical context, a breach of confidentiality occurs when a physician discloses to a third party any nonpublic information that a patient has revealed in the course of their professional relationship (McNairn and Scott, 2001). A breach of confidence harms the relationship, as the bonds of trust between the parties are eroded. As a further consequence, the more vulnerable party may also suffer a violation of her right to privacy.[6]

Court orders to produce confidential documents held by mental-health and counseling professionals, in sexual-assault cases, have the potential to threaten both aspects of the right to privacy and to damage the trust built up in confidential relationships. However, because production may enable the accused to mount a full answer and defense and protect his right to a fair trial, a difficult question arises: how can the interests of complainants and the rights of the

---

[4] Section 7 of the *Charter* enunciates these rights; it states: "Everyone has a right to life, liberty, and security of the person and the right not to be deprived thereof except in accordance with the principles of fundamental justice" (*Canadian Charter of Rights and Freedoms,* 1982).

[5] For an analysis of the relationship between confidentiality and privacy, see Dawson (1998).

[6] It has been suggested that a breach of confidentiality necessarily entails a violation of the right to privacy. In the view presented here, information in which there is no expectation of privacy, and whose disclosure therefore does not harm the dignity of the more vulnerable party in a fiduciary relationship will not, if disclosed by the more powerful party, result in a breach of confidentiality (*R. v. Spidell,* 1996).

accused be balanced? Before I move to a discussion of the particular means by which this balance has been achieved in Canada, I would like to describe briefly the recent history of equality rights in Canadian law and to show why it is impossible to exclude equality concerns from the present discussion.

Equality in Canada: Dignity with a Difference

In its early Charter jurisprudence, the Supreme Court of Canada recognized the foundational importance of the value of equality to any society where justice is more than a mere hope. Justice MacIntyre, in *Andrews v. Law Society of British Columbia* (1989), noted that: "[t]he promotion of equality entails the production of a society in which all are secure in the knowledge that they are recognized as human beings equally deserving of concern, respect and consideration."

In the years since that endorsement, our Court has wrestled with the meaning and significance of equality in a wide variety of contexts. It has come to be recognized that the achievement of equality requires more than reliance on formal definitions of equality, which equate identical treatment with equal treatment. Such definitions ignore the lived experience of those who suffer economic and social disadvantage, of those who are excluded from full participation in Canadian society and its institutions (see, e.g., *Eldridge v. British Columbia,* 1993). To invest equality with a meaning that responds to citizens' experience of injustice, courts must be attentive to certain groups' histories and continuing stories of disadvantage.[7]

In addition, our Court has moved away from a model of equality that focused on intent or fault toward one that is remedial, purposive, and focussd on discriminatory effects.[8] Such an analysis has required our Court to uncover stereotypes that influence both behaviors and standards and to examine requirements, neutral on face

---

[7] In an attempt to give life to this substantive, contextually sensitive understanding of equality, in *Moge v. Moge* (1992), I drew on an analysis of the disadvantages experienced by women on the breakdown of marriage to interpret the spousal-support provisions of the Divorce Act.

[8] In an early enunciation of this shift, Justice McIntyre in *Ontario (Human Rights Commission) v. Simpson-Sears Ltd* (1985), held that the approach of a particular piece of human rights legislation "is not to punish the discriminator but rather to provide relief for the victims of discrimination. It is the result or the effect of the action complained of which is significant."

value, that disproportionately and unjustifiably have negative effects on vulnerable groups.[9]

These trends in equality jurisprudence have long informed my analyses of cases involving sexual assault. Over a decade ago, I noted that women are disproportionately the victims of sexual assault. In *R. v. Seaboyer* (1991), I wrote:

> Sexual assault is not like any other crime. In the vast majority of cases the target is a woman and the perpetrator is a man (98.7 percent of those charged with sexual assault are men: Crime Statistics 1986, quoted in T. Dawson, "Sexual Assault Law and Past Sexual Conduct of the Primary Witnesses: The Construction of Relevance" (1988), 2 C.J.W.L. 310 at note 72, p. 326). Unlike other crimes of a violent nature, it is for the most part unreported. Yet by all accounts, women are victimized at an alarming rate and there is some evidence that an already frighteningly high rate of sexual assault is on the increase. The prosecution and conviction rates for sexual assault are among the lowest for all violent crimes. Perhaps more than any other crime, the fear and constant reality of sexual assault affects how women conduct their lives and how they define their relationship with larger society. Sexual assault is not like any other crime [para. 137].

Because women suffer disproportionately from sexual assault, they also bear the brunt of any unfairness that may result from the criminal-justice system's treatment of victims of sexual assault. Unfairness may enter into the system in a variety of ways. Those charged with administering the system may hold stereotypical beliefs and may, as a result, exercise their discretion in an unfair manner. Again in *Seaboyer* (1991), I described a variety of myths that plague the conduct of criminal prosecutions of sexual assault. The myths include:

1. *Struggle and Force: Woman as Defender of Her Honor.* There is a myth that a woman cannot be raped against her will, that if she really wants to prevent a rape she can. . . .
2. *Knowing the Defendant: The Rapist as a Stranger.* There is a myth that rapists are strangers who leap out of bushes to at-

---

[9] For example, in *British Columbia (Public Service Employee Relations Commission)* v. *British Columbia Government and Services Employees' Union (BCGSEU)* (1999), our Court held that physical-fitness requirements for becoming a firefighter disproportionately excluded women and that this exclusion was not shown to be justified. The requirements were neutral of face value because they did not explicitly target women, although this was their effect.

tack their victims. . . . the view that interaction between friends
or between relatives does not result in rape is prevalent. . . .
3. *Sexual Reputation: The Madonna-Whore Complex.* . . .
Women . . . are categorized into one-dimensional types. They
are maternal or they are sexy. They are good or they are bad.
They are madonnas or they are whores [para.141].

In *Seaboyer* (1991), I found that such myths are pervasive and
deeply held. I further found that these myths may affect a wide variety of actors in the criminal-justice system and that stereotypical images may infect legal rules. I wrote:

This mythology finds its way into the decisions of police regarding their "founded"/"unfounded" categorization, operates in the
mind of the Crown when deciding whether or not to prosecute,
influences a judge's or juror's perception of guilt or innocence of
the accused and the "goodness" or "badness" of the victim, and
finally has carved out a niche in both the evidentiary and substantive law governing the trial of the matter [para. 144].

The last point raises the concern that unfairness also results when
legal standards ignore women's experiences. In the particular context of a criminal trial, as in all situations of systemic gender discrimination, a rule that is neutral on face value may adversely affect women.

The particular and somewhat technical issues surrounding the
production of confidential information held by mental-health professionals and counselors in cases of sexual assault have posed a challenge to all who are concerned about equality. In Canada, the legislature
and judiciary have answered that challenge. We have signaled through
changes to a narrow set of legal rules our broad commitment to the
dignity and equality of women, and we have expressed our continuing
concern for some of the most vulnerable members of our society.

From *O'Connor* to *Mills*: Making a Difference

As befits a discussion that grounds itself in a substantive approach to
equality, I will in this section weave together narratives of the relevant
concrete facts and analyses of the legal issues at stake. The starting
point will be the case of *R. v. O'Connor* (1995) and there, as in all
cases involving sexual assault, the allegations are embedded in stories
of sorrow.

R. v. O'Connor: *Voicing Dissent*

H. P. O'Connor, a bishop of the Catholic Church and the principal of a native residential school during the 1960s, was charged with two counts of rape and two counts of indecent assault that were alleged to have taken place in the mid-1960s. The complainants were former students under the direct supervision of the accused. In the course of a preliminary inquiry, counsel for the accused applied for an order requiring disclosure of the complainants' entire medical, counseling, and school records. The Crown did not have in its possession the records of those who treated the complainants. The accused was granted the court order, which required, inter alia, that the Crown produce the contact information of therapists, counselors, psychologists, or psychiatrists who had treated the complainants; that the complainants authorize the same professionals to produce to the Crown copies of their complete files pertaining to the complainants, and that the Crown provide copies of these materials to counsel for the accused. At trial, it was shown that the Crown failed to comply with the order, and, subsequently, the trial judge entered a stay of proceedings. The Court of Appeal allowed the Crown's appeal, and a new trial was ordered. The Supreme Court of Canada heard the accused's appeal on February 1, 1995.

The disagreement between the majority and the dissenting opinions in the Supreme Court on the issues surrounding production centered on the mechanism governing the production of medical records that are outside the control of the Crown. The mechanism has two stages. The first governs the disclosure of the documents to the court, and here the accused must show that the documents sought are likely to be relevant either to an issue in the proceeding or to the competence of the witness to testify. At the second stage, the court, in reviewing the documents to determine whether they should be produced to the accused, must determine whether not producing them would adversely affect the accused's ability to make full answer and defense (*R. v. O'Connor*, 1995).

The majority held that the threshold for establishing relevance at the first stage should be low and should only prevent the defense from engaging in "speculative, fanciful, disruptive, or unmeritorious, obstructive and time-consuming requests for production." The majority found that to impose a higher burden would place the accused in a catch-22 position. According to the majority, the accused would have to satisfy a high burden without knowing what the records contained; such a burden, it was held, would frustrate the search for truth. Moreover, the majority held that information contained in counseling records had the potential to be relevant in sexual assault cases. In support of this claim, the majority pointed to the significant number of past cases in which the production of third-party records was ordered, and set out a variety of scenarios in which such records would be relevant (*R. v. O'Connor*, 1995).

The dissenting opinion, which I wrote on behalf of Justices LaForest and Gonthier, with Justice McLachlin (as she then was) concurring, held that the threshold for showing relevance at the first stage should be a significant one, and my reasoning tracked one of the lines of equality analysis set out here; I undertook an analysis that was sensitive to the particularities of context.

After rejecting a set of bare, unsupported assertions as insufficient to meet the threshold, I noted that it is unlikely that counseling records would ever be relevant. I held (*R. v. O'Connor*, 1995):

> The focus of therapy is vastly different from that of an investigation or other process undertaken for the purposes of the trial. While investigations and witness testimony are oriented toward ascertaining historical truth—namely, the facts surrounding the alleged assault—therapy generally focuses on exploring the complainant's emotional and psychological responses to certain events after the alleged assault has taken place. Victims often question their perceptions and judgment, especially if the assailant was an acquaintance. Therapy is an opportunity for the victim to explore her own feelings of doubt and insecurity. It is not a fact-finding exercise. Consequently, the vast majority of information noted during therapy sessions bears no relevance whatsoever or, at its highest, only an attenuated sense of relevance to the issues at trial. Moreover, as I have noted elsewhere, much of this information is inherently unreliable and, therefore, may frustrate rather than further the truth-seeking process [para. 144].

In addition, I rejected the majority's reliance on past practice as a means of demonstrating the potential relevance of therapeutic records. I held that rather than looking to the past judges should be sensitive to the therapeutic context in which the records were taken and that it is the absence of this sensitivity that would frustrate the pursuit of truth and needlessly harm the privacy interest of the complainant.

Additional concerns militate against a low threshold of relevance.

I set out earlier the stereotypes and myths that have plagued the administration of justice in sexual-assault cases. Here is another. If we permit relatively uninhibited disclosure of complainants' private lives, we "indulge the discriminatory suspicion that women's and children's reports of sexual victimization are uniquely likely to be fabricated." Moreover, such a level of access to complainants' records *assumes* that "personal and psychological backgrounds and profiles of complainants are relevant as to whether or not the complainant consented to the sexual contact or whether the accused believed that she consented." To permit this assumption to flourish under a low threshold for relevance represents an instance of systemic bias against the complainant.

Finally, in its analysis of the first stage, the dissent stressed that a legal system can be considered fair only if it seeks always to respect the dignity of the complainant. In the present context, this respect requires always keeping the privacy rights of the complainant in view. The majority disagreed when it held that the only relevant question at the first stage is "whether the right to make full answer and defense is implicated by information contained in the records." On behalf of the dissenting justices, I held that at the first stage the question of whether the salutary effects of producing the documents outweigh the deleterious effects should be contemplated. Disclosure to the court of the intimate details of a complainant's life is in all cases an infringement of her privacy interests. Although in border-line cases, production to the court should be the default position at the first stage, the complainant's right to privacy must always be weighed. Fairness requires nothing less (*R. v. O'Connor*, 1995).

The majority and dissenting opinions again diverged at the second stage. Although we were in agreement that there should be a balance struck between the rights of the accused and the complainant and we accepted that the trial judge should take five factors into consideration when making the determination about whether to order the production of therapeutic records to the accused,[10] we disagreed over two factors (*R. v. O'Connor*, 1995):

---

[10] The five factors were: the extent to which the record is necessary for the accused to make a full answer and defense, the probative value of the record in question, the nature and extent of the reasonable expectation of privacy vested in that record, whether production of the record would be premised on any discriminatory belief or bias, and the potential prejudice to the complainant's dignity, privacy, or security that would be occasioned by production of the record in question (*R. v. O'Connor*, 1995).

The extent to which production of records of this nature would frustrate society's interest in encouraging the reporting of sexual offenses and the acquisition of treatment by victims, and the effect on the integrity of the trial process of producing, or failing to produce, the record [para. 156].

The majority held that the first should not be a paramount consideration, and that the second should not be considered at all. The dissenting justices strongly disagreed with the majority's stance on the first factor. Production to the accused of a complainant's most intimate thoughts is a serious invasion of the complainant's privacy, and the prospect of such an invasion may deter victims of sexual assault from reporting offenses or seeking treatment (*R. v. O'Connor*, 1995). Again, because women are disproportionately the victims of sexual assault, measures that fail to protect complainants' right to privacy in sexual-assault cases will disproportionately result in violations of women's right to privacy; if such violations deter victims of sexual assault from seeking counseling, women will bear the brunt of this harm also. When deciding whether to disclose complainants' confidential records, courts' consideration of these potential harms will increase their attentiveness to the equality claims of women who have suffered, or are vulnerable to, sexual assault. I am of the opinion that such consideration is of paramount importance.

Bill C-46 and R. v. Mills: *Engaging in Dialogue*

The metaphor of dialogue, as an expression of the post-*Charter* relationship between legislatures and courts, has been the subject of academic debate (Hogg and Bushell, 1997; Manfredi and Kelly, 1999) and has entered into the Court's reasons (e.g., *Vriend v. Alberta*, 1998; *R. v. Mills*, 1999). For those who are sympathetic to the metaphor, it expresses the creative possibilities that legislatures and courts can exploit together in shaping legislation that is consistent with "Charter" values. I am among those who feel that the metaphor is suggestive, and I feel that the legislative and judicial sequels to *O'Connor* are instances in which the promise of dialogue was fulfilled.

Legislative Review

The story of the legislative response to *O'Connor* has been well told by Jodie van Dieen (1997). Six months after our Court rendered its decision in *O'Connor*, Bill C-46 was tabled in the House of Commons, and, as van Dieen notes, it was "crafted in an attempt to rectify many of the perceived inadequacies of the majority decision" (van Dieen, 1997).

The concerns of the dissent suffuse the legislative text. The preamble speaks the language of substantive equality when it recognizes that sexual violence has a "particularly disadvantageous impact on the equal participation of women and children in society and on the rights of women and children to security of the person, privacy, and equal benefit of the law as guaranteed by Sections 7, 8, 15, and 28" (van Dieen, 1997).

Sections 278.5(2) and 278.7(2) of the Criminal Code were introduced by Bill C-46 (1996), and require judicial consideration of the complainant's privacy interest at both stages in the *O'Connor* test for production. The legislature included, as relevant considerations for both stages, all the factors that the dissent listed as guiding principles for the second-stage analysis. In addition, the legislature reproduced the list of bare, unsupported assertions, which the *O'Connor* dissent held that a court should find to be insufficient to establish the relevance of the documents in question. In so doing, the legislature limited the scope of what courts can consider to be relevant at the first stage and sought to challenge stereotypical assumptions about victims of sexual assault (van Dieen, 1997). With each of these changes, the legislature echoed and confirmed the concerns expressed by the dissent in *O'Connor*, and with each the legislature affirmed its commitment to the privacy, confidentiality, and equality rights of women and of victims of sexual assault.

R. v. Mills: *The Judicial Coda*

This brief review of judicial and legislative history on the matter should answer the charge that under the Charter judicial review necessarily distorts the legislative will (Manfredi and Kelly, 1999). Central to the charge is the claim that legislatures alter their policies to accord with "judicially articulated norms." If the argument against judicial review is to be coherent, however, such alteration must be undertaken under the threat of review. Because the legislative alterations that responded to *O'Connor* echoed the dissent and implicitly critiqued the majority, it is evident that the legislature did not act in response to such a perceived threat. If anything, the legislature reviewed the Court.

More than this, the majority reasons of *R. v. Mills* (1999) articulate a position on production that is at odds with the majority reasons
of *O'Connor* and that defer to the legislature's choices. In *Mills,* the
Court concurred with the legislature: protection of a complainant's
right to control her own information, to liberty and security of the
person, and to equality complement, rather than detract from, the
right to a fair trial.

Brian Mills was charged with one count of sexual assault and
one count of unlawful sexual touching. The offenses are alleged to
have occurred on July 12, 1995, when the complainant was 13 years
old. At trial, counsel for the accused applied for production of therapeutic records and notes pertaining to the complainant, which were
held by a counseling organization, a psychiatrist, and a child-and-
adolescent-services association. In the course of the trial, Bill C-46
came into force. Counsel for the accused challenged the constitutionality of the provisions of the Criminal Code introduced by Bill C-
46. The provisions challenged included those that imposed a relatively
high threshold for relevance, required a balancing of the complainant's
and accused's interests at the first stage of the *O'Connor* test, and
required a judge to weigh factors that the majority in *O'Connor* explicitly rejected. The trial judge held that Bill C-46 infringed the
accused's rights under Sections 7 and 11(d)[11] of the *Charter.* Our
Court granted the complainant leave to appeal.

The majority of our Court, in reasons written by Justice McLachlin
(as she then was) and Justice Iacobucci on behalf of Justices Gonthier,
Major, Bastarache, Binnie, and me, upheld the constitutionality of the
impugned legislation. The majority took the opportunity to affirm
the importance of the right to privacy, in both its aspects. Moreover,
the majority reasons linked the privacy interest to the trust fostered
by confidential therapeutic relationships. The majority also spoke
clearly about the significance of gender equality in cases involving
sexual assault. And the majority held that the rights of the accused
were not infringed by the impugned legislation because inter alia,
the "accused is not permitted to distort the truth-seeking function of
the trial process." The majority found that the purpose of the list of
bare assertions, which cannot on their own establish likely relevance,

---

[11] Section 11(d) states: "Any person charged with an offence has the right to be
presumed innocent until proven guilty according to law in a fair and public hearing
by an independent and impartial tribunal."

is to prevent stereotypes and myths "from forming the entire basis of an otherwise unsubstantiated order for production of private records" (*R. v. Mills,* 1999).

Conclusions

Having explored the narrow pathways of the law of evidence and examined the concrete particulars of the case law and legislation, I would like to close by presenting some broad views of the law of privacy.

The right to privacy, like all other rights, is enriched when its interpretation and application are informed by equality considerations, and in the end the dialogue between the legislature and the judiciary on the question of production was a conversation about equality. As in all such conversations where the exchange is more than idle chatter, the participants were sensitive to the particularities of the contexts in which unfairness can arise. More than simply applying the legal tests of equality, they listened to the moral imperatives of equality. Equality demands empathy, and in the present context the only adequate response to this demand is a constant sensitivity to the privacy interests of the complainant, as well as the rights of the accused. Equality demands courage. It asks that we speak truth to power and that we recognize that truth can take a variety of forms. It can involve challenging untruths that are embedded in stereotypes and myths, and it can entail bringing to light the biases against the vulnerable that are shaded by apparently neutral standards.

My sincere thanks to Hoi Kong, my law clerk at the Supreme Court of Canada, whose valuable assistance made this chapter possible.

References

Andrews v. Law Society of British Columbia, 1 SCR 143 (1989).
Bill C-46, *An Act to Amend the Criminal Code (Production of records in sexual offence proceedings),* 2d. Sess., 35th Parl. (1996), proclaimed in force 12 May 1997, SC 1997, c. 31.
British Columbia (Public Service Employee Relations Commission) v. British Columia Government and Services Union (BCGSEU), 3 SCR 3 (1999).
Canadian Charter of Rights and Freedoms, Constitution Act (1982), Section 7, I. Canada Act 1982, U.K. (1982), c. Schedule B, 11.

Criminal Code, RSC (1985), c. C-46, as am. By SC 1997, c.31.

Dawson, J. (1998), Compelled production of medical reports. *McGill Law J.,* 43:25–65.

Eldridge v. British Columbia, 2 SCR 872 (1993).

Hogg, P. W. & Bushell, A. A. (1997), The charter dialogue between courts and legislatures (or perhaps the charter of rights isn't such a bad thing after all). *Osgoode Hall Law J.,* 35:75–105.

M.(A.) v. Ryan, 1 SCR 157 (1997).

Manfredi, C. P. & Kelly, J. B. (1999), Six degrees of dialogue: A eesponse to Hogg and Bushell. *Osgoode Hall Law J.,* 37:513–527.

McNairn, M. & Scott, S. (2001), *Privacy Law in Canada.* Toronto: Butterworths.

Moge v. Moge, 3 SCR 813 (1992).

Ontario (Human Rights Commission) v. Simpsons-Sears, 2 SC. 536 (1985).

Oxford Dictionary of Law (2002). Oxford: Oxford University Press.

R. v. Dyment, 2 SCR 417 (1988).

R. v. Mills, 3 SCR 668 (1999).

R. v. Morgantaler, 1 SCR 30 (1988).

R. v. O'Connor, 4 SCR 411 (1995).

R. v. O'Connor, 30 CR, 4th, 33 BCCA (1994).

R. v. Plant, 3 SCR 281 (1993).

R. v. Seaboyer, 2 SCR 577 (1991), online: QL(SCC).

R. v. Spidell, 151 NSR, 2d., 290 (1996).

Rodriguez v. British Columbia (Attorney General), 3 SCR 519 (1993).

Schafer, A. (1980) Privacy: A philosophical overview. In: *Aspects of Privacy Law: Essays in Honour of John M. Sharp,* ed. D. Gibson. Toronto: Butterworths, pp. 1–20.

Sopinka, J., Lederman, S. N. & Bryant, A. W. (1999), *Law of Evidence in Canada.* Toronto: Butterworths.

van Dieen, J. (1997), *O'Connor* and Bill C-46: Differences in approach. *Queen's Law J.,* 23:1–65.

Vriend v. Alberta, 1 SCR 493 (1998).

Epilogue

Introduction to Epilogue

❧

A Psychoanalyst Looks
at the Witness Stand

Anne Hayman's legendary statement in the British medical journal *The Lancet* (1965) on her successful refusal to testify in court about an alleged analysand is widely considered a landmark in the history of psychoanalytic confidentiality. Invited to review this experience and its aftermath for the present volume, Hayman has extended her reflections to provide a detailed analysis of the current state of British and European privacy law, and the prospects for the future. Her chapter concludes with thoughtful meditations on the most difficult and troubling aspects of the confidentiality ethic.

CHAPTER 21

❧

A Psychoanalyst Looks at the Witness Stand

Anne Hayman

*I*t is 36 years since I was subpoenaed to give evidence about some-one alleged to have been a patient. I chose to give none and subse-quently published an anonymous account in *The Lancet* (Anonymous [Hayman, A.], 1965). Enough time has passed to justify some comment on later developments around this issue and to consider whether the passage of time has produced any change in the view I so strenuously held then.

When subpoenaed, I anxiously sought advice from a senior col-league, who eventually referred me to another, who did likewise, and so on, until I had spoken to five of them. All of their ideas were different, apart from the fact that they were all uncertain what to do. So I had to work it out for myself, and in court the judge accepted my explanation (Anonymous [Hayman], 1965) and did not imprison me. I was of course pleased with my effort, and in writing up and pub-lishing my reasoning I naively hoped my example would be hailed and followed.

But there were no such grand hurrahs. There was no response when *The Lancet* referred to the case twice in the following months, and the event appeared to have sunk into obscurity, though it did reemerge a few times in the following decades. The first was when Joseph Goldstein, a professor of law at Yale who had been visiting London at the time, arranged for my article to be reprinted in an American publication (Katz, Goldstein, and Dershowitz, 1967). A few years later, when Joseph Lifschutz, a psychoanalyst in California, was actually jailed for refusing to give evidence about an analysand, Joe

Goldstein briefly considered flying me there to give expert evidence on Lifschutz' behalf. *The Handbook of the British Psycho-Analytical Society* sought and gained permission to reprint the article, and it has appeared there ever since. Much later, Christopher Bollas and David Sundelson (Bollas and Sundelson, 1995) applauded my stand in their 1995 book, and it has been quoted as authoritative in some counseling journals (Bond, 1993; Jenkins, 1997). There were also the very rare occasions when colleagues sought my advice because *they* had been asked for evidence about analysands. I have no way of knowing whether the paucity of these requests reflects the lack of knowledge about psychoanalysis among English lawyers or whether there were other cases not known to me because some colleagues quietly complied with the request or demand for information. I know of no other British colleague taking the ultimate stand taken by me and by Joseph Lifschutz.[1] I did once have the impression that my stand was unwelcome, perhaps because it provoked a fantasy of a frightening or degrading example to be avoided, or because it may have invited unwarranted guilt feelings in someone who, for whatever reason, could not follow a similar course. If such perceptions have been a factor—admittedly a small one, as the crisis cannot be all that frequent among psychoanalysts in private practice—then sadly my stand has little value as an example.

When considering the views of colleagues (helpful or not), I concentrated on psychoanalytic ones. Although I was qualified medically and psychiatrically, it somehow never occurred to me when subpoenaed to seek help or advice from the authority of those professional bodies (resources that would of course never be available to my nonmedical analytic colleagues). I probably believed they would not at all see the situation as I did, which was somewhat confirmed when I rang the Medical Defence Society with which I was perforce insured. A bored voice reeled out some justificatory statement for me to give in court, explaining that having thus complied with medical ethics, I should then give evidence. Patently, I was expected to do just this, which presumably was the generally accepted practice. The

---

[1] According to Henning Paikin, a colleague in Denmark, a private practicing psychiatrist (not an analyst) was recently ordered by the Danish Supreme Court to break professional secrecy by revealing the names of five of his patients. He refused and was jailed, being released temporarily after 11 days while an appeal was to be considered. There has been protest by lawyers and the Danish medical association. The background was that the psychiatrist wrote to a newspaper that five of his patients independently gave the same description of assaults by the police while under arrest. At the time of writing the outcome is unknown.

tone changed abruptly to excitement when I said that was not my intention, and a barrister to plead in mitigation of sentence was found for me within the hour.

There appears to have been an important change of expectation since then, to judge by the following statement of the General Medical Council 2000 that "patients have a right to expect that you will not disclose any personal information which you learn during the course of your professional duties, *unless they give permission*" (italics added). This phrase is italicized by me specifically because it is the one with which, as a psychoanalyst, I could not concur. This is explained in the following quotation from my *Lancet* article (1965):

> To the Judge's query whether I would still object (to giving evidence) if "the patient" gave permission, I answered with an example: suppose a patient had been in treatment for some time and was going through a temporary phase of admiring and depending on me; he might therefore feel it necessary to sacrifice himself and give permission, but it might not be proper for me to act on this.
>
> This example involves a vital principle. Some of the United States have a law prohibiting psychiatrists from giving evidence about a patient without the patient's written permission, but this honourable attempt to protect the patient misses the essential point that he may not be aware of unconscious motives impelling him to give permission. It may take months or years to understand things said or done during analysis, and until this is achieved it would belie all our knowledge of the workings of the unconscious mind if we treated any attitude arising in the analytic situation as if it were part of ordinary social interchange. If we allow and help people to say things with the ultimate aim of helping them to understand the real meanings underlying what may well be a temporary attitude engendered by the transference, it would be the crassest dishonour and dishonesty to permit unwarranted advantage to be taken of their willingness to avail themselves of the therapeutic situation. It would be as if a physician invited a patient to undress to be examined, and then allowed the Law to see him naked and to arrest him for exhibiting himself [Anon (Hayman), 1965, p. 785–6].

Given the same circumstances, apart possibly from finding some phrase less gung ho and more related to meanings than "crassest dishonour and dishonesty" (it was a shorthand that seemed appropriate then to my expected readers), I would abide by that statement today. I will come later to whether this assertion might ever be varied, given some different circumstances.

My court experience reflected the situation then regarding the effective rights of a witness in an English court to retain confidentiality—namely, none whatsoever. It was totally within the power of a judge to sentence a silent witness to imprisonment for contempt of court. The question is whether the position would be any different today, and, essentially, that judicial right has not changed. Equally discouraging is at least one judicial pronouncement made in 1979[2] on the legal concept of "privacy," under which the issue of confidentiality per se appears to fall, that "it is well known that in English law there is no right to privacy" (Lester and Pannick, 1999). However, since then the picture has been somewhat more variable.

It might have been hoped that our right to retain confidentiality would be specifically protected by the rules supporting "privacy" in the new Human Rights Act of 1998, which came into force in October 2000 and which derives from the European Convention for the Protection of Human Rights (1950). Article 8(1) states, "Everyone has the right to respect for his private and family life, his home and his correspondence." There are various ways in which this has been, and doubtless will be interpreted (Bowers and Lewis, 2000, referring inter alia to employment law vis-à-vis the Data Protection Act 1998). Indeed, it has been said that the concept of "private life" is open-ended (*Lopez Ostra v. Spain*, 1994). To note a few examples: one instance was the judgment of there being "no reason in principle why . . . [private life] should be taken to exclude activities of a professional or business nature" (*Niemetz v. Germany*, 1991). Housing laws (*Larkos v. Cyprus*, 1999), nuisance (*Lopez Ostra v. Spain*, 1994), harassment (*Whiteside v. UK*, 1994), and search of premises (*Chappell v. UK*, 1990), have all come within the scope of Article 8 because of the inclusive definition of "home." In some respects, according to one authority,[3] "the judiciary has indicated a willingness to create a 'law of privacy,' by developing the common law of breach of confidence,"

---

[2] In Lord Lester and David Pannick (1999). *Human Rights Law and Practise.* London: Butterworths. For illustration of different versions, see *Malone v. Metropolitan Police Comn* (1979) and *Kaye v. Robertson* (1991) FSR 62 at 66 per Glidewell LJ; at 70 (per Bingham LJ) and at 71 (per Leggatt LJ), and the Report of the Younger Committee, Cmnd 5012, 1972, especially paras 74-97. See, however, *Morris v. Beardmore* (1981) and *R v. Khan* (1997) AC 558, 582-3A (Lord Nicholls of Birkenhead).

[3] See *Chappell v. UK*, 1990, quoting Lord Keith observing "the right to personal privacy is clearly one which the law . . . should seek to protect" in *AG v. Guardian Newspapers (no. 2)* 1 AC 109 (1990), at 255 H (the "Spycatcher" case).

with "a system of specific civil and (although more rarely) criminal remedies for . . . breach of confidence, copyright, trespass . . . nuisance, defamation, malicious falsehood, and harassment" (*Chappell v. UK*, 1990).[4]

Indeed, on one occasion (*Kontakt-Information-Therapie and Hagen v. Austria*), the protection of confidentiality was sought elsewhere in the Human Rights Act, namely under Article 3, which prohibits "torture . . . inhuman . . . or degrading treatment," on the grounds of treating breach of confidentiality as "inhuman or degrading." This was unsuccessful; however, it was stated (Simor and Emmerse, 2000), about the "obligation to give evidence in breach of confidence, that

> The (European) Commission has held that Article 3 is not violated by a court order requiring an individual, who has received information from someone in confidence and in their professional capacity, to give evidence against that person in criminal proceedings despite any anxiety this may cause.

Unfortunately, even the Human Rights Act might well not help us, for two reasons. First, it has no special protection for the silent psychoanalyst. Article 10, which protects freedom of expression, reads, "Confidentiality of journalists' sources is considered to be a necessary precondition for press freedom . . . affirmed in several international instruments" (Simor and Emmerse, 2000). No analogous protection is provided for psychoanalysts acting in their profession.

The second reason is that, in general, the protections afforded by the aforementioned Act are for persons or bodies suffering wrongs at the hands of a public authority.[5] Consequently, they might not be accepted as applicable in cases where no such authority is involved— as, for example, a psychoanalyst practicing privately. There are cases where "the collection of medical data and the maintenance of medical records fall within the sphere of private life" (Bowers, 2001), thereby engendering the "right to respect" of privacy. But this kind of case law would not benefit the silent psychoanalyst who is not involved with a public authority. Furthermore, this protection seems not to have taken a secure foothold in jurisprudence. Some cases (*Z v. Finland*, 1998; *MS v. Sweden*) indicate that this right is limited to protection against the infringement of medical-records disclosure re-

---

[4] ibid.
[5] Thanks to Professor Costas Douzinas of Birkbeck College, London, for alerting me to this.

garded as "unnecessary," whereas disclosure that is administratively or legally "required" is not regarded as an infringement of privacy rights.

But despite these discouraging findings, it is a relief to remember that the law is not an exact science. There have in fact been cases where personal privacy has been upheld, partly by using the Human Rights Act, even though the opposing party was not a public authority. A recent instance was a case of much-publicized entertainers who had sold the rights to their wedding pictures exclusively to one magazine and were suing another that had obtained some and published them. They won their case, the court using inter alia Article 8 to "recognise privacy itself as a legal principle, drawn from the fundamental value of personal autonomy" (*Hello v. Douglas*, 2001). (As the pictures were being published anyway, "the couple had already sold most of the privacy" to their chosen publication, but what remained to them was "a right of veto."[6]) At the time of writing, two somewhat similar cases are in the offing, and there is currently some pressure for the protection of privacy in law (Wadham, 2001). That this could invoke a contradiction between Articles 8 and 10 of the Human Rights Act, that is, between the rights of privacy and of freedom of expression, is another complication, the future testing of which is anticipated.

An even better-known case was that of the two young men who, as children, had murdered a toddler and whose time within secure units was about to expire (*Thompson and Venables v. Newsgroup Newspapers Ltd*, 2001).[7] At the time of their trial, comprehensive injunctions restricted publication of further information about them. Anticipating their reintegration into the community, and in view of "widespread public interest," certain newspaper groups "sought further injunctions"; in other words, they wanted the freedom to publish on the matter. It was eminently likely that such publication would have continued and extended the consistently virulent and hostile publicity over the case, and there was real fear of promoting actual violence. The court ruled that the freedom of the media to publish could be restricted.[8] "The court had jurisdiction, in exceptional cases, to extend the protection of confidentiality of information where

---

[6] Lord Justice Sedley in *Hello v. Douglas*, reported in the *Times*, June 12, 2001.

[7] Thanks to Professor Costas Douzinas of Birkbeck College, London, for alerting me to this.

[8] Under Article 10(2) of the European Convention for the Protection of Human Rights.

not to do so would be likely to lead to serious physical injury or death." The "claimants' rights under Articles 2[9] and 3[10] of the Convention, from which there could be no derogation . . . met the requirement of proportionality" and supported the exception. So in this case, an injunction protecting confidentiality (of the future whereabouts, identity, and appearance of the young men) was ordered by the court.

Whether these examples using the Human Rights Act could be helpful precedents for the silent psychoanalyst in England is open to question. Consequently, it is worth pursuing another remedy that might possibly afford limited protection for our written records, though not against the obligation to testify in court. The Police and Criminal Evidence Act of 1984 (PACE) has quite powerful legal rules about confidentiality in some specific circumstances. These might be claimed as analogous to psychoanalytic confidentiality. The Act includes "personal records . . . relating to . . . purposes of personal welfare. . . ."[11] Although I am not able to quote any case where the situation has been similar to the "silent psychoanalyst," it would be worth citing the Act in the legal defense of a psychoanalyst who refuses to communicate confidential material.

The above possibilities could relate to psychoanalysts generally. Additionally, there are possibilities for psychoanalysts who see and treat patients within government organizations. I take the example of psychiatrists working within the National Health Service. They have relied on guidelines issued by the Royal College of Psychiatrists (2000) on "good practice in information-sharing." These are detailed and considered, and in some ways almost certainly owe much to the presence of psychoanalysts in the higher echelons of psychiatry here. To quote a few items selected from many: "the report notes the statutory right courts have to order disclosure of documents but also that ultimately a court would take careful account of the opinion of fellow doctors . . . as to whether . . . disclosure was . . . within reason-

---

[9] Protecting the right to life.
[10] Prohibition of torture.
[11] Psychoanalytic material just might be taken as sufficiently akin to "excluded material." PACE 11.(1) (a) and/or "personal records" 12.(a) & (c) to be subject to the protection afforded them, that of the requirement of a warrant issued by a judge or justice of the peace. This is not an absolute protection, the power residing with the court, but the existence of the protective rulings could militate favorably toward confidentiality.

able practise." There are various places where the emphasis is on conditions under which the doctor may disclose, in contrast with the fewer ones where this is deemed not justifiable. Concern is mainly with the reports psychiatrists should make, but the problem of confidentiality—of not reporting—is not ignored.

My main reservation with the otherwise-welcome statement that "patients have a right to expect that doctors will keep confidential information they acquire during . . . their professional duties," is with the phrase "unless permission to disclose is given," which immediately follows. I have indicated earlier why I might well find reliance on permission inappropriate in our professional circumstances. Nonetheless, there is much of value within this document.

Unfortunately, there is a significant new problem for colleagues in the Health Service and other organizations. In May 2001, the new Health and Social Care Act was passed in Parliament. This Act has aroused great concern and opposition because it is seen inter alia as imposing a grave danger to medical privacy. Under its terms, the Secretary of State can make regulations controlling patient information (Health & Social Care Act, 2001) requiring or authorizing disclosure. "[W]here . . . patient information is processed . . . in accordance with the regulation . . . [a]nything done . . . shall be taken [as] lawful . . . despite any obligation of confidence." Further, this law includes "creating offences punishable on summary conviction of a fine," that is, creating offences for opposing its terms. This Act is widely perceived as undermining medical confidentiality, arousing "overwhelming anger and opposition by doctors and patients," according to a health-privacy survey released on April 24, 2001. It appears that this Act could in some circumstances make it illegal for a psychoanalyst to maintain confidentiality.

How this very new Act will be applied is yet to be determined, but it does appear that there are new grounds for concern by our colleagues in government and allied services. Worry has been expressed lest planned future legislation inflict similar constraints on psychoanalysts in private practice. Nonetheless, the position of the silent analyst in private practice could become marginally more hopeful. Though the situation remains uncertain, it is mitigated by the fact that the legal demand for information from psychoanalysts is not a common occurrence.

I come finally to the extraordinarily difficult subject of whether the psychoanalyst's professional duty of confidentiality must ever

give way to a greater duty. I was first confronted with the suggestion
when talking with friends soon after my court appearance. In my
statement to the court, I had never divulged whether or not I had
treated the person in question. In my article, I had assumed that it
was likely that this was the only potential exception to other psychoanalysts' thinking as I did on the matter. I thought most analysts
would be unlikely to give evidence, but possibly more inclined to
divulge whether the person in question was or had been an analysand.
This particular refusal worried a lawyer friend. As far as I recall,[12] he
imagined the example of a case of murder, in which my analysand's
being with me at a certain time would provide the only available
alibi for someone. Was it really true, he wondered, that I would think
it right not to give evidence to establish an alibi? Another difficult
example came from a senior colleague who argued for the existence
of situations where it may be mandatory to betray confidentiality. He
told of having once rung the police to protect someone's safety, in
serious anxiety over what an analysand had said on the couch. This
example falls within one category of ethical problems that might
beset the analyst as a consequence of his allegiance to confidentiality.[13] There is also a different category, which might overlap with the
first, and to which I will come later.

The first category encompasses situations where danger seems
threatened by the analysand, or to the analysand, or to others in the
knowledge of the analysand. If an analysand spoke, perhaps in a
terribly frightened or in a very destructive manner, about impending
"real" disaster, the first need would be to try to understand the ramifications of what unconsciously or consciously underlay the fact that
the analysand communicated these disturbing and frightening ideas
at just that time. This understanding might well be difficult with an
analysand in a very disturbed state. Simultaneous with this need to
understand the immediate transference, there is the essential task of
assessing whether the danger is located in the outer world or in the
analysand's mind. A conclusion at this level dictates the next steps.
Tricky situations like this are sometimes encountered by analysts of
very disturbed perverted and aggressive patients. On one hand, the
analyst has to learn to tolerate the enormous anxiety of *not* doing

---

[12] The details have become foggy with time!
[13] Somewhat analogously, the Royal College of Psychiatrists recommends disclosure, where nondisclosure risks death or serious harm.

anything, other than simply analyzing. On the other hand, if whatever emerges leads to the conclusion that clarification of transference and other interpretations are not addressing the situation and that some protective action has to be taken, it is in my view essential to make every effort to communicate and explain this in the session. Indeed, a discussion like this might actually help to resolve the situation.

I have heard expressed the radically different view that any action taken by the analyst to protect someone outside the analysis should not or need not be divulged to the analysand. To my mind, acting protectively on the information without telling the analysand could establish a climate ripe for mistrust and self-doubt on the part of the analysand.

However much I try, I cannot believe that breaking confidentiality will not interfere with the analysis. This seems likely even when careful attention is paid to the transference, including the likely effect on the analysand of speaking and behaving "realistically." There are, of course, too many different possibilities to allow for adequate generalizations. Alas, both silence and telling will have every chance of interfering in one way or another with the analysis. There are likely to be mistakes and sufferings whatever one chooses to do in this desperate sort of situation. If one has to face making a decision between two bad choices, it is, of course, simpler and easier to stick to the rules (including those of confidentiality): but one can imagine circumstances where this might almost be an indulgence.

The second category of ethical problems that can arise with allegiance to confidentiality is the one that involves psychoanalytic colleagues. Life as a psychoanalyst begins with training, which in most societies of the International Psychoanalytical Association (IPA) means beginning with personal analysis. This is the one place where it should in theory be possible to say anything and everything. Although this does not apply in quite the same way anywhere else, the fact that all students and analysts go through the same type of experience supports whatever feelings exist[14] among colleagues of amity and sharing; and as with any professional group, this certainly includes one or another shared professional language and body of ideas. In certain ways, one can talk more freely to one's colleagues than to any other type of friend or acquaintance. The question arises as to where the line should be drawn to limit this.

---

[14] There are, of course, rivalries, disagreements, dislikes, and so on, but a basic awareness of professional linkage remains.

The practice of psychoanalysis is inherently lonely. The analysands with whom we spend our professional days are the very people on whom we cannot and must not lean for friendly professional support and understanding. Consequently, we rely heavily for the latter on our colleagues, as a valuable concomitant of clinical discussions, Society management, and so on. This reliance probably has a double result. On one hand, we are sometimes accused of being the biggest gossip shop ever; on the other hand, the habit of not saying important things because they belong only in an analysis can perhaps spread to not speaking to anyone, not breaking confidentiality in the few exceptional circumstances when it might be the one thing that ought to be done. It might be embarrassment or fear of "grassing"[15] (as I've heard it expressed) that can interfere with finding just that right person to whom to speak, in those dreadfully painful situations where there might be reason to worry about the professional behavior of a colleague for whom one has no direct responsibility. The particular worry is, of course, when it concerns behavior likely to do harm to analysands. The anguish of decision in this situation is magnified, and all the more problematic, when the worrying information has been learned in the course of an analysis. In such a situation, the analyst could be faced with a choice between two dreadfully "wrong" decisions—either of doing nothing to prevent an anticipated harm somewhere or of mistreating and damaging an analysand by some relaxation of the rule of confidentiality.

Obviously, the particular details of the situation influence this decision, but in practical terms it would be helpful to have some general rulings about where the line ought to be drawn between silence and breaching it. One suggestion I have heard that some claim avoids this dilemma is to routinely warn, before starting analysis, that in some circumstances confidentiality might, to put it politely, "be shared." That is not a view with which I concur. I would need a great deal of convincing that this "off-putting" introduction to an analysis could do anything other than make most of those seeking help simply go elsewhere. Its only possible value lies in the attempt to short-circuit ahead of time the whole problem of betraying confidentiality.

A completely different way of trying beforehand to prevent or minimize the harm has been promoted in the one specific area of relationships between colleagues. If followed, this measure might

---

[15] As with one criminal betraying another to the police, for his own protection.

just contribute to finding some protection for individuals in danger, without breaching confidentiality. Many years ago, I was part of a small group of youngish analysts, not attached to the Society's management but independently dissecting and discussing it; ultimately, we produced a memorandum.[16] As part of our thinking, I promoted in the memorandum a view about our ethic that seems not irrelevant today. My suggestion was for the creation of an Ethical and Disciplinary Committee (we had no ethical committee then) that would have the task of exploring and seeking to work out a *specifically psychoanalytic* ethic. The Committee's dicta would include the various rulings of bodies like the General Medical Council (GMC), covering things like honesty, good practice, no sex with patients, and so on, but it would have additional rulings particularly relevant just to psychoanalysis. To illustrate the difference, the GMC would not preclude warm friendships between doctors and patients and their relatives, but we would preclude them for analysts and analysands, due to what we know about the power and timelessness of the unconscious transference.

The next step in this formulation would be to introduce an idea concerning an element we all know about, which is sometimes called countertransference—namely, the unconscious transference of the analyst to the analysand. This exists for all analysts, part of whose work is to understand it. Because of the two transferences—analysand to analyst and vice-versa—social interchange is necessarily avoided in the analytic relationship. Moreover, though it is obvious that these transferences diminish and fade after analysis ends, I stressed the point that they never completely disappear. Focusing on the countertransference of the former analyst, the point was made that limits need to be maintained on postanalytic social contact, even though former analytic couples may develop friendly and ordinary relationships in time. Specifically, to quote a phrase I've heard, training analysts should never behave toward trainee analysands and ex-analysands as if they were protégés. I formulated it in terms of never playing an active part in promoting (or preventing) their professional advancement. Such extraanalytic behavior, even after analysis, can never really be in the same category as behavior with all other colleagues. If one has cases to refer, one can surely send them to ex-supervisees, rather than to ex-analysands. This special reservation avoids the failure of all-around confidentiality, in what I now dare to

---

[16] Privately circulated to the British Society in 1967.

stigmatize as "psychoanalytic incest." By this term, I mean an overly intense, overfriendly, overtalkative, gossipy, "helpful" involvement (which can actually be truly destructive) of the sort with which some earlier, senior analysts have appeared to embroil their former analysand-candidates.

An additional protective measure is in no sense new. It is the vital necessity for analysts to continue clinical discussions with colleagues. It is important that analytic societies cater to this need in every way possible. Side by side with each analyst's ever-present self-analysis, the ongoing learning and development implicit in such discussions (checking and noticing mistakes and hiatuses, constantly seeking the views of others) is of incalculable value. It is now increasingly felt that regular forums of this sort should be mandatory. It is less likely that such discussions could address those painful anxieties about colleagues in difficulty. Fortunately, we in the British Society now have another resource. Our Ethical Committee, which has the task of enforcing discipline where necessary, has also developed a pastoral function, with the aim of advising and helping any member who might be struggling with an ethical dilemma. It is to be hoped this attitude will make it possible for the analyst anxious about possible defalcations of a colleague to confide in the Ethical Committee.

It remains to discuss whether my present views on psychoanalytic confidentiality differ in any way from those I held formerly. But before entering on this, I must communicate something affecting the validity of my current ideas. I have retired from active psychoanalytic practice, so for me it is no longer a practical matter. With this demurrer, I declare unequivocally that from the point of view of the analysand, the security of uncontested analytic confidentiality is essential. Without believing it assured, no one could be expected to produce and permit the free-associations essential to the psychoanalytic process. In my experience, analysands took strict confidentiality for granted: unless I actually said it was not the case, I would be tacitly confirming it as an agreement between us. As I put it in 1965, the fact that it "may not be explicit is no excuse. Part of our work is to put into words things that are not being said." In this respect, my 1965 attitude remains unchanged. My stand then has sometimes been understood as "being silent in order not to betray a patient's secrets," but this was not so. As I never revealed whether or not the person in question had ever been my patient, the question of "secrets" simply could not arise. My stand was to protect, not a particular person, but the very principle of confidentiality. On this my view has not changed.

The painful question is whether this declaration is contradicted when I acknowledge the existence of extremely rare occasions where I could imagine I just might think differently. I cannot begin to work out the philosophical dilemma of these conflicting values: between the absolute clinical, moral, and ethical ruling of confidentiality on one hand and, on the other hand, the equally absolute humane, moral, and ethical insistence on protecting someone in real danger. In simple practical terms, I *think* the essential difference between the two is that my tacit promise and undertaking to analysands and analysis for silence would always be an ingrained principle; I would be unable to abandon it in order to save myself from discomfort, interference in life, and so on, even if I wanted to.[17] Protecting someone from real danger should be the only possible circumstance that might override this strong super-ego ruling.

But these brave words do not answer the question of how to resolve, in principle, and in practice, conflict between confidentiality and protection. The only general answer is that I do not know the answer. Sometimes there are irresolvable dilemmas that we have to live with and somehow manage. Our only resource (apart from reading) is the much-valued availability of colleagues, with whom, continually and continuously, we may argue, discuss, exchange views, investigate, and be used by and use and on whose shared professional awareness, understanding, and forgiveness we will always need to rely.

References

Anonymous (Hayman, A.) (1965), Psychoanalyst subpoenaed. *The Lancet,* October 16:785–786.

Bollas, C. & Sundelson, D. (1993), *The New Informants: Betrayal of Confidentiality in Psychoanalysis and Psychotherapy*. Thousand Oaks, CA: Sage Publications.

Bond, T. (1993), *Standards and Ethics for Counselling*. Thousand Oaks, CA: Sage Publications.

Bowers J. (2001), *The Right to Private Life and the Employment Relationship*. Liberty Annual Conference, 7 D.R. June 6, 2001, London.

———— & Lewis, J. (2000), *Employment Law and Human Rights Special Report*. London: Sweet & Maxwell.

Chappell v. UK, 12 EHRR 1 (1990).

European Convention for the Protection of Human Rights and Fundamental Freedoms, Rome, November 4,1950: TS 71 (1953): Cmnd 8969.

---

[17] I could do no other.

Health & Social Care Act (2001), Part 5, 60.

Hello v Douglas (2001) reported in *The Lawyer,* 12 March.

Jenkins, P. (1997), *Counselling, Psychotherapy and the Law.* Thousand Oaks, CA: Sage Publications.

Katz, J., Goldstein, J. & Dershowitz, A. M. (1967), *Psychoanalysis, Psychiatry, and Law.* London: The Free Press & Collier-MacMillan.

Kontakt-Information-Therapie and Hagen v. Austria, App. no 11921/86; 57 D.R. 81.

Larkos v. Cyprus (1999).

Lopez Ostra v. Spain (1994).

Lester, L. & Pannick, D. (1999), *Human Rights Law and Practise.* London: Butterworths.

MS v. Sweden, 3 BHRC 248.

Niemetz v. Germany (1992) 16 EHRR 97.

Prevention of Professional Abuse Network (POPAN) (2001), Press release, April 25.

Royal College of Psychiatrists (2000), Good psychiatric practise: Confidentiality. *Council Report CR85 2000.*

Simor, J. & Emmerse, B. (2000), *Human Rights Practise.*

Thompson and Venables v. Newsgroup Newspapers Ltd., Associated Newspapers Ltd. and MGN Ltd. 1 FLR 791 (2001).

Wadham, J. (2001), *The Politics of Injustice,* by The National Council of Civil Liberties (Liberty). July.

Whiteside v. UK, 76A DR 80 (1994).

Z v. Finland, 25 (1998) EHRR 371 (1997).

Index